Political scientists have often assumed that communities severely divided by cleavages such as religion and ethnicity will also be unstable. The civil strife experienced by Northern Ireland seems to confirm this assumption. Yet other communities, no less divided than Northern Ireland, have maintained political stability in spite of serious tensions created by religious and ethnic differences. The Canadian province of New Brunswick is an example of such a community.

In Search of Political Stability offers a detailed comparison of society and politics in New Brunswick and Northern Ireland. It reveals the fragmented nature of the two communities by comparing the distinctive cultures and separate social institutions of the major blocs, whether English or French, Protestant or Catholic. It documents the contrasting experiences of stability and instability by assessing the durability of each community's political institutions, the legitimacy and efficacy of their governments, and the prevalence or absence of civil strife.

The search for the causes of stability and instability focuses on the nature of the social conflicts and the behaviour of the political elites. In New Brunswick major conflicts have cut across the division between the English and French blocs. In Northern Ireland conflicts have tended to reinforce the division between the Protestant and Catholic blocs. The effects of these differing patterns are consistent with the theory of crosscutting cleavages. An examination of the elite political cultures, including such specific elements as campaign strategies, cabinet formation, and civil service composition, shows a pattern of elite cooperation in New Brunswick and elite confrontation in Northern Ireland. These results are broadly consistent with Lijphart's theory of consociational democracy, although significant revisions are made to this theory.

Edmund A. Aunger teaches economics and political science in the Faculté Saint-Jean of the University of Alberta.

In Search of Political Stability

A Comparative Study of New Brunswick and Northern Ireland

Edmund A. Aunger

McGill–Queen's University Press
Montreal

© McGill-Queen's University Press 1981
ISBN 0-7735-0366-8

Legal deposit 1st quarter 1981
Bibliothèque Nationale du Québec

This book has been published with the help of a grant from the Social
Science Federation of Canada, using funds provided by the Social Sciences
and Humanities Research Council of Canada

Design by Naoto Kondo
Printed in Canada

For my parents
Edmund Thomas Aunger
Peggy Cameron Aunger

ontents

Tables

Figures

Acknowledgements

In the course of writing this book, I have incurred a large number of debts, both personal and professional. William R. Schonfeld of the School of Social Sciences at the University of California, Irvine, supervised the work from the early stages of research until the completion of the first draft, and it is to him that I owe my greatest debt. He introduced me to the study of comparative politics; and he challenged me with his own standards of academic excellence. His constant encouragement, his sensitive advice, and his rigorous critiques have been of invaluable assistance.

The book also benefited from the help of many others who read the manuscript and provided constructive suggestions for its improvement. James N. Danziger and M. Ross Quillian of the University of California, Irvine, provided insightful criticisms of the theoretical framework. Robert A. Young of Oxford University contributed a detailed and very helpful commentary, based on his own extensive research in New Brunswick politics. Two anonymous referees, who evaluated the manuscript on behalf of the Social Science Federation of Canada, also gave very useful advice for its revision. Joan Harcourt judiciously edited the text. Others who offered helpful comments during earlier stages of the research were Douglas M. Amedeo, W. Lance Bennett, Jerome Kirk, Denis P. Barritt, Ruth Ann Pitts, and William J. Reeves. I am also grateful to Gerard Grobben of the University of Alberta for his assistance in obtaining access to the survey data from the Northern Ireland Loyalty Study and the Canadian National Election Survey.

A special debt of gratitude is due to the many people of New Brunswick and Northern Ireland who gave freely of their time and energy to assist me during my stay in these two communities. I would particularly like to express my appreciation to Benoît Duguay of Radio-Canada, P. J. Fitzpatrick and Earl Walter, both of the University of New Brunswick, and Eric L. Swanick of the Legislative Library; and to Tom Smyth and Daniel Crawford, both of the Union of Construction Allied Trades and Technicians, Sydney Elliott of Queen's University (Belfast), Frances Pinter of the Richardson Institute, and Frank Hanna, former member of Parliament.

The research was supported by fellowships from the University of California, Canada Mortgage and Housing Corporation, and the Canada Council. The Faculté Saint-Jean of the University of Alberta has provided a congenial and supportive environment for the completion of this book. It has provided me with both moral and material support. Jocelyne Desbiens efficiently retyped the bulk of the manuscript.

Finally, I would like to express my deep appreciation to my wife, Elizabeth Sovis, for her unfailing support and encouragement throughout the long period of writing this book.

Introduction:
Fragmentation and Instability

The communities of New Brunswick and Northern Ireland are characterized by striking, yet paradoxical, similarities.[1] Both are divided along a dominant cleavage into separate and self-contained segments. In New Brunswick there is a British-origin majority and a French minority; in Northern Ireland there is a British-origin majority (the "Protestants") and an Irish minority (the "Catholics"). Each of these segments has a separate identity with its own political symbols, flags, anthems, and heroes. There is only intermittent contact across the ethnic divide at the mass level; social structures are relatively segmented and residential patterns, segregated. Each segment within the community possesses its own educational institutions, communication media, leisure associations, and pressure groups. Further, each of the major subcultures is

---

1. New Brunswick and Northern Ireland will be described as "communities" throughout this study. Since this term has many different connotations, it is appropriate to clarify the sense in which it is used here. A community is taken to be a territorially bounded social system with a set of common political institutions. In conventional terms, a community is frequently considered to be a geographic subdivision of a society. For New Brunswick and Northern Ireland, the corresponding societies are Canada and the United Kingdom, respectively. The use of the term "community" is not intended to imply that there are shared norms or sentiments. Nor is it intended to convey any of the meanings implicit in Tonnies' (1887/1957) distinction between *Gemeinschaft* and *Gesellschaft*.

strongly identified with one or the other of the two dominant political parties in the community. In short, both New Brunswick and Northern Ireland represent *fragmented* communities—they contain competing networks of interconnected social organizations divided along a dominant cleavage.

Such fragmentation has been frequently held by social theorists to be conducive to the development of severe conflict and political instability. Yet it is on this dimension—that of political stability—that the similarity between New Brunswick and Northern Ireland breaks down. Political stability refers essentially to the ability of a system's political institutions to endure without losing their basic pattern or form. The existence of organized movements fundamentally opposed to the constitution of the state and the frequent recourse to violence in order to effectuate change are both powerful indicators of political instability. The collapse of the state's constitution is the ultimate confirmation of this instability. On the basis of these criteria, it becomes evident that Northern Ireland is unstable and that New Brunswick is stable.

Only in Northern Ireland has the fragmented social structure perpetuated intercommunal violence into the twentieth century. New Brunswick, like Northern Ireland, had incidents of violent conflict throughout much of its early history but these did not extend past 1875, the year in which clashes between French Catholics and English Orangemen resulted in two deaths (Stanley, 1972). By contrast, since its creation as a separate entity in 1920, Northern Ireland has continued to experience cyclical waves of increasingly intense violence. Between 1920 and 1922, an estimated 544 deaths occurred in Belfast alone as a result of intercommunal violence which was "far more terrifying than all the disturbances of the nineteenth century" (Boyd, 1970, p. 176). During the summer of 1935, sectarian riots claimed the lives of eleven persons. A much more serious outbreak of violence began in 1969, when a series of confrontations between civil rights demonstrators and security forces escalated into a limited civil war. From 1968 through 1974, factional conflict brought about the deaths of almost 1,100 persons, most of whom were civilians. During this same period, there were more than 20,000 shooting incidents and more than 4,000 bomb explosions ("Countering the Violence," 1974). The failure of the provincial government to maintain law and order in the community led finally to the collapse of the existing constitution: in 1972 the British government suspended the Northern Ireland Parliament and imposed direct rule.

The frequency and intensity of sectarian violence in Northern Ireland is the most salient, but not the only, indication of its political instability. From its creation, the constitution of Northern Ireland has been actively opposed by a nationalist movement which consistently receives between a quarter and a third of the votes cast at each election. Following the first election of 1921, the members of the Nationalist Party abstained from taking up their seats in the Northern Ireland House of Commons. While they later sat in the House, they nevertheless refused to recognize the legitimacy of the government for several decades—it was not until 1965 that the party formally accepted the title of official opposition. During this time an extremist branch of the nationalist movement, the Irish Republican Army (IRA) led sporadic guerrilla attacks against the existing regime, its security forces, government officials, and public installations. In direct contrast, the government of New Brunswick has been accepted as fully legitimate by all segments of the population. The overwhelming majority of the population has consistently supported the two parliamentary parties, the Liberals and the Conservatives. Although a nationalist and socialist party, the Parti Acadien, was formed in recent years, this party has been committed to working within the existing political system—its avowed goal being to improve the quality of the minority group's representation within the New Brunswick Legislative Assembly (*Le Parti Acadien*, 1972, p. 19).

New Brunswick and Northern Ireland are particularly appropriate as subjects for analysis because they represent "comparable" cases: they are "similar in a large number of important characteristics (variables) which one wants to treat as constants, but dissimilar as far as those variables are concerned which one wants to relate to each other" (Lijphart, 1971a, p. 687). The characteristic that is being treated as a constant, in this case, is the social fragmentation of the two communities. That which will represent the dependent variable, and which is considerably dissimilar in the two communities, is political stability.

The application of the comparative method to the study of these two communities will serve as a means of testing the value of pluralist theory which relates social fragmentation to political instability. This theory can be used to illuminate the specific cases, just as these cases may suggest revisions to the theory. The benefit of combining a theoretical study and a case study has been aptly summed up by Eckstein (1966): "Theories are generalizations pertaining to a 'universe of cases,' case studies interpretations of one unit in such a universe, and theoretical case studies a kind of synthesis of the two. Their object is to interpret specific cases through established generalizations and, by so doing, to cast a sharper light on the cases and to confirm or modify the theories or, if necessary, to generate new ones" (p. 177). The task of this chapter is to define the theoretical model that will guide our analysis of the two communities.

THE PLURALIST PROPOSITION[2]

The term "fragmentation," used in its current context, was introduced by Almond (1956) in his proposed typology of political systems. Almond classes western democracies as either "Anglo-American" or "Continental European." In spite of the connotations of the labels, the two classes are defined according to cultural rather than geographic criteria: the former have *homogeneous* political cultures while the latter have *fragmented* political cultures. The primary feature of the fragmented "Continental European" systems is their self-contained, mutually exclusive subcultures. Each subculture possesses its own subsystems of roles—for example, schools, unions, press, and political parties. One of the most important contributions of Almond's typology is the link he traced between social fragmentation and political instability. The normal characteristic of fragmented societies is, in Almond's view, "immobilism" and such societies are in constant danger of a "Caesaristic breakthrough."

The basis for this proposition is found in the theory of overlapping memberships proposed by group theorists, notably Truman. Truman (1971) describes multiple, overlapping memberships as the balance wheel which maintains the stability of societies such as the United States: "In the long run a complex society may experience revolution, degeneration, and decay. If it maintains its stability, however, it may do so in large measure because of the fact of multiple memberships" (p. 168). Verba (1965) interprets "an overlapping pattern of organizational affiliation" as being "a way of *managing* the strains that arise from patterns of cleavage in a society" (p. 469). In the opposite situation where there are no overlapping memberships, the political system is made up of closed, hostile camps: "Politics comes to resemble negotiations between rival states; and war or a breakdown of negotiations is always possible" (p. 470). Kornhauser (1959) similarly argues the importance of membership in independent associations because they create the "crosscutting solidarities" necessary for the maintenance of liberal democracy: these solidarities "constrain associations to respect the various affiliations of their members lest they alienate them" (p. 60).

These conclusions are directly relevant to the study of fragmentation because, in the terms of the group theorists, the fragmented society is one in which there are cumulative rather than overlapping member-

---

2. There may be some disadvantages in using the adjective "pluralist" to describe this proposition because of its many and varied connotations. However, since this is the description commonly given to this proposition in other studies (e.g., Di Palma, 1973; Lijphart, 1968a; Powell, 1970), there seems to be little sense in inventing a new terminology.

ships. Lijphart (1968b), for example, has argued: "In political culture terminology, overlapping memberships are characteristic of a homogeneous political culture, whereas a fragmented culture has little or no overlapping between its distinct subcultures" (p. 12). Overlapping memberships exist where an individual simultaneously belongs to organized groups which are independent of each other and, often, in competition.[3] On the other hand, cumulative memberships exist where an individual belongs to groups which are interdependent and, often, in concurrence.

The group theorists' model of stability, particularly as presented in the work of Truman, centres upon the effect of overlapping memberships on group cohesion (Mitchell, 1963). Where individuals are members of many competing groups, conflicts of interests, which weaken cohesion, are created within each group. The group's leadership must accommodate these various interests without alienating important segments of the membership. The result is a process of internal compromise and adjustment which leads the group to moderate its public demands. Truman (1971) sums up part of this process: "The internal political situation in a group is affected by the extent to which its membership overlaps that of other groups because of the varying effects that such overlapping has, and can have, upon cohesion. Cohesion in turn...is a crucial determinant of the effectiveness with which a group may assert its claim. It is a constantly operating influence that limits the activities of a group and its leaders" (p. 159). The effect of this weakened group cohesion and moderated group demands is a reduction in intergroup conflict and, consequently, greater socio-political stability. Truman does not discuss in detail the opposite situation—where group memberships do not overlap—since his primary concern is to give an explanation for the stability of societies such as the United States. However, it may be inferred that where memberships are cumulative, as in fragmented communities, the consequences are the reverse: the cohesion of each group and the conflict between groups are increased (see Table 1).

3. The term "overlapping membership" is not without ambiguity. In its simplest sense, any person who belongs to more than one group is a member of groups which overlap—even if they overlap only in that person. The pressures which such groups impose on the individual may be either consistent or inconsistent. It is clear, however, that Truman (1971) had the latter in mind from his references to "memberships in competing groups" and the "divided loyalties of the individual" (p. 210). Thus, it is important to restrict the definition of overlapping groups to groups which do not simply reinforce each other. The feature of the society characterized by many overlapping memberships is not simply that the citizens belong to multiple groups but that they simultaneously belong to groups which often have inconsistent aims and which compete across the major societal divisions.

Table 1

Group Theory and Political Stability

Homogeneous community	Fragmented community
1. All individuals are members of competing, overlapping groups.	1. All individuals are members of interconnected, cumulative groups.
2. Overlapping memberships create crosscutting allegiances and solidarities between groups.	2. Cumulative memberships create reinforcing allegiances and solidarities within groups.
3. Crosscutting allegiances weaken the cohesion of each group.	3. Reinforcing allegiances strengthen the cohesion of each group.
4. Weakened cohesion results in a reduction of each group's demands on the socio-political system.	4. Strengthened cohesion results in an increase in each group's demands on the socio-political system.
5. Reduced group demands attenuate conflict between the groups.	5. Increased group demands intensify conflict between the groups.

The proposition that social fragmentation leads to political instability is also supported by research dealing with individual behaviour. On the one hand, membership in competing groups is held to create psychological crosspressures in the individual members which tend to moderate their political commitment. Lane (1959), for example, concludes that such a situation could result in a moderation of attitudes, a generalized apathy, a minimization of conflict, or even a failure to "see" the conflict (p. 209). Kriesberg (1949), in a study of the crosspressures on a group of trade unionists—resulting from the inconsistent demands of membership in a Communist-led union and in the Roman Catholic Church—found that the effects were a reduction of interest in, and a moderation of attitudes toward, relevant political issues. On the other hand, there is evidence that cumulative memberships, by eliminating exposure to diverse group pressures, contribute to the development of extremist attitudes and, ultimately, to political instability. Verba (1965) postulates that "cumulative memberships should result in increased political involvement, increased commitment to a particular point of view, increased hostility to political opponents, and so forth" (p. 471). This postulate is supported by Powell (1970), who finds that membership in cumulative organizations is associated with increased levels of political hostility.

In sum, the proposition that social fragmentation is conducive to the development of political instability is based on two principal assertions. First, it is claimed that fragmentation increases the cohesion of social organizations, produces more militant leadership and demands, and consequently intensifies the conflict between the subcultures of the community. Second, fragmentation tends to reinforce the views of individual group members, to raise the level of their political commitment, and to strengthen their political antagonisms.

THE PLURALIST PROPOSITION REVISED

When it is observed that a fragmented community possesses cumulative group memberships, it should be made clear that the term "group" is used to refer only to "associational" and not to "non-associational" groups. It does not include what Truman (1971) describes as "potential" groups, where individuals share only a mutual interest or a similar attitude (p. 511). Such a definition would be so broad that the use of the term "group" would lose much of its value and, indeed, would pose very real operational difficulties.

By explicitly limiting the concept of fragmentation (and cumulative memberships) to formal social organizations, it is possible to introduce an additional concept, that of social cleavages, as an independent variable. A cleavage is defined as a division along which there is sociopolitical opposition. While a great many divisions exist within any society, usually based upon either categoric or value differences between individuals, these become cleavages only insofar as the differences are recognized as being the basis for competition and dispute. Thus, for example, the distinctions between male and female, rural and urban, Protestant and Catholic, all represent possible social divisions; but they will be described as cleavages in this study only if they have political significance as a basis for conflict. Cleavages may be thought of as "crosscutting" when these lines of conflict intersect each other.

While our definition of fragmentation in terms of the pattern of social organization is consistent with the common usage, it departs from other studies by explicitly distinguishing the concept of fragmentation from that of cleavage. This contrasts with the frequent assumption—based on a failure to differentiate between the concepts of overlapping memberships and crosscutting cleavages—that fragmented communities are inevitably accompanied by congruent cleavages. Such an assumption often leads to confusion and contradiction in the study of fragmented communities.[4]

---

4. The difficulties which may arise with such an assumption are illustrated in Lijphart's (1968a) study of the Netherlands. Lijphart describes the Netherlands as a fragmented society, using as his criteria the separate networks of social organizations (e.g., political parties, labour unions, newspapers, schools). Having thereby demonstrated that the Netherlands has cumulative "organizational patterns," Lijphart also interprets this as proof

Powell (1970) is one of the few authors to draw attention to the differences between the organizational structure and the cleavage patterns in a fragmented society. In a study of political attitudes in an Austrian community, Powell discovered that the position of an individual, when measured by social cleavage and then by organizational membership, is not necessarily the same—some individuals belonging to cumulative organizations are nevertheless in "mixed cleavage positions" (p. 16). He observes further that the "failure to distinguish between specific formal groups and generalized cleavage groups (or subcultures), such as those differentiated by class, religious identification, and ethnicity, greatly weakens the validity of present pluralist formulations" (p. 33).

This problem can be largely avoided by the revised formulation of the original proposition—by defining fragmentation only according to the organizational structure of the society, and by adding cleavage patterns as a separate independent variable. Thus, the revised proposition acknowledges that fragmentation is conducive to political instability, but proposes that crosscutting cleavages will tend to counteract this tendency. The corollary to this revision is that congruent cleavages in a fragmented society greatly increase the likelihood that political instability will develop.

The theoretical support for the effects of crosscutting cleavages—as distinct from overlapping memberships—has its origins most particularly in the writing of Georg Simmel. Simmel (1908/1964) argues that conflict, rather than playing a destructive and dysfunctional role, frequently serves to hold society together. While he cites a variety of positive functions performed by conflict, that most relevant to the problem of fragmentation is its ability to unify segments which were previously completely separated and opposed: "The character...of unification appears of course most pointed when it is composed of elements who at other times or in respects other than the one at issue are not only indifferent but hostile to one another. The unifying power of the principle of conflict nowhere emerges more strongly than when it manages to carve a temporal or contentual area out of competitive or hostile relationships" (Simmel, 1908/1964, p. 102). While Simmel's contention was, implicitly, that conflict on one dimension is conducive to the containment of conflict on other dimensions, it was left to Edward Ross to make an

---

that the Netherlands has congruent cleavages (p. 15). Later, however, he acknowledges that "the basic cleavages in Dutch society—religion and class—do cut across each other at an almost perfectly straight angle" (Lijphart, 1968a, p. 205).

explicit formulation of the principle of crosscutting cleavages. Ross (1920), taking Simmel's observation one step further, presented the principle in its contemporary form:

> Every species of conflict interferes with every other species in society at the same time, save only when their lines of cleavage coincide; in which case they reinforce each other.... A society, therefore, which is riven by a dozen oppositions along lines running in every direction, may actually be in less danger of being torn with violence or falling to pieces than one split along just one line. For each new cleavage contributes to narrow the cross clefts, so that one might say that society *is sewn together* by its inner conflicts. (pp. 164–65)

Williams (1947), in an influential monograph which consolidated the major research hypotheses relevant to the study of conflict, reasserted this principle, noting that "a society riven by many minor cleavages is in less danger of open mass conflict than a society with only one or a few cleavages" (p. 59). More recently, Dahl (1967) has employed the concept of cleavages as a prominent variable in constructing a paradigm of conflict: "The more conflicts accumulate along the same lines of cleavage, the more severe they are likely to be; conversely, the more conflicts intersect along different lines of cleavage, the less severe they are" (pp. 279–80).

The means by which crosscutting cleavages contribute to the maintenance of stability in a fragmented society may be summarized by noting two principal effects. First, there is what Simmel (1908/1964) has described as the "collectivizing effect," which refers to the establishment of links between segments that are in opposition to each other (p. 101). Since, in simple terms, one must unite in order to fight, a conflict that cuts across a line of fragmentation brings these fragments closer together. It creates new bonds of alliance that may serve, in the future, to regulate potentially severe conflict. This is, in part, the sense of the general rule suggested by Gluckman (1969) that "divisions in the ranks of any group, which link its members with its enemies in other relationships, exert pressure to prevent open fighting" (p. 138).

Second, there is what could be described as the "dispersing effect," which refers to the diffusion of conflict throughout the society. T. S. Eliot (1949), for example, observes that "numerous cross-divisions favour peace within a nation, by dispersing and confusing animosities" (p. 134). Rather than concentrating all antagonism along the line of fragmentation, the crosscutting pattern of conflicts permits them to be vented along a diverse number of cleavages. Coleman (1957) has a simi-

lar process in mind when he proposes that crosscutting cleavages allow
the absorption of discord within the various levels of the community:
"Part of the conflict is located within each person, part within each small
group of friends, part within larger organizations, and only the remainder
at the level of the community itself" (p. 22). On the other hand, when the
cleavages are congruent, the various conflicts will, in Dahrendorf's
(1959) word, be "superimposed": "The energies in all of them will be
combined and one overriding conflict of interests will emerge" (p. 215).
This "overriding conflict" would, however, be an "inclusive" conflict,
dominating the total community and encompassing both the issues and
the antagonisms of the other conflicts.

In addition, it should be noted that crosscutting cleavages, like overlapping memberships, may create crosspressures on the members and
leaders of each segment within the fragmented community. A cleavage
which cuts through an organized group weakens its cohesion and tem-
pers its demands. This is illustrated by Lijphart's (1969a) conclusion
that the crosscutting class and religious cleavages in the Netherlands
are a set of factors "conducive to prudent leadership": they create
crosspressures which predispose the leadership to pursue a policy of
moderation and compromise (p. 205).

THE ELITE PROPOSITION

In recent years, the pluralist proposition that social fragmentation leads
to political instability has been criticized by some political scientists as a
simplification which lays too much emphasis on sociological factors and
not enough on political factors. Di Palma (1973) argues that pluralist
theory "underplays the role of institutions and elites"; therefore it is
necessary "to return comparative politics to the study of government"
(p. 19). Nordlinger (1972) justifies his own study of political elites by
pointing to an imbalance in democratic theory, resulting from the fact
that "the mainstream of recent literature emphasizes attitudinal and
socio-economic explanations at the expense of political ones" (p. 2). Both
authors argue that there is little evidence that either overlapping memberships or crosscutting cleavages have a decisive influence on the management of conflict within a society. The predominant role is played by
the political elite: "Conflict group leaders are alone capable of making a
direct and positive contribution to conflict regulation" (Nordlinger,
1972, p. 42).

Substantial support for this view is found in recent studies of fragmented countries which are, in terms of pluralist theory, "deviant cases."
These countries—notably, the Netherlands, Belgium, and Austria—
while fragmented, are nevertheless stable democracies. According to

Lijphart (1968b), the crucial factor in the maintenance of their stability is that political leaders, cognizant of the instability that could result from fragmentation, consciously adopt accommodative policies in order to counter this possibility. Lijphart (1968b) asserts: "The leaders of rival groups may take actions to counter the unstabilizing effects of fragmentation, if they are aware of the dangers involved and desire to avoid them, and thus turn the overlapping memberships proposition into a self-denying hypothesis" (p. 18). The particular importance of the elite role in the management of conflict is summed up by Verba (1965) in this description of severe fragmentation: "One can conceive of a political system made up of two closed camps with no overlapping membership. The only channels of communication between the two camps would be at the highest level—say when the leaders of the two camps meet in the governing chambers—and all conflict would have to be resolved at this highest level" (p. 470).

Lijphart (1968a) proposes an important revision to the overlapping memberships proposition, specifically, that "overarching cooperation at the elite level can be a substitute for crosscutting affiliations at the mass level" (p. 200). Where memberships do not overlap, as in fragmented societies, conflict can nevertheless be regulated if elites "bridge" the segments. This is done most frequently through the formation of a grand coalition of the political leaders of each segment. However, any device which brings about cooperative behaviour is equally acceptable: the essential characteristic "is not so much any particular institutional arrangement as overarching cooperation at the elite level with the deliberate aim of counteracting disintegrative tendencies in the system" (Lijphart, 1968b, p. 21).

The pluralist proposition acknowledges the role of group leaders in moderating conflict between groups but states that this is effected as a consequence of the crosspressures resulting from overlapping memberships (Truman, 1971). The elite proposition is strikingly different because it emphasizes the autonomy of the political leaders. Their responses are influenced by the pattern of organizational memberships, but are not determined by them. In the words of Di Palma (1973) "elites follow a variety of strategies in responding to mass conditions, which are largely independent of the latter" (p. 9). In fact, in the fragmented society, the elites are consciously able to reject the pressures resulting from cumulative group memberships which, according to pluralist theory, should lead them to adopt hostile, conflictual behaviour.

The fact that they do not in some cases adopt such behaviour is attributed to the existence of two primary conditions. First, there will be a strong commitment by the elites to the maintenance of stability within the society. This motivates them to take action that leads to the prevention of potentially severe conflict between the major segments. Lijphart (1968b) cites as two of the prerequisites of consociational democracy, the recognition of the destabilizing effects of fragmentation and the commitment to maintaining the stability of the social system. This commitment could be rooted in a variety of motives, one of the most likely being the desire to avoid civil disorder. Nordlinger (1972) proposes that the elites' desire to avoid "bloodshed and suffering" and to preserve the "economic well-being" of their segment may inspire conflict-regulation (pp. 46–51). Lehmbruch (1975) implicitly suggests a similar motive in putting forth, as a condition for elite accommodation, the requirement that "past violence among the subcultures is perceived as a traumatic experience" (p. 380).

Second, there will be a separate elite political culture which favours the adoption of accommodative policies. Nordlinger (1972) describes the need for a "culturally defined predisposition to behave in a conciliatory manner" (p. 55). This predisposition develops historically when, as in Switzerland, earlier attempts at conciliation are rewarded, leading to the emergence of amicable agreement as a general norm. Lehmbruch (1975) describes this as "learning through success" (pp. 379–80). Lijphart (1968a), in his study of the Netherlands, concludes that particular cultural characteristics, notably the "habits of pragmatism and prudence in politics," enables the political elite to govern successfully in spite of the socially fragmented system (p. 207). This characteristic is partially derived from a common set of rules which are "a part of the 'role culture' developed by and instilled in the elite, and not of the mass culture" (Lijphart, 1968a, p. 122). Di Palma (1973), on the other hand, points to the advantages of a "socioeconomic" elite—rather than a "partisan" elite—which, because of its professional training in technical matters, is likely to favour the adoption of non-competitive procedures of government based on "expertise" and the "balancing of interests" (p. 15).

An essential feature of the elite theorists' revision to the pluralist proposition is the provocative suggestion that intersegmental conflict can be reduced by the leadership's introduction of specific policies which will minimize political competition. The fundamental premise of Lijphart's (1968a, 1968b, 1969, 1971b) work is that stability may be maintained in a fragmented community by the removal of situations most likely to be the scenes for dispute. In its simplest form, this means discouraging frequent intersegmental contact at the mass level: "When different groups in society have widely divergent interests and values, self-containment and mutual isolation can be more conducive to stable democracy than a high incidence of overlapping affiliations" (Lijphart, 1968a, p. 200). In a more advanced form, it means removing issues with serious segmental implications from the arena of partisan debate. A number of political procedures have been proposed for achieving this end, variously described as the "rules of the consociational game" (Lijphart, 1968b) and as "conflict-regulating practices" (Nordlinger, 1972). The most frequently cited practices may be summarized here.

1. *Grand coalition.* Where the leaders of the major segments govern through the formation of a coalition, the result is to establish effective links between the major segments. Further, coalition government will tend to protect contentious political issues from public interparty dispute, substituting instead, private intragovernmental negotiation.

2. *Proportionality.* The policy of allocating scarce resources and positions of influence proportionately between the major segments tends to eliminate these matters as the focus for intersegmental conflict. Instead, competition for these resources is concentrated within the segments.

3. *Depoliticization.* Issues may be depoliticized either by their transformation into technical problems requiring particular expertise or by their avoidance as a result of norms limiting partisan discussion. In either case, political competition on sensitive issues is restricted.

4. *Mutual veto.* Where the leaders accept that all decisions on matters of major contention must be made on the basis of agreement between the blocs, compromise may be facilitated. The mutual veto principle moderates competition by offering assurance, especially to the minority subculture, that important segmental preferences will be respected.

NEW BRUNSWICK AND NORTHERN IRELAND COMPARED

These two apparently inconsistent propositions—the elite proposition and the revised pluralist proposition—form the basis of the theoretical framework for our comparison of New Brunswick and Northern Ireland. The goal, as proposed by Eckstein (1966) in his description of the "theoretical case study" method, will be to apply these propositions to New Brunswick and Northern Ireland in order (1) to cast a sharper light on the two communities and (2) to confirm or modify the propositions.

Our first task will be to demonstrate that New Brunswick and Northern Ireland are indeed comparable cases. Thus, it must be clearly shown that both communities have quite similar levels of social fragmentation, but considerably different degrees of political stability. The second step will be to examine the major social cleavages in each community in order to determine whether the patterns are congruent or crosscutting. Finally, the elites will be compared to establish whether their behaviour may be described as either cooperative or confrontative.

If, as we have supposed, New Brunswick is both socially fragmented and politically stable, our hypothesis is that New Brunswick will be characterized by both crosscutting cleavages and cooperative elites. That is, both of these variables are necessary conditions for political stability. If Northern Ireland is both socially fragmented and politically unstable, our hypothesis is that Northern Ireland will be characterized by either congruent cleavages or confrontative elites, or both. That is, either of these variables is a sufficient condition for political instability.

2. Two Fragmented Communities

Both New Brunswick and Northern Ireland share the two characteristics which define a fragmented community. First, both are divided into separate subcultures based on differing cultural values. They thus conform to Almond and Powell's (1966) description of fragmentation as "a fundamental division in the values of different groups in the society" (p. 110). Second, and most important, each of these subcultures contains its own network of interconnected social organizations. That is, there are schools, leisure groups, newspapers, and political parties particular to each subculture. In operational terms, this is the most salient characteristic of a fragmented community. When Almond (1956) gives a specific example of fragmentation in a society divided between Communist and Catholic blocs, he notes: "The Catholic sub-culture has the Church itself, the Catholic schools, propaganda organizations, a Catholic party or parties, and a Catholic press. The Communist sub-culture... similarly has a complete and separate system of roles" (p. 407). The term "fragmentation" may be likened to that of "segmented pluralism" employed by Lorwin (1971), although the latter term is limited to communities divided along the religious cleavage: "A political system is one of segmented pluralism when its cleavages have produced competing networks of schools, communication media, interest groups, leisure time associations, and political parties along segmented lines, of both religious and anti-religious nature" (p. 142).

MAJOR SUBCULTURES

It is the ethnic cleavage that defines the subcultures in both communities, and most particularly in New Brunswick. In New Brunswick the division is between those of British origin (commonly referred to within the province as the "English") and those of French origin. In Northern Ireland, the division is between those of British origin ("Protestants") and those of Irish origin ("Catholics"). In both cases, the British-origin population is in a majority of almost two-thirds, although its proportions have shown a gradual decline from decade to decade (see Table 2).

The nucleus of the English majority in New Brunswick is formed by the descendants of the United Empire Loyalists who fled the American colonies with the outbreak of the War of Independence in 1775. The Loyalists—largely English and Scottish—were later joined by new immigrants coming, first, from Scotland and then, later, from Northern Ireland (Ganong, 1904; Hunter, 1971). A recent census shows that one-half of those of British descent originate in England, one-quarter in Scotland, and one-quarter in Ireland.[1] The French minority, on the other hand, is largely descended from the inhabitants of the original French colony of Acadia, established in 1610. Other French-speaking settlers, *Canadiens* from the region that is now Quebec, subsequently settled in the northwest corner of New Brunswick; however, these are a relatively small group. A recent estimate sets the proportion of *Acadiens* at four-fifths of the French-origin population (Baudry, 1966, p. iv–2).

In Northern Ireland, the British-origin majority is predominantly descended from Scottish and English Protestants who settled in the region during the seventeenth century. An estimated 90 percent of these colonists were Scots, although this proportion declined over the next two centuries as a result of emigration to North America (Heslinga, 1962, p. 161). The Irish minority, on the other hand, originates from the native Gaelic-speaking Catholic population living in Ulster at the time of the British plantations. They are thus of the same ethnic origin as the Irish in the Republic of Ireland, although historically they possessed a separate identity and a more Gaelic culture.

---

1. In the Canadian census, no distinction has been made between those originating in Northern Ireland and those in the Republic of Ireland: until 1961, those originating in the British Isles were classed simply as English, Irish, or Scottish. (See Canada, Dominion Bureau of Statistics, 1871–1971.) Since 1971, however, not even this breakdown has been given. The use of the broad term "British Isles" by the census, without any further detail, reflects the extent to which the various groups from the United Kingdom and Ireland have been assimilated into a common English-speaking group in Canada.

Table 2

Size of the Major Subcultures

| Census year[a] | New Brunswick | | | Northern Ireland | | |
	% English[b]	% French	N	% Protestant	% Catholic	N
1931	66	34	408,219	67	33	1,256,561
1941	64	36	457,401	66	34	1,279,745
1951	62	38	515,697	66	34	1,370,921
1961	61	39	597,936	65	35	1,425,042
1971	63	37	634,555	65	35	1,519,640[c]

Note: The New Brunswick data are from Canada, Dominion Bureau of Statistics, 1873–1971; and Canada, Statistics Canada, 1973–77. The Northern Ireland data are from Northern Ireland, Information Service, 1973.

a The first Northern Ireland censuses were held at irregular years, rather than decennially. The first census was in 1926 (rather than 1931) and the second in 1937 (rather than 1941).

b The English category has been used as a residual category to include all those who were not French. In 1971 only 5 percent of the New Brunswick population was of neither British nor French origin.

c In the 1971 census an unusually high proportion (10 percent) of the Northern Ireland respondents refused to state their religious preference. The percentages are based on the total of those who indicated their religion.

Differences in ethnic origin are not always translated into differences in cultural values. In both New Brunswick and Northern Ireland, however, the major ethnic groups also constitute subcultures. Partial evidence of this can be seen in the differing national identities and the differing communal symbols of each ethnic group (see Table 3).

The English subculture in New Brunswick, while defining itself as Canadian, maintains nevertheless a continuing sentimental attachment to the United Kingdom. The Loyalist tradition, including as its main elements attitudes of elitism, loyalty to the Crown, reverence for British institutions, and support for a united Anglo-Saxon race, has made the English subculture a bastion of support for the symbols of British nationality—the Commonwealth, the monarchy, and the Union Jack (M. Barkley, 1971). In contrast, the members of the French subculture most commonly identify themselves as Acadians, or in some cases—depending upon the region—as French Canadians. Since the late nineteenth century, the Acadian identity has been given formal expression by the adoption of a variety of exclusive national symbols, including an anthem and a flag. The cultural distinctiveness of the Acadians is evi-

Table 3

Communal Symbols of National Identity

Category	New Brunswick		Northern Ireland	
	English subculture	French subculture	Protestant subculture	Catholic subculture
National identity	Canadian	Acadian	British	Irish
National origin	United Kingdom	France	United Kingdom	Ireland
National day	8 October Loyalist Day	15 August Assumption Day	12 July Orange Day	15 August Assumption Day
Celebrated event	1783 Arrival of Loyalists	1755 "Le Grand Dérangement"	1690 Battle of the Boyne	1916 Easter Rebellion
Traditional flag	Union Jack	French tricolour étoilé	Union Jack	Irish Tricolour
National anthem	God Save the Queen	Ave Maris Stella	God Save the Queen	A Soldier's Song
Patron	Queen	Virgin Mary	King William	Saint Patrick

dent in their references to themselves as the "Acadian people" and the "Acadian nation." The anthropologist Marc-Adélard Tremblay (1962) observes: "They signify by this that they have the same socio-cultural characteristics, that they have in common the same traditions, that they are inspired by the same ideological sources, and that they share the same aspirations" (p. 145).

Like the English of New Brunswick, the British-origin majority in Northern Ireland still distinguishes itself by its attachment to the symbols of British nationality: the British flag, the British anthem, and the British Crown. Hence the frequent assertion that the Northern Ireland Protestants are "more British than the British." Nevertheless, this British identity coexists with a more exclusive local identity which is variously described as "Scots-Irish," "Ulster Scot," or simply "Ulsterman." A leading Orangeman sums up this self-identification: "Neither wholly English nor wholly Scots, they have become a third race, the Ulster Protestants, distinct from both, as from the Irish of the South and the West" (Dewar, Brown, and Long, 1967, p. 50). In direct contrast, the Catholic minority describes itself as "Irish," an identity which finds expression in the political symbols associated with the Republic of Ireland, notably the Irish flag (the Tricolour) and the Irish anthem (A Soldier's Song). A former prime minister of Northern Ireland has therefore described the Catholics as disloyal, noting: "They won't do anything about the Union Jack, they won't take their hats off, they won't stand up when 'God Save the Queen' is played, and naturally with severe frictions as a result" (Rose, 1971, p. 273).

These differing national identities have had important political implications because both communities adjoin larger political entities ethnically related to the minority bloc. The possibility of annexation by this neighbouring state has always been a serious political issue, particularly in Northern Ireland, where it has received substantial support from the minority bloc. A 1974 survey, for example, found that 46 percent of the Catholic population favoured the creation of a united Ireland (that is, the uniting of Northern Ireland and the Republic of Ireland) while 37 percent were opposed (National Opinion Polls, 1974). In New Brunswick, a 1965 survey found that 25 percent of the French population favoured annexation of the French-speaking regions by Quebec, while 41 percent were opposed (De la Garde, 1966).

The fragmentation of the two communities also has a geographic dimension: the subcultures are separated from each other along lines which reflect the original settlement patterns. In New Brunswick, the British colonists arriving from the American colonies settled first in the southern section of the province and then later moved north from Saint

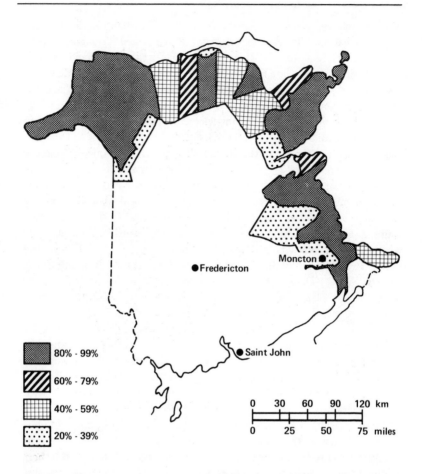

Fig. 1.   Distribution map of the French population in New Brunswick, 1971, by census subdivisions. (The data are from Canada, Statistics Canada, 1973–77.)

John, while the Acadians, returning from exile and finding the land in the south taken, settled predominantly along the eastern coast. This explains the contemporary distribution which shows the French largely in the north and the east while the English are concentrated in the southwest (see Fig. 1). In Northern Ireland, similarly, the British colonists settled first in the most accessible areas. Since they originated largely in Scotland, the Ulster Protestants concentrated primarily in the east. Nevertheless, the Irish Catholic minority was never completely

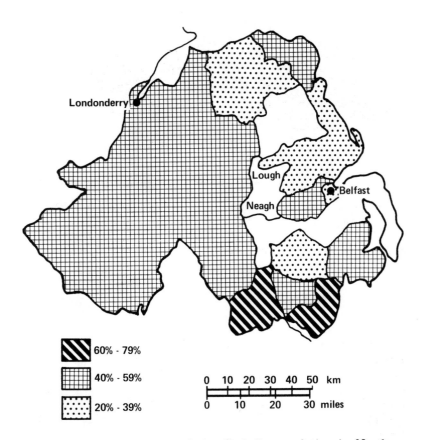

Londonderry

Lough

Neagh

Belfast

◼◼◼ 60% - 79%

▦ 40% - 59%

⋮⋮⋮ 20% - 39%

0   10   20   30   40   50   km

0   10   20   30   miles

Fig. 2. Distribution map of the Catholic population in Northern Ireland, 1971, by rural districts. (The data are from Northern Ireland, General Register Office, 1973–74.)

driven from the region and there is still considerable geographic mixing (see Fig. 2).

In spite of the many similarities, the subcultures in New Brunswick differ from those in Northern Ireland because of their linguistic basis. Those New Brunswickers of British origin have English as their mother tongue, while those of French origin have French (see Table 4). In Northern Ireland, at the time of the colonization, the native Irish were Gaelic-speaking (or "Irish"-speaking) while the Scottish settlers were English-speaking. This distinction, however, rapidly disappeared as Gaelic gave way to English: as early as 1851, the year of the first com-

Table 4

Subculture and Mother Tongue in New Brunswick, 1971

Mother tongue	% of English bloc ($N = 399,530$)	% of French bloc ($N = 335,025$)	% of Total ($N = 634,555$)
English	96	12	65
French	2	88	34
Other[a]	2	0	1
Total	100	100	100

Note: $\chi^2(2) = 481,344$, $p < .0001$; $V = .871$. The data are from Canada, Statistics Canada, 1973–77.

a The largest "other" language is native Indian, followed distantly by German and Dutch.

prehensive census, only 7 percent of the population of Ulster still spoke Gaelic (O'Cuiv, 1951). Nevertheless, it is claimed by some that Irish Catholics are distinguishable from Ulster Protestants by "an accent with slightly longer vowel-sounds and softer consonants" (Fraser, 1973, p. 89).

POLITICAL PARTIES

Like most social organizations in the two communities, the political parties correspond closely to the fragmented subcultures. In effect, each culture can claim to have its own party. This is particularly true in Northern Ireland where religious denomination and political party have been historically almost perfectly linked. It is less true in New Brunswick where there has been some overlapping of ethnic group and partisan preference.

In New Brunswick, the two major parties—the Liberal Party and the Progressive Conservative Party—have been closely matched, with each receiving nearly a half of the vote in recent years. In the 1970 election, the Liberals received 48.6 percent and the Conservatives 48.4 percent of the total vote. Both parties received similar proportions in the elections of 1974 and 1978 when, again, there was less than one percentage separating them. Since the turn of the century, the Liberals have appeared as the party of the French, and the Conservatives as the party of the English. Nevertheless, the Liberals have obtained a sufficiently large number of cross-over votes from the English population to show an edge over the Conservatives (see chapter 8). An examination of the party standings in the New Brunswick Legislative Assembly illustrates the extent to which the two parties coincide with the major subcultures.

Table 5
Political Party Representation by Constituency, 1971

Party of MLA	New Brunswick[a]		
	English constituencies	French constituencies	Total constituencies
Conservative	30	2	32
Liberal	6	20	26

Party of MP	Northern Ireland[b]		
	Protestant constituencies	Catholic constituencies	Total constituencies
Unionist	39	0	39
SDLP	0	6	6
Nationalist	0	5	5
Labour[c]	1	1	2

Note: The constituencies were classed according to their majority subculture at the 1971 census. The party standings are for January 1971. The most recent elections were February 1969 in Northern Ireland, and October 1970 in New Brunswick.

a $\chi^2(1) = 27.5$, $p < .0001$; $\phi = .724$.
b $\chi^2(3) = 49.2$, $p < .0001$; $V = .973$.
c Includes one Protestant member of the Northern Ireland Labour Party and one Catholic member of the Republican Labour Party.

Following the 1970 election, 94 percent of the Conservative members of the Legislative Assembly (MLAs) represented English constituencies, while 77 percent of the Liberal MLAs represented French constituencies (see Table 5). While other parties have contested the elections, none have succeeded in electing an MLA since 1920. The two minor parties, the New Democratic Party (NDP) and the Parti Acadien, are both socialist parties, but they nevertheless conform to the ethnic division. The NDP is chiefly an English party, while the Parti Acadien is dedicated to serving the French population.

For much of its history, Northern Ireland has similarly been a two-party-dominant system. The two major parties—the Unionist Party and the Nationalist Party—have corresponded almost perfectly to the two religious blocs. However, between the election of 1969 and the prorogation of the Northern Ireland Parliament in 1972, the two parties splintered and assumed new forms. Divisions within the official Ulster Unionist Party led to the formation of new factions, including the Vanguard Unionist Progressive Party (VUPP), the Democratic Unionist Party (DUP), and, later, the Unionist Party of Northern Ireland (UPNI). Nevertheless, while differing on various policies, each of these parties continued to represent exclusively the Protestant bloc. The links between these unionist factions have been sufficiently strong for the three largest subsequently to form an electoral alliance, the United Ulster Unionist Coalition (UUUC). The party representing the Catholic bloc, the Nationalist Party, began to break up at the 1969 election and was eventually replaced by a new party, the Social Democratic and Labour Party (SDLP). While describing itself officially as a non-sectarian labour party, the SDLP has, since its formation in 1970, become the chief political spokesman for the Catholic minority. An examination of the party standings in the Northern Ireland House of Commons, before it was suspended, shows clearly the relationship between the political parties and the two religious blocs. All of the Ulster Unionist members of Parliament (MPs) represented Protestant constituencies while all the SDLP and Nationalist MPs represented Catholic constituencies (see Table 5).

The relationship of the political parties with the two blocs in New Brunswick is due to the development of an "ethnic vote," rather than any formal institutionalized link. A strong bond between the Liberal Party and the Acadian group was forged during the 1920s when a prominent Acadian leader, Peter Veniot, was selected as the head of the party and prime minister of the province. While Veniot's success within the Liberal Party led to an Acadian bloc vote for that party, the Conservatives won a substantial victory at the subsequent 1925 election on the basis of an English backlash (Finn, 1972, p. 89). Consequently, in terms of the public images of the parties, the Liberals became associated with the French and the Conservatives with the English. In direct contrast to this development, the political parties in Northern Ireland were formally linked to the major blocs from a very early period. The Protestant secret society, the Orange Order, played a major role when the Ulster Unionist Party was first organized as a wing of the Conservative Party in 1904 and, from its inception, the governing council of the party included representation not only from the local party associations but also from the local Orange lodges (Lyons, 1948). Until the present, it has been customary for all Unionist political candidates to be members of the Orange Order, a requirement which has effectively blocked Catholic participation. Similarly, the Nationalist Party has been closely linked both to the Ancient Order of Hibernians (AOH) — a Catholic sectarian society — and the Roman Catholic Church itself. Eamonn McCann (1974), describing the Nationalist Party in Londonderry during the 1950s and 1960s notes: "Its basic unit of organization was not the electoral ward but the parish. The local parish priest would, in most cases automatically, be chairman of the convention called to select a candidate" (p. 12).

In both communities, the political parties are connected closely enough to the major blocs for voting to be frequently an expression of cultural loyalty rather than policy preference. Political allegiance becomes entwined with cultural identity. Fitzpatrick (1972) observed that "to a British Protestant New Brunswicker of United Empire Loyalist stock... the idea of voting Liberal might well be unthinkable, an act of cultural treachery equivalent to conversion to Roman Catholicism" (p. 119). In a similar vein, Conor Cruise O'Brien (1972) concludes: "In Northern Ireland a person who adheres to the politics of the other religion—a Protestant Nationalist, or Catholic Unionist—is for most practical purposes deemed, by the group he has left, to have gone over to the other religion; which of course is worse than having been born in it" (p. 13).

EDUCATION

The effects of the subcultural divisions in both New Brunswick and Northern Ireland are most evident in the educational system where parallel structures have been developed to meet the needs of each bloc. There is a significant contrast between the two communities, however. In Northern Ireland, the division between Protestant schools and Catholic schools corresponds to the division between state schools and private schools. In New Brunswick, both the English and the French schools have been accommodated within the state educational system.

The New Brunswick Schools Act guarantees that the students of each subculture will receive instruction in their mother tongue, a provision which has in practice led to a system of separate schools. Although "bilingual" schools—schools containing both English and French students—were provided for, these proved to be unpopular among the Acadian minority who feared that contact with English students would lead to assimilation. A brief presented to a local school board in 1975 by the Association des Enseignants Francophones noted: "When two languages such as English and French coexist daily in an atmosphere of so-called *bonne entente*, above all in our schools, one of these languages will have to give way to the other" (Landry, 1975). Consequently, only 9 percent of the New Brunswick pupils attended bilingual schools in 1975 (see Table 6), and this proportion has diminished in each subsequent year.[2]

2. Even this relatively low figure underestimates the extent to which pupils are segregated into separate English and French schools. Within some "bilingual" schools, the students are separated by either physical or temporal

Table 6
Separate School Systems

	New Brunswick (1974)[a]		
Type of school	% of English pupils ($N = 110{,}991$)	% of French pupils ($N = 57{,}065$)	% of Total pupils ($N = 168{,}056$)
English	94	0	62
French	0	87	29
Bilingual	6	13	9
Total	100	100	100

	Northern Ireland (1964)[b]		
Type of primary school	% of Protestant pupils ($N = 101{,}084$)	% of Catholic pupils ($N = 89{,}181$)	% of Total pupils ($N = 190{,}265$)
County	96	1	51
Voluntary	1	98	42
Four-and-Two[c]	3	1	2
Total	100	100	100

Note: The New Brunswick data are compiled from New Brunswick, Department of Education, 1974; while the Northern Ireland data are adapted from Lawrence, 1965.

a $\chi^2(2) = 151{,}824$, $p < .0001$; $V = .950$.
b $\chi^2(2) = 180{,}140$, $p < .0001$; $V = .973$.
c This is a voluntary school managed by a committee which has four representatives from the body providing the school, and two representatives from the local government.

To administer this parallel system of schools, the New Brunswick Department of Education itself has a dual structure, being divided into English and French sections, each headed by a deputy minister. The local school boards—with few exceptions—are also separated such that each board is responsible for the schools of only one language group. In only four of the thirty-three school districts are the local school boards responsible for both English and French schools. (In most cases the jurisdiction of the school boards is defined geographically; but because

barriers (e.g., at the Polyvalent Thomas-Albert French pupils attend in the morning and English pupils in the afternoon); at others there is only an insignificant number of pupils from one ethnic group (e.g., at Fredericton High School there are 2,600 English pupils and only nine French pupils).

of the territorial segregation of the two blocs, this is usually consistent with the linguistic division.)

In Northern Ireland, the division of the school system into Protestant and Catholic schools coincides with the distinction between voluntary and county schools. Before 1923, education in Northern Ireland was provided by private or "voluntary" schools, usually established and operated by the various religious denominations. The Northern Ireland government subsequently established a system of public or "county" schools. Only the Protestant denominations, however, chose to transfer their schools into the public system and then only after guarantees that religious instruction would be continued (Akenson, 1973, p. 103). As a consequence, the present educational system is divided between county schools which are almost entirely Protestant, and voluntary schools which are virtually all Catholic. The former are fully supported by the state and the latter only partially. According to a recent estimate, 98 percent of the children in Northern Ireland attend schools which are segregated on religious grounds (Fraser, 1973, p. 131). It is only in a small number of rural areas that there is a mixed system of elementary education.

This dual system of education is continued at the post-secondary level in New Brunswick, but not in Northern Ireland. In New Brunswick, there are two principal English universities (University of New Brunswick and Mount Allison University) and one French university (Université de Moncton). Each of these possesses its own Faculty of Education for the training of teachers. The New Brunswick Institute of Technology is similarly divided between a French college (Bathurst) and an English college (Moncton). By contrast, in Northern Ireland, both the two universities (Queen's University and the New University of Ulster) and the technical colleges provide higher education in an integrated environment. The only exception to this is the training of teachers, which is the responsibility of a Protestant college (Stranmillis) and two Catholic colleges (St. Mary's and St. Joseph's).

The parallel structure of the educational system is particularly important for the perpetuation of the major cleavage within the two communities. On the one hand, it tends to restrict contact and hence friendships to members of the same bloc; on the other hand, it maintains the cultural distinctiveness of the two blocs. The students learn different languages, different histories, and different values. This is particularly true in Northern Ireland where the Catholic schools promote the Irish identity from texts published in the Republic of Ireland and the Protestant schools promote the British identity from texts published in Great Brit-

ain. Bernadette Devlin (1969), a Catholic and former member of Parliament, notes:

> We learned Irish history. People who went to Protestant schools
> learned British history. We were all learning the same things, the
> same events, the same period of time, but the interpretations we were
> given were very different. At the state school they teach that the Act
> of Union was brought about to help strengthen the trade agreements
> between England and Ireland. We were taught that it was a malicious
> attempt to bleed Ireland dry of her linen industry which was affecting
> English cotton. (p. 62)

Jack Magee (1970) concludes: "Here, I'm afraid, are some of the roots
of our present problem—different ancestors, different anniversaries,
different wars" (p. 6).

The New Brunswick school system has also fostered separate identities, but to a lesser extent. While the French schools contribute to the
maintenance of Acadian culture, their role has been limited by the centralized control of the state. Both English and French schools follow the
same curriculum and frequently use the same texts. It is, in fact, only
since 1955 that French texts have been fully used in the French schools,
and many of these are simply translated from the English. Consequently, many Acadian leaders believe that the "neutrality" of the
educational system is biased toward the ideology of the dominant subculture. Jean Hubert, for example, has complained: "The school which
should teach the youth to respect the values recognized by the adults...
offers only an education with an Anglo-Saxon and Protestant orientation
under the cloak of a vague neutrality" (Hautecoeur, 1972, p. 217).

COMMUNICATION MEDIA

The daily newspapers in both New Brunswick and Northern Ireland are
each aligned with one of the major subcultures. In the case of the largest
dailies, however, this alignment is not sufficiently close to exclude a
mixed readership. In general, the largest papers in each community are
associated with the dominant bloc but take a relatively independent
position; the smallest papers are integrally linked to the minority bloc
and take a strongly partisan stance.

In New Brunswick, the daily paper of the French minority is *L'Evangéline*, a nationalistic paper which features news relevant to the
Acadian community and which crusades for French-language rights.
However, because of distribution problems, the influence of the newspaper is restricted to the southeast of the province, where it is pub-

Table 7
Daily Newspaper Circulation, 1973

Newspaper	City	Orientation	Circulation	% of Total circulation
New Brunswick				
Telegraph-Journal[a]	Saint John	English	57,689	47
Times-Transcript	Moncton	English	37,064	30
Daily Gleaner	Fredericton	English	18,575	15
L'Evangéline	Moncton	French	9,880	8
Northern Ireland				
Belfast Telegraph	Belfast	Protestant	190,687	57
News-Letter	Belfast	Protestant	89,034	26
Irish News	Belfast	Catholic	57,648	17

Note: The circulation data are from Editor and Publisher Co., 1974.
a Includes the Evening Times-Globe.

lished. In the northern part of New Brunswick, many Acadians read newspapers from the neighbouring province of Quebec. Thus, while the circulation of L'Evangéline itself is not large (see Table 7), nevertheless more than two-thirds of the French newspaper readers read a French-language paper (Dion, Even, and Hautecoeur, 1969, p. 92). In Northern Ireland, the daily paper of the Irish-Catholic minority is the Irish News, a paper which features reports on Gaelic sports and news on Catholic religious activities. The paper has also been closely allied with the Nationalist Party. The results of the Northern Ireland Loyalty Survey (see Appendix A) show that 49 percent of Catholic newspaper readers read the Irish News, while an additional 11 percent read papers published in Dublin.

Of the remaining daily newspapers, only the Belfast News-Letter, a strongly Unionist paper, has a readership which is restricted to the members of the majority bloc. The largest daily in Northern Ireland, the Belfast Telegraph, is widely read by both religious groups, in spite of its associations with the Unionist Party (see Table 8). Nevertheless, with the intense polarization of the major subcultures over the past decade, the readership of the Belfast Telegraph has consistently declined, while that of the more partisan News-Letter has more than doubled. In New Brunswick, all the English-language daily newspapers are owned by the same publisher, although they are based in different cities. In spite of their English and Conservative orientation, they have a wide Acadian readership, notably in Moncton, where twice as many Acadians read the

Table 8
Daily Newspaper Readership

	Moncton, New Brunswick (1971)[a]		
Newspaper	% of English readers ($n = 606$)	% of French readers ($n = 212$)	% of Total readers ($n = 818$)
Times-Transcript	97	90	95
L'Evangéline	3	42	13

	Belfast, Northern Ireland (1968)[b]		
Newspaper	% of Protestant readers ($n = 185$)	% of Catholic readers ($n = 124$)	% of Total readers ($n = 309$)
Belfast Telegraph	82	64	75
News-Letter	27	6	18
Irish News	1	64	26

Note: Columns may total more than 100 percent since some respondents read more than one newspaper. The Moncton data are from Sunderland, Preston, Simard and Associates Ltd., 1972. The Belfast data are from the Northern Ireland Loyalty Survey (see Appendix A).
a Corrected $\chi^2(1) = 148$, $p < .0001$; $\phi = .412$.
b $\chi^2(2) = 126$, $p < .0001$; $V = .584$.

Times or the *Transcript* as read *L'Evangéline* (see Table 8). Thus, the editor of *L'Evangéline* has commented sardonically to his Acadian readers: "Read the English press of the province, don't have any scruples, most Acadians have been drinking their anti-French poison there in small doses for years" (Hautecoeur, 1972, p. 211).

In addition to the daily newspapers, both New Brunswick and Northern Ireland have a large number of weekly papers which serve local regions and which correspond to the bloc divisions. In the west of Northern Ireland, the *Derry Journal* is read by the Catholic population, while in County Antrim the *Ballymena Observer* caters to Protestant opinion. In New Brunswick, the largest weekly paper is *Le Madawaska*, a French-language paper based in the northwest of the province; however, other major weeklies, such as the *Miramichi Press* and the *Saint Croix Courier*, serve the English population.

The radio and television networks follow the subcultural divide in New Brunswick but not in Northern Ireland. In both communities the programs available are the same as those at the national level: there is only a small proportion of local content. In New Brunswick, the publicly owned Canadian Broadcasting Corporation (CBC) is divided into separate English and French networks, providing radio and television service in both languages. The private Atlantic Television network (ATV) supplies additional English-language service. According to the available evidence, a significant majority of Acadians watch French rather than English television but they show a slight preference for English radio (Dion, Even, and Hautecoeur, 1969, p. 94). This cross-over can likely be accounted for by the greater availability of English-language service. In Northern Ireland, the public British Broadcasting Corporation (BBC) and the private Ulster Television network provide service to both subcultures, without distinction.

VOLUNTARY ASSOCIATIONS

The pattern of membership in voluntary associations conforms closely to the general pattern of fragmentation already observed. In both communities, the subcultures have separate organizations and there is little mixed membership. Interpersonal relations occur within, rather than across, the major subcultures. The trade unions, however, are a partial exception to this general rule.

The proportion of individuals who are members of voluntary associations (exclusive of unions or churches) is significantly higher in New Brunswick than in Northern Ireland (see Table 9).[3] There are also important differences in the extent of memberships within each of the two communities. In Northern Ireland, 41 percent of the Protestants, but only 20 percent of the Catholics are members of a voluntary association. Similarly, in New Brunswick, 52 percent of the English, but only 36 percent of the French are members (Dion, Even, and Hautecoeur, 1969). In both communities, it is likely that these differences can be accounted for by the breadth of activities provided within the Catholic Church; these offer a substitute for the functions of the various clubs to which Protestants belong.

The most prominent associations in both New Brunswick and Northern Ireland tend to be those formed for a specific ethnic or religious

---

3. It is likely that this difference would be considerably reduced if trade union membership were also considered. In New Brunswick, only 30 percent of the employed population belongs to a trade union (New Brunswick, Department of Labour and Manpower, 1974), while in Northern Ireland the figure is 55 percent (Northern Ireland, Review Body on Industrial Relations, 1974). This variance is representative not so much of differing local conditions as of the broader differences between Canada and the United Kingdom.

Table 9
Association Membership in Selected Countries

Country	Year	n	% Association members	% Multiple members
Canada	1968	2,767	51	31
United States	1960	960	50	29
NEW BRUNSWICK	1968	518	46	23
Germany	1959	955	34	9
Great Britain	1959	963	33	11
NORTHERN IRELAND	1968	1,291	32	13
Italy	1959	955	25	4
Mexico	1959	1,007	15	1

Note: Membership in a union or church is not included. The data for New Brunswick are from Dion, Even, and Hautecoeur, 1969, while the Northern Ireland data are from the Northern Ireland Loyalty Survey. Data for all other countries are from J. Curtis, 1971.

function. The Orange Order in Northern Ireland, for example, is directed specifically toward the majority bloc, as evidenced by the ordinances of the society which note that the "institutions is composed of Protestants, united and resolved to the utmost of their power to support and defend the rightful Sovereign, the Protestant Religion, the Laws of the Realm, and the Succession to the Throne of Windsor, BEING PROTESTANT" (Gray, 1972, pp. 193–94). Related to the Order are a large number of affiliated organizations, such as the Ladies' Orange Benevolent Association (LOBA), the Junior Boys' Orange lodges, and the more exclusive Royal Black Institution. The Orange Order originated in Northern Ireland, and almost a third of the male Protestant population are members (Rose, 1971, p. 383). While New Brunswick is one of the very few areas outside the British Isles where the Orange Order has been a significant force, its role has declined considerably; membership is now largely confined to rural areas in the south of the province. In its stead, the Masonic Lodge—a secret, largely-Protestant fraternal organization—has a much larger membership, probably because of its reputation as a more respectable and less extreme organization. Both the Orange Order and the Masonic Lodge are supplemented in New Brunswick by a variety of specifically "ethnic" associations, such as the United Empire Loyalist Association, the Imperial Order Daughters of the Empire (IODE), and the English-Speaking Association, but these have smaller memberships.

The minority blocs in both New Brunswick and Northern Ireland have separate, and comparable, organizations, but these are generally less influential. In Northern Ireland, the Ancient Order of Hibernians parallels the Orange Order, but only about 6 percent of the male Catholic population are members (Rose, 1971, p. 383). Among the French-Acadian population of New Brunswick, the Ordre de Jacques-Cartier functions similarly to the Masonic Lodge, but its membership is restricted to prominent Acadians. Much more widely based is the Société des Acadiens du Nouveau-Brunswick (SANB) which, while fulfilling some social functions, acts primarily as the chief spokesman and lobby for Acadian interests. The SANB claims a membership of 50,000 ("Acadian society to consider steps for 'equality' in N.B.," 1976), more than a third of the French-Acadian adult population. In addition, there are a large number of other organizations, such as the Dames de l'Acadie and the Cercle Français, which cater to more particular cultural needs.

Although there exist many associations whose functions are not tied intrinsically to one bloc, membership in these, nonetheless, tends to be consistent with the fragmented structure of the communities. Social clubs, for example, while in principle open to members from both subcultures, in practice attract members disproportionately from only one. In New Brunswick, the Lions clubs and the Rotary clubs are predominantly English while the Richelieu clubs and the Boishébert clubs are almost wholly French. A similar pattern is visible in Northern Ireland where the Rotary clubs are largely Protestant; and where only one in six of the major boys' clubs has a mixed Protestant and Catholic membership (Barritt and Carter, 1972, p. 146). In sum, memberships are cumulative rather than overlapping and, as Table 10 demonstrates, only a minority of the population belong to associations with mixed memberships.

The major exception to this general pattern are the trade unions, which are not generally organized along religious or ethnic lines. This may be largely accounted for by the fact that the union locals in both communities belong to large national and international unions, and thus their structure is determined by conditions outside the region. In Northern Ireland, 93 percent of the union members belong to unions whose headquarters are in Great Britain (Northern Ireland, Information Service, 1973, pp. 208–9). In New Brunswick, 62 percent belong to Canadian unions, and 38 percent to American-based unions (New Brunswick, Department of Labour and Manpower, 1974). With few exceptions, the unions are distinguished from each other by the criteria

Table 10

Membership in Voluntary Associations, 1968

| Associations, by language | New Brunswick[a] | | |
	% of English members (n = 151)	% of French members (n = 107)	% of Total members (n = 258)
English	98	22	66
French	2	65	28
Both	0	13	5
Total	100	100	99

| Associations, by religion | Northern Ireland[b] | | |
	% of Protestant members (n = 297)	% of Catholic members (n = 102)	% of Total members (n = 399)
Protestant	69	8	53
Catholic	0	44	11
Mixed	31	48	35
Total	100	100	99

Note: The New Brunswick data are calculated from Dion, Even, and Haute-coeur, 1969, while the Northern Ireland data are from the Northern Ireland Loyalty Survey.

a $\chi^2(2) = 164$, $p < .0001$; $V = .798$.
b $\chi^2(2) = 191$, $p < .0001$; $V = .691$.

of occupation and industry, rather than religion and ethnicity. Nevertheless, because in many instances certain occupations are dominated by the members of one subculture, there are a significant number of unions with fairly homogeneous memberships. In Northern Ireland, for example, the Amalgamated Union of Engineering Workers is almost entirely Protestant while, in New Brunswick, the Canadian Seafood Workers' Union is overwhelmingly French in membership. It should also be noted that the teachers' associations, consistent with the separate systems of education, have parallel organizations. New Brunswick has both the (English) New Brunswick Teachers' Association and the (French) Association des Enseignants Francophones du Nouveau-Brunswick; while Northern Ireland has a (Protestant) Ulster Teachers' Union and a (Catholic) Irish National Teachers' Organization.

Less formal social organizations, outside the framework of the organized associations, also reveal a segregated pattern. Athletic activities in Northern Ireland show a striking dichotomy, with Protestants playing "British" sports, such as rugby football and field hockey, and Catholics playing "Irish" sports, such as Gaelic football and hurley. In shopping activities, there is a distinct tendency for the members of each subculture to patronize only those shops which are operated by coreligionists, a practice which leads to considerable duplication of services, particularly in smaller neighbourhoods. Rosemary Harris (1972), in her study of a rural Northern Ireland community, has observed: "The advantages offered by one shop over its rival had to be very considerable before a Protestant could attract Catholic customers, or vice versa" (p. 6).

The separation of commercial activity is, in some respects, more institutionalized in New Brunswick as the result of the Acadian cooperative movement. For example, while the English use the financial services of banks, the Acadians have developed a separate system of credit unions, the Fédération des Caisses Populaires Acadiennes. In 1973, the *caisses populaires* had over 107,000 members (New Brunswick, Department of Agriculture, 1973), a membership equal to more than three-quarters of the Acadian adult population. The cooperative principle has been extended by the Union Coopérative Acadienne into a variety of other domains and now includes grocery stores, department stores, and fishing cooperatives. One of the largest cooperative enterprises is an insurance company, Assomption Mutuelle-Vie, which for many years restricted membership only to Acadians who were also practising Catholics. It is likely that the differing linguistic preferences of the major blocs also carries the division into areas not served by the cooperative movement. A 1968 survey of the French population noted that 78 percent use the French language in their dealings with small shops (see Table 11); this is highly suggestive evidence that each bloc patronizes the establishments of its colinguists.

The clearly separated networks of interaction in both New Brunswick and Northern Ireland have had a predictable effect on friendship patterns. In New Brunswick, for 91 percent of the population, most friendships are formed with others of the same mother tongue (Dion, Even, and Hautecoeur, 1969, p. 102). In Northern Ireland, similarly, for 70 percent of the population, most friendships are formed with others of the same religion (Rose, 1971, p. 496). The description of social relations in Moncton, New Brunswick, made in a study conducted for the Royal Commission on Bilingualism and Biculturalism, is equally applicable to Northern Ireland:

Table 11
*Language Usage of the French-speaking Population
in New Brunswick, 1968*

Sector of usage	% Speaking French (n = 294)	Sector of usage	% Speaking French (n = 294)
With friends	88	With employers	68
At home	86	At the garage	68
At church	85	At the restaurant	65
With the doctor	82	At the supermarket	64
With workmates	79	At the bank	64
In small shops	78	With the Power	
At work	73	Commission	54
With postal employees	71	With governments	54
		With telephonists	48

Note: The data are from Dion, Even, and Hautecoeur, 1969.

Table 12
Degree of Fragmentation by Sector of Activity

Sector	New Brunswick	Northern Ireland
Education		
Primary	High	High
Secondary	High	High
University	High	Low
Mass media		
Press	Medium	Medium
Electronic	Medium	Low
Voluntary associations		
Labour	Medium	Medium
Leisure	High	High
Political parties		
Representation	High	High
Voting	Low	High

Note: In measuring the degree of fragmentation, the values of phi (or Cramer's V), as given in the preceding tables, have been used as a guide. The values were simply trichotomized into low (.00–.33), medium (.34–.68), and high (.69–1.00). Where the data were incomplete (e.g., labour unions), however, the measure given here is only an estimate. The various sectors of activity adopted in this table are modelled after those used by Lorwin (1971) and McRae (1974) for Austria, Belgium, Holland, Switzerland, Canada, and Quebec.

At the level of social activities it seems that there is not much "social inter-play"; it seems rather that there exist two worlds living side-by-side which meet for their normal needs but do not succeed in integrating themselves. If it is not a question of two solitudes, it may be a question here of two worlds almost separated, living a bit on the border of each other without any real exchange, in sum, undergoing a sort of "cultural isolationism." (Cadieux, 1966, p. 2)

Thus, when the structural organization of the two communities is closely compared, sector by sector, there are striking parallels. First, both New Brunswick and Northern Ireland are divided—in approximately the same proportions—into two subcultures, each with its own distinctive history, national symbols, and cultural identity. Second, there are separate networks of interconnected social organizations for each of these subcultures: separate political parties, schools, newspapers, shops, clubs, and pressure groups (see Table 12). In short, New Brunswick and Northern Ireland have a remarkably similar degree of social fragmentation.

3. Stability and Instability

Political stability refers to the ability of a system's political institutions to endure without abrupt modification. Eckstein (1966), for example, describes a stable democracy as one "which has demonstrated considerable staying power, a capacity to endure, without great or frequent changes in pattern" (p. 227). Lijphart (1968b) similarly defines stability as "the system's ability to survive intact" (p. 8). These conclusions do not imply that the political system is static but rather that it is able to adapt to changes in its environment without abruptly losing its essential form. There is thus a continuity over time in the major institutions of the state.

In applied terms, the durability of a political regime, and of its institutions, may be measured by evaluating the endurance of the constitution. A constitution, whether codified or uncodified, is the set of principles which define the basic political institutions of the state, the relationships between each of these institutions, and the relationships between these institutions and the citizenry (cf. Cairns, 1971). The stable political system maintains a consistent set of political institutions: the constitution may be modified to meet changing needs, but the political institutions it describes remain essentially the same. The evidence of an unstable political system, however, lies in the collapse of its political institutions and the failure of its constitution: the pressure of changing demands leads, not to adaptation, but to the replacement of the existing political structures.

While constitutional durability is the fundamental measure of political stability, it is nevertheless a measure which has certain limitations. Principally, it is not finely graduated; it provides only gross distinctions, most useful when the evaluation pertains to an extensive period of time. It does not tap the intimately related components whose presence indicates political health, and whose absence heralds an imminent breakdown. These secondary components, which must be considered in any evaluation of political stability, include political legitimacy, governmental efficacy, and civil order.[1] Expressed negatively, they address the following questions: first, is the state's constitution opposed by significant portions of the community; second, is government decision-making immobilized because of intra-elite conflict; third, is political change accomplished by the resort to violence? If these conditions exist, then the community is not fully stable: a politically stable community not only endures, its endurance is not threatened.

CONSTITUTIONAL DURABILITY
The operational definition of durability proposed by Gurr and McClelland (1971) is based on "the length of time a polity endures without abrupt, major change in the pattern of authority relations among its basic elements" (p. 11). The basic elements include executive-legislative relationships, state organization, and government-citizen relations. The definition is essentially, therefore, a measure of constitutional change; and when the two communities are ranked, New Brunswick is extremely high in terms of durability, and Northern Ireland relatively low.

In New Brunswick, the major area of constitutional change has been that of executive-legislative relations, but this has been gradual rather than abrupt; the province has moved slowly from an executive-dominant government, to a legislature-dominant government and then back again to an executive-dominant government. This changing pattern has been almost imperceptible because, while the focus of power has shifted, the original institutions of government have remained largely unchanged.

---

1. The elements of political stability proposed here correspond closely to those employed by Eckstein (1971) and by Gurr and McClelland (1971) as the four "axiomatic" dimensions of political performance: durability, civil order, legitimacy, and decisional efficacy. Gurr and McClelland point to durability as the principal dimension and argue that the three other dimensions have an "interacting, time-dependent relationship" with durability (pp. 6, 71). The definitions and operational measures developed by these authors will be useful, not only in precisely evaluating the stability of New Brunswick and Northern Ireland, but also for situating it in the context of other nations.

When New Brunswick was established as a separate colony in 1784, the government was based on the "royal" model exemplified by Virginia, in that political power was vested in a governor (or a lieutenant-governor) who was empowered to appoint a council and to summon an elected assembly (cf. Dawson and Ward, 1963, p. 6). The twelve-member council had extensive executive powers and many of its members held appointed public offices, including those of provincial secretary, attorney-general, solicitor-general, surveyor-general, and chief justice. In addition, the council also possessed legislative powers by virtue of its function as an upper house. The assembly, first elected in 1784, exercised little check on the authority of the lieutenant-governor and his council but, nevertheless, enjoyed the exclusive right to impose taxes on the colony and to apportion the money so raised (MacNutt, 1963, pp. 55, 226–27).

During the first half of the nineteenth century, the division between the lieutenant-governor-in-council and the assembly was the basis for a lengthy power struggle which ended only with the winning of responsible government. The eventual victory of the assembly, with the transfer of power from the executive to the assembly, was gradual, however, stretching over a period of decades. A significant step was taken in 1837 when the control of revenues from Crown lands—previously the major source of the lieutenant-governor's financial independence—was turned over to the assembly. Two years later, the tenure of the principal government offices, which until then had been for life ("during good behaviour"), became dependent upon the will of assembly ("during pleasure"). But this principle was not fully implemented until 1848 when the lieutenant-governor asked one of the leading assembly members, Edward Chandler, to form an executive council composed of members of the assembly and possessing its confidence (MacNutt, 1963, p. 318). The test of the government's responsibility came in 1854 when the council resigned, following a vote of non-confidence, and the lieutenant-governor called upon the leader of the opposition to form a new administration.

In the century since the winning of responsible government there has been a slow but sure transfer of power back to the executive. This began particularly in the 1880s when Prime Minister Blair, through the shrewd use of patronage, succeeded in establishing an omnibus government party which held power for twenty-five years. It continued in the post-World War I era, when the growth of party discipline assured the executive of majority support in the assembly. And it reached a peak in the 1960s as the rapid growth of the civil service gave the executive new strength. Nevertheless, while this transfer of power has been important, it has also been gradual, and not abrupt.

A second area of important constitutional change has been that of state organization, specifically, the transformation of New Brunswick from a British colony to a Canadian province. However, the inclusion of New Brunswick within a new federal state in 1867 resulted in much less political change than might at first be supposed. First, the British North America Act—the act which established the new Dominion of Canada— expressly provided that the New Brunswick constitution, as it affected the executive and legislature, would continue unchanged. Second, the power to appoint and to remove the lieutenant-governor became the prerogative of the central government, "thereby placing the Dominion in the position occupied by the Imperial Government in relation to the administration of the individual colonies" (Dawson and Ward, 1963, p. 31). The imperial powers of the central government meant that the new Canadian state was only "quasi-federal." It took several decades more before the imperial-colonial relationship became a federal-provincial relationship, that is, before the New Brunswick government became fully autonomous and coordinate in its legislative authority.

In contrast to the clearcut pattern of constitutional durability in New Brunswick, constitutional development in Northern Ireland has been severely disjointed. Whether the period under study is the past decade or the past two hundred years, Northern Ireland has experienced repeated constitutional upheaval, combining changes in executive-legislative relations, state organization, and government scope. The instability of the Northern Ireland state, founded in 1920, is simply a modern reflection of the centuries-old instability of colonial Ireland.

Eighteenth-century Ireland had a governmental structure not too unlike that of New Brunswick. Executive authority in Ireland was vested in a lord lieutenant advised by a Privy Council, whose members included the chancellor of the exchequer, chief secretary, attorney-general, and lord high treasurer. Legislative powers were vested in an Irish Parliament, composed of a House of Commons and a House of Lords, but were extremely limited since the initiation of legislation was the prerogative of the lord lieutenant and his council. As in New Brunswick, the struggle between the Privy Council and the elected Commons resulted in the victory of the latter. Unlike New Brunswick, however, the change was abrupt. Backed by the armed force of thousands of Irish Volunteers, the new "Constitution of 1782" gave the Irish Parliament the power to initiate legislation and removed the veto power previously possessed by the lord lieutenant.

This new constitution was also subject to abrupt and radical change. In 1798 an insurrection led by the United Irishmen, inspired by the French Revolution and aided by French military forces, attempted to overthrow the constitution and construct a new and fully democratic state. When the rebellion had been successfully suppressed three years later, the British government decided upon the legislative union of Ireland and Great Britain in the hope of establishing a more durable political arrangement. The Act of Union which took effect in 1801 abolished the Irish Parliament but gave Ireland representation in the British Parliament: Ireland was permitted one hundred members in the House of Commons and thirty-two peers in the House of Lords. The lord lieutenant and his Privy Council continued to exercise executive power in Ireland, but were now responsible to the Parliament of Westminster.

These political arrangements did prove to be more durable and the union survived more than a century, in spite of continuous opposition. The survival had its costs, however, and this included major constitutional change. The Emancipation of 1829, which permitted Catholics to hold public office signalled the beginning of the end of the Protestant ascendancy in Ireland, although the act was accompanied by the massive disenfranchisement of Catholic electors because the property qualification for voting was revised. A much more fundamental change was threatened in 1886 when Gladstone introduced the first Irish Home Rule Bill; however, the bill was narrowly defeated in the House of Commons and the government fell. A second such bill was defeated in the House of Lords in 1893. In Ireland there was massive opposition to the union from a wide range of parliamentary and paramilitary organizations but it was not until 1916, following an insurrection led by the Irish Volunteers and the Irish Citizen's Army, that the British prime minister, Asquith, concluded in the House of Commons that "the system under which Ireland has been governed has completely broken down" (De Paor, 1971, p. 83).

The government's eventual solution was the 1920 Government of Ireland Act establishing two Irish Parliaments, one in the North and the other in the South. The Northern Parliament was to legislate for the newly created province of Northern Ireland and was endowed with a constitutional structure similar to that of the Dominions. Executive authority was vested in a governor (appointed by the monarch on the advice of the British government), advised by a Privy Council. Legislative powers were given to a Parliament composed of a House of Commons and a Senate, the latter elected by the Commons. While the division of powers between the Northern Ireland and British Parliaments resembled that of the Canadian federal system, the political arrangements deviated from the federal principle by retaining for the British Parliament supreme authority in *all* matters.

In spite of extensive opposition to this new constitutional structure, the Northern Ireland Parliament continued in existence until 1972. In that year, following the breakdown of law and order as a result of rapidly escalating civil violence, it was prorogued by the British government. Executive authority was vested in a newly created office, the Secretary of State for Northern Ireland, assisted by three junior ministers. The Secretary of State was also advised by a "commission" made up of persons appointed by him from the Northern Ireland community. Legislative authority was returned to the British Parliament.

A year later, the Parliament of Northern Ireland and the post of governor were formally abolished by the passage of the Northern Ireland Constitution Act (1973). The act provided for the establishment of a unicameral assembly elected on the basis of the single transferable vote and an executive which received its warrant of appointment from the Secretary of State. The powers envisaged for the Northern Ireland Assembly included many of those possessed by the former provincial Parliament, with the exception of security matters and judicial appointments. The devolution of executive and legislative authority to the assembly and its executive was dependent upon several conditions, however, the most important of which was the formation of an executive which, "having regard to the support it commands in the Assembly and to the electorate on which that support is based, is likely to be widely accepted throughout the community" (Lawrence, Elliott, and Laver, 1975, p. 51). When this condition was met, the Northern Ireland Executive formally took office in January 1974. A general strike opposing the new constitutional arrangement brought the downfall of the executive less than four months later, and responsibility for the government of the province reverted to the Secretary of State for Northern Ireland.

From the first meeting of the Northern Ireland Parliament in 1921 until the collapse of the Northern Ireland Assembly in 1974, the community has undergone major and abrupt constitutional change no less than three times. While the first Parliament lasted more than fifty years, the constitutional arrangements of the past decade are more appropriately measured in months. The duration of each constitution in Northern Ireland between 1921 and 1974 thus averages eighteen years, considerably below the cross-national average of forty-five, calculated by Gurr and McClelland (1971), but approximately the same as pre-Fifth Republic France. New Brunswick, on the other hand, would rank with Sweden and the Netherlands—extremely durable polities with life spans of more than a century.

The constitutional impasse in Northern Ireland since 1974 strongly suggests a continuing state of instability. In May 1975, a seventy-eight-member constitutional convention was elected with a directive to consider "what provision for the government of Northern Ireland is likely to command the most widespread acceptance throughout the community" (Lawrence, Elliott, and Laver, 1974, p. 51). Unable to reach a satisfactory consensus on the matter, the convention was later dissolved in March 1976. The reins of government have thus remained with the Secretary of State for Northern Ireland.

POLITICAL LEGITIMACY

A second, more sensitive, component of political stability is the extent to which a constitutional system is perceived as legitimate by its citizens. Such legitimacy implies, to borrow the definition of Lipset (1963), "the capacity of the system to engender and maintain the belief that the existing political institutions are the most appropriate ones for the society" (p. 64). A community lacking this capacity is less stable than one possessing it: the former may appear to be durable, but its durability is threatened. Measurement of political legitimacy is facilitated by focusing on negative indicators, that is, by looking for manifestations of illegitimacy, such as organized opposition to a state's constitution, or severe government repression in response to such opposition. When these two criteria are applied, the political institutions in New Brunswick can be described as politically legitimate, and those in Northern Ireland as comparatively illegitimate.

In New Brunswick, one of the most salient features of provincial politics has been the absence of any major movement opposing the constitutional system. In recent history, only two political parties, the Liberals and the Progressive Conservatives, have been serious contenders for power, and both have been strong supporters of the status quo. No other party has elected a representative to the Legislature since 1920 when the United Farmers achieved temporary success by electing nine members. The lack of success of such third parties has been attributed by Thorburn (1961) to the fact that "New Brunswickers, influenced by Acadian and Loyalist traditions, are conservative and give a cool reception to any doctrine that seeks to upset the established pattern in the province" (p. 103). A recent exception to this general tendency is the Parti Acadien, a socialist party founded in 1971 and dedicated to defending Acadian interests. The party proclaims in its political manifesto that it "works within the 'established system'" and that its candidates "still believe in the effectiveness of our parliamentary system" (*Parti Acadien*, 1972, p. 19). However, the party, which in 1972 demanded simply a better deal for Acadians, had by 1977 adopted a program calling for the creation of a separate province for the Acadians of northern New Brunswick.

In contrast to New Brunswick's legitimacy, Northern Ireland has been troubled since its foundation in 1920 by substantial opposition to its

Table 13

Attitude to the Constitutional Position of Northern Ireland, 1968

Attitude	% of Protestants (n = 749)	% of Catholics (n = 526)	% of Total (n = 1,278)
Approve	69	34	54
Disapprove	10	35	20
Don't Know	22	32	26
Total	101	101	100

Note: $\chi^2(2) = 178$, $p < .0001$; $V = .374$. The data are from the Northern Ireland Loyalty Survey.

very existence. The Northern Ireland Loyalty Survey, conducted just prior to the current civil disturbances, showed that a fifth of the population disapproved of the existing constitutional arrangements (see Table 13). The bulk of this opposition has come from the minority Catholic population which has traditionally favoured union with the Republic of Ireland. The traditional political representatives of this opposition have been the Nationalist Party and the Republican Party—the former espousing peaceful means to achieve union, the latter openly advocating the use of physical force. Between 1921 and 1969 these two parties averaged approximately 23 percent of the vote in the Northern Ireland elections.

In the first election of 1921, the two parties elected twelve members of Parliament; all twelve refused to take their seats in the House of Commons. When, several years later, members of the Nationalist Party did sit in the House, they declined to accept the designation of official opposition. This policy was not reversed until 1965 when the Nationalist leader, Eddie McAteer, formally became leader of the opposition. In 1971, however, the members of the opposition, composed principally of the Nationalist Party and the Social Democratic and Labour Party (SDLP), withdrew from the House of Commons to create a dissident parliament, the "Assembly of the Northern Irish People" (see H. Kelly, 1972, pp. 51–55). While the new assembly provided a temporary forum for the leaders of the Catholic minority, it was largely ineffectual and of short duration.

Opposition to the constitutional system has also been reflected in various mass protests, including strikes, work stoppages, and boycotts. In 1971, for example, more than 26,000 largely Catholic households engaged in a political strike against the regime by withholding their payments of rents and rates (Deutsch and Magowan, 1973/1974, p. 133). This strike did not end until December 1973, when introduction of a new constitution led the way to a coalition government including the Catholic SDLP. During this same period Protestant workers also protested the possibility of constitutional changes with a series of work stoppages. During the first stoppage in March 1973, organized by the Loyalist Association of Workers, approximately 190,000 workers stayed at home, thereby closing down transportation services, power supplies, and many factories. A second one-day general strike, in February 1973, resulted in a total electrical blackout, in addition to the closedown of schools, shops, and factories. Much more serious, however, was the general strike in May 1974, organized by the Ulster Workers' Council against the new executive. The strike, lasting more than a week and bringing the province to a standstill, resulted in the collapse of the new government and, with it, the new constitution. In Britain, the lord chancellor called the strike a "conspiracy against the state," noting that judges in previous times "would have had no difficulty in describing it as high treason because it's an attempt to overthrow the authority of the Queen in Parliament" (Fisk, 1975, p. 223).

The application of repressive measures by the Northern Ireland government in order to maintain its authority is a further indication of the rather weak legitimacy of that political system. Frequent recourse to such measures has been necessary because the usual democratic processes, based on the due process of law, have not been adequate to ensure the continued existence of the state. Since 1922 the Northern Ireland government has possessed "special" powers which have enabled the minister of home affairs to "take all such steps and issue all such orders as may be necessary for preserving the peace and maintaining the order" (Calvert, 1968, p. 381). The application of this act, instituted largely in response to the threat of terrorist attacks from the military wing of the Republican Party, the Irish Republican Army, resulted in measures which deviated from traditional democratic practices: arrest without charge, imprisonment without trial, search without warrant, and the banning of public assembly. The most notorious of these practices, "internment,"—the imprisonment without trial of those suspected of acting "in a manner prejudicial to the preservation of the peace and maintenance of order" (Boyle, Hadden, and Hillyard, 1975, p. 8)—has been used at regular intervals (see Fig. 3). During the period 1971–75 alone, approximately 2,200 orders leading to internment were issued in less than four years (Rose, 1976, p. 24).

The size of the security forces in Northern Ireland provides a partial indicator of this government repression and, by implication, of the opposition to the state. In 1960, several years before the outbreak of the

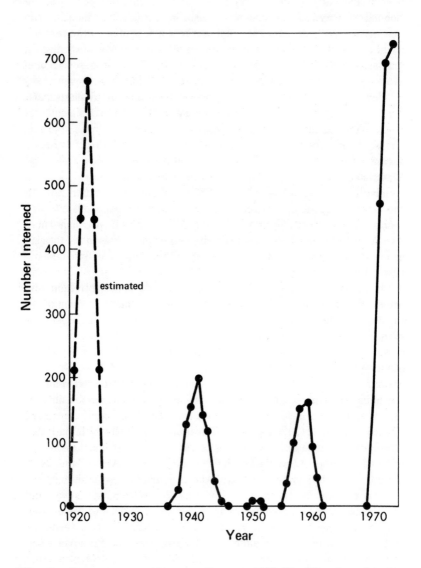

Fig. 3. Internment in Northern Ireland, 1920–73. (The data for the three year moving averages are from Barritt and Carter, 1972; Boyle, Hadden, and Hillyard, 1975; Deutsch and Magowan, 1973, 1974; and "Does detention curb violence?" 1973.)

recent episodes of civil disorder, the members of the police force—
including both the Royal Ulster Constabulary (RUC) and the part-time
Ulster Special Constabulary (USC) — already amounted to an impres-
sive 111 per 10,000 population (Rutan, 1965, pp. 384–85). This must be
compared with New Brunswick where, at the 1971 census, policemen
numbered only 14 per 10,000 population. By 1976, after several years of
violence, the size of the security services in Northern Ireland had grown
considerably and included: 5,123 members of the RUC, 4,711 members
of the RUC Reserve, 7,700 members of the Ulster Defence Regiment,
and 22,000 members of the British Army (Northern Ireland, Information Service, 1976). Taken together, the Northern Ireland security
forces thus numbered 259 members per 10,000 population.

The relative legitimacy and illegitimacy of the two communities can
be situated in a broader context by applying the political illegitimacy
scale proposed by Gurr and McClelland (1971). The scale is constructed
by coding manifestations of illegitimacy according to their object, form,
scope, and persistence, for a ten-year period. On this scale, with a maximum score of thirty possible, Northern Ireland would receive a twenty-
three, for the period 1965–74, higher than any of the nations studied by
Gurr and McClelland, including pre-Civil War Spain. New Brunswick,
on the other hand, would receive a score of one, placing it at the low end
of the scale with the Netherlands.

GOVERNMENTAL EFFICACY

A further component of political stability is the extent to which a government can "make and carry out prompt and relevant decisions in
response to political challenges" (Eckstein, 1971, p. 65). Government
efficacy contributes to constitutional durability: it is the initial variable
in a causal sequence which links efficacy to legitimacy, legitimacy to
civil order, and civil order to durability (see Gurr and McClelland, 1971,
p. 79). Operational measurement of efficacy is not an easy task, particularly because of the difficulty in evaluating the "relevant decisions" and
"political challenges" which define efficacy. A useful indicator of such
efficacy, however, is the frequency and circumstances of government
turnover. Frequent changes in executive personnel, particularly when
such changes are the consequence of elite dissension, may be assumed to
indicate a lack of decisional efficacy. Support for this assumption may be
found in the very high .91 correlation between this indicator and an
efficacy summary score, constructed by Gurr and McClelland (1971)
from seven measures of efficacy.

When compared with other western countries, the executives in both
New Brunswick and Northern Ireland have had a relatively low rate of

Table 14

*Indices of Government Change-over for
Selected Countries, 1921–72*

Country	Cabinet	Chief executive	Governing party	Mean
France	123	106	n.a.	115
United Kingdom	48	29	17	31
Canada	29	17	13	20
Ireland	31	15	10	19
United States	23	17	8	16
NEW BRUNSWICK	21	17	10	16
NORTHERN IRELAND	21	12	1	11

Note: Each index was constructed by calculating $G/Y \times 100$, where G represents the number of government change-overs and Y the number of years. The index measures, therefore, the number of government change-overs per hundred years. A cabinet change-over is defined as a change in the chief executive or at least half of the cabinet ministers. A change-over of the governing party is defined as a change in the party affiliation of the chief executive. The data are calculated from Banks, 1971; *Canadian Parliamentary Guide*, 1898–1975; Chubb, 1970; Pierce, 1973; *Statesman's Year-Book*, 1864–1975; and Whitaker, 1869–1976.

turnover (see Table 14). Major cabinet changes—defined as the turnover of the prime minister or half of his ministers—have occurred, on average, only slightly less than every five years; and in many cases, these changes have amounted only to a shuffle of the existing ministers to new posts, rather than a wholesale injection of new blood. The prime ministers have generally been more secure than the cabinet as a whole, particularly in Northern Ireland, where the prime ministers have averaged almost nine years in office. In New Brunswick, the average has been slightly more than five years.

If the rate of cabinet turnover in both communities has been similar, the causes of these turnovers have been considerably different. In New Brunswick, the major mechanism has been the decision of the electorate at the polls. The constitution provides that the legislatures are elected for a period of five years unless earlier dissolved, and the New Brunswick voters have traditionally re-elected each government at least once. Since 1925, this has resulted in an average tenure for each political party of eleven years in government; and, in recent years, each prime minister has continued in office as long as his party was re-elected. It is the changing electoral returns which have ensured a changing cabinet by returning the opposition party to power about once each decade (see Fig. 4). The Liberal leader, John McNair, became prime minister in

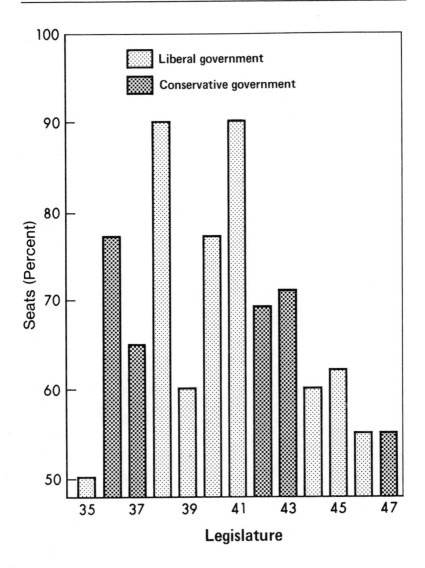

Fig. 4. Government support in the New Brunswick Legislative Assembly, 1921–72. (The data are from Scarrow, 1962; and *Canadian Parliamentary Guide*, 1898–1975.)

1939 and held office until his defeat by the Conservatives, led by Hugh John Flemming, twelve years later. Flemming, in turn, was replaced by the Liberal, Louis Robichaud, when his party was defeated at the polls in 1960. Robichaud continued as prime minister for ten years before giving way to Richard Hatfield in 1970, when the Conservatives were again returned to power. As well, those cabinet changes which took place during each party's tenure were often the consequence of the electoral defeat of incumbent cabinet ministers.

Northern Ireland, however, has been essentially a one-party-dominant political system: the Unionist Party held power continuously for more than fifty-one years, from the first election of the Northern Ireland Parliament in 1921 until its prorogation in 1972 (see Fig. 5). Cabinet changes have not, therefore, been the consequence of the changing preferences of the electorate, as in New Brunswick. They have been, rather, the result of the ill health of incumbent ministers or of internal party strife. During the early period of Northern Ireland's government, cabinet office appeared largely to be a lifelong sinecure. But in the more recent period, the tenure of cabinet office became very unstable as internal government conflict and external political pressure resulted in rapid turnover of ministers, particularly in the key positions.

The first prime minister of Northern Ireland, James Craig (later Lord Craigavon), governed for nineteen years without a major cabinet change, until his death in office. As early as 1936, Nicholas Mansergh commented on the "static" character of the Northern Ireland ministry: "It is discouraging to the younger members of the party, it deadens the party policy and it destroys the benefit of change in departmental administration" (p. 235). Critics within the party demanded the inclusion of younger members in the cabinet and one parliamentary secretary observed: "This Government has been too long in office and is in the main composed of tired and jaded men" (Lawrence, 1965, p. 65). In spite of this, John Andrews, Craig's successor, continued to govern with a virtually identical cabinet to that of Craig, until internal party strife forced his resignation. The new prime minister, Basil Brooke (later Viscount Brookeborough), upon his entry into office in 1943, was obliged to make the declaration that: "The office of a Cabinet Minister is not, and should not be, a life appointment" (Lawrence, 1965, pp. 70–71). Nevertheless, Brooke himself went on to establish a new United Kingdom record by holding cabinet office continuously for more than thirty-three years, including twenty years as prime minister (Harbinson, 1973, p. 145). First elected to the Northern Ireland House of Commons in 1929, Brooke was forced to retire from Parliament in 1968 because of ill health, at which time he was succeeded by his son, John Brooke.

If the early years of cabinet government were marked by an absence of change, the last years of the Northern Ireland Parliament were distinguished by an accelerated turnover of ministers, until the demise of the constitutional system in 1972. In contrast to the long terms in office

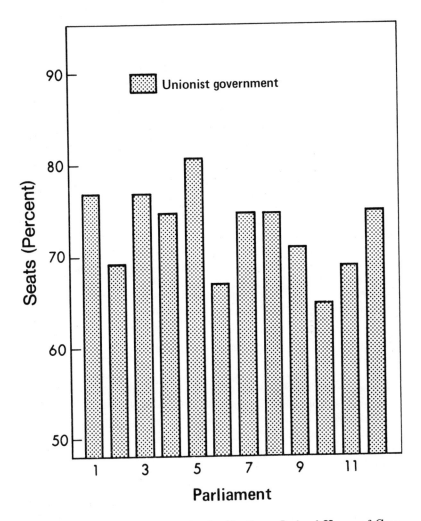

Fig. 5. Government support in the Northern Ireland House of Commons, 1921–72. (The data are from Elliott, 1973.)

of Craig (nineteen years) and Brooke (twenty years), the last two prime ministers governed for only brief periods: Chichester-Clark for only two years, and Faulkner for only one. The crucial Ministry of Home Affairs, which had responsibility for domestic security, had only four ministerial changes between 1921 and 1955, as compared to eleven between 1956 and 1972. Of all the major cabinet changes between 1921

Table 15
Ministerial Change-overs, 1921–72

Ministry[a]	1921–37	1938–55	1956–72	Total
New Brunswick				
Cabinet	5	3	2	11
Prime Minister	5	2	2	9
Attorney-General	5	1	5	11
Treasurer	2	3	2	7
Public Works	2	2	4	8
Northern Ireland				
Cabinet	0	4	7	11
Prime Minister	0	2	4	6
Home Affairs	0	4	11	15
Finance	1	3	5	9
Labour	1	6	6	13

Note: The data are from *Canadian Parliamentary Guide*, 1898–1975, and Whitaker, 1869–1976.

a In recent years some of these ministries have changed name. For example, in New Brunswick, the treasurer became the minister of finance (1963), the attorney-general became the minister of justice (1967), and the minister of public works became the minister of highways (1968). In Northern Ireland, the Ministry of Labour was superseded by the Ministry of Health and Social Services (1965).

and 1972, almost two-thirds occurred during the last sixteen years (see Table 15). During the final years of the Parliament, each successive prime minister found himself incapable of constructing a cabinet that could withstand either the internal or external political pressures.

Internal strife became particularly evident with the government of Prime Minister Terence O'Neill when, in 1966, a petition calling for his resignation was signed by twelve Unionist members of Parliament. Disputes over policy matters led to the dismissal of two cabinet ministers (Harry West in 1967, and William Craig in 1968) and the resignation of three others (William Morgan, Brian Faulkner, and James Chichester-Clark in 1969). At a meeting of the parliamentary party in 1969, only twenty-three of the thirty-six Unionist MPs were willing to give their leader a vote of confidence, while ten others walked out before the vote. O'Neill's successor, Chichester-Clark, survived less than two years, resigning when he too was unable to get the necessary backing for his policies. Brian Faulkner took office as prime minister in 1971 but, in the face of a rapidly worsening security situation and the government's inability to cope with the civil violence, the Northern Ireland Parliament was suspended one year later. Following the introduction of a new constitution in 1973, Faulkner took on the new post of chief minister, but was confronted with mounting Protestant opposition—both inside and outside the assembly—and the executive was forced to resign less than five months later. This most recent failure of the executive to sustain itself in office is perhaps the clearest indication of the lack of governmental efficacy in Northern Ireland.

The contrast between the two communities may be summarized by comparing their scores on the scale of government changes with that of other nations ranked on the same scale by Gurr and McClelland (1971). Taking the period 1965–74, Northern Ireland ranks lower in governmental efficacy than any of the modern-day polities, except Italy. On a scale which ranges from a low of -2.0 to a high of $+2.0$, Northern Ireland receives a score of -0.8. New Brunswick, on the other hand, ranks near the top of the scale, just ahead of the Philippines, with a score of $+1.4$.

CIVIL ORDER

A final component of political stability is civil order or, quite simply, "the absence of collective resorts to violence" (Eckstein, 1971, p. 32). The resort to violence as a means of bringing about political change is a symptom of malfunction. It implies a lack of political legitimacy and governmental efficacy. Civil order signals the continued endurance of a society just as civil violence, described by Marx as the midwife of an old society pregnant with a new one, heralds its imminent demise. Thus, the escalating violence of the late 1960s in Northern Ireland was the harbinger of the political system's collapse in 1972. The recurrent cycles of violence in that community indicated its intrinsic instability, just as the continuous pattern of civil order in New Brunswick reflects its inherent stability.

Since its establishment in 1784, New Brunswick has experienced neither civil war nor rebellion, nor indeed any attempt to bring about constitutional change by violent means. Major political changes have been achieved peacefully. The attainment of responsible government, although aided by the 1837 uprisings in Upper and Lower Canada, excited no great clamour in New Brunswick. Similarly, the entry of New Brunswick into the Canadian Confederation, although the subject of two bitter election campaigns, was accomplished peacefully and accepted with "uncheerful resignation" (MacNutt, 1963; Baker, 1974). The exceptions to this general pattern are found in three instances of sectarian violence. In 1847 an armed party of Catholics impeded an Orange procession near Woodstock, leading to a shooting battle between

Table 16

Major Civil Disturbances since 1800

Initial year	Primary location	Conflict behaviour	Precipitating event	Approximate duration	Known casualties
New Brunswick					
1849	Saint John	riot	Orange procession	1 day	12 dead
1875	Caraquet	riot	School tax	3 days	2 dead 2 injured
Northern Ireland					
1813	Belfast	riot	Orange procession	1 day	2 dead 4 injured
1832	Belfast	riot	Parliamentary election	1 day	4 dead
1852	Belfast	riot	Parliamentary election	1 day	1 dead
1857	Belfast	riots	Orange procession	2 months	undetermined
1864	Belfast	riots	Nationalist celebration	2 weeks	12 dead 100 injured
1872	Belfast	riots	Nationalist celebration	1 week	5 dead 243 injured
1880	Belfast	riot	Catholic procession	4 days	2 dead 8 injured
1886	Belfast	riots	Home Rule Bill	4 months	32 dead 371 injured
1907	Belfast	riot	Unknown	3 days	2 dead 11 injured
1920	Belfast Londonderry	riots assassinations guerrilla war	Partition of Ireland	2 years	544 dead

Year	Location	Conflict behaviour	Event	Duration	Casualties
1932	Belfast	riot	Hunger march	1 day	2 dead 35 injured
1935	Belfast	riots	Orange processions	3 weeks	11 dead 574 injured
1956	Fermanagh Armagh	guerrilla war	IRA campaign	5 years	19 dead
1968[a]	Belfast Londonderry	demonstrations riots general strikes assassinations guerrilla war	Civil rights marches	more than 8 years	1,691 dead 18,312 injured

Note: The table includes only those disturbances which resulted in death. The definitions of conflict behaviour used are those proposed by Rummel (1963) and include assassination, general strike, guerrilla war, purge, riot, anti-government demonstration, and revolution. The data are calculated from Barritt and Carter, 1972; Bell, 1974; Boyd, 1970; Budge and O'Leary, 1973; "December fatalities," 1977; MacNutt, 1963; De Paor, 1971; Rose, 1971; Senior, 1972; and Stanley, 1972.

a The data for this period are based on events up to and including 31 December 1976 only.

the two groups. Although there were no fatalities, thirty-nine persons were subsequently sentenced and imprisoned (MacNutt, 1963, p. 347). A more serious disturbance occurred in 1849 when an Orange parade through a Catholic neighbourhood of Saint John led to a street battle which the city's police force was unable to control. According to Senior (1972), "about fifty shots were fired and perhaps a dozen people killed before troops restored order" (p. 64). A further outbreak of violence occurred in 1875 as a result of opposition to the Common Schools Act, an act which had established a non-sectarian school system supported from public funds. Catholic resistance to the act culminated in bloodshed in Caraquet when a party of constables and "volunteers" — including Orangemen — attempted to arrest a group of Acadian demonstrators. In the shooting which followed, one "volunteer" and one Acadian were killed. The violence of the "Caraquet riots," if not accidental, was certainly unexpected in the New Brunswick context: "No one had ever anticipated that two men might die by gunfire while arrests were being made" (Stanley, 1972, p. 31).

When compared with the long history of recurring violence in Northern Ireland, these New Brunswick events appear relatively inconsequential. Beginning with the first religious riot in 1813, violent clashes between opposing political and religious groups have been a regular feature of Northern Irish life. Since the beginning of the nineteenth century, the intensity of these confrontations has increased, reaching a peak with the civil disturbances which began in 1968. In general, the incidents of violence have centred around particular political events which have tended to exacerbate religious differences in the population. In typical cases, clashes between opposing groups during an election or procession have been sufficient to set off serious rioting, involving "street fighting, burning of houses and schools, and conflicts with the police" (Budge and O'Leary, 1973, p. 91). The frequency of these disturbances is illustrated by Table 16, although only those events which resulted in deaths are included.

Among the worst of the nineteenth-century disturbances were the riots of 1886 which developed in response to the introduction of the Irish Home Rule Bill by the Liberal government at Westminster. The bill met with vehement opposition from the Protestants of Northern Ireland — opposition which was fanned by the inflammatory oratory of a leading Conservative politician, Lord Randolph Churchill. Churchill's visit to Belfast, followed later by the defeat of the Home Rule Bill on the second reading, sparked sustained rioting with attacks by Protestant mobs on Catholic homes and on the Irish constabulary. Winston Churchill, in the biography of his father, notes: "Firearms were freely used by the police and combatants. Houses were sacked and men and women killed. The disturbances were savage, repeated and prolonged" (Boyd, 1970, p. 123). The riots, which began on 3 June, the day after the defeat of the Home Rule Bill, continued sporadically until 25 October. During this time, thirty-two people were killed and 371 injured.

Far more serious disturbances occurred between 1920 and 1922, following the creation of Northern Ireland as a semi-autonomous state. The Irish Republican Army (IRA) engaged in guerrilla warfare against the new regime, striking sporadically at military and police barracks. In response to the terrorist tactics of the IRA, the British government in 1920 created the Special Constabulary, an auxilliary police force with an exclusively Protestant membership, which led violent attacks on the Catholic population. The violence of these armed forces was more than matched, however, by the mob violence on the streets. On one day in July 1921, 161 homes were burned, fifteen persons killed, and sixty-eight wounded in attacks by Protestant mobs on Catholic districts in Belfast. Bowyer Bell (1974) describes the mob violence: "Mobs, unrestrained by the police or army, ran loose firing and beating. Homes were burned. Men, women, and children were shot down in the streets. Vengeful Catholics struck back with counter-terror" (p. 29). The total number of deaths during this period was 544, and included the assassination of two members of Parliament. In 1922 alone, 232 people were killed and nearly 1,000 wounded (Arthur, 1974, p. 11).

The most recent disorders, beginning in 1968 and continuing until the present time, have been the most bloody of the disturbances in the modern history of Northern Ireland. These disturbances began with the peaceful marches of civil rights demonstrators protesting political discrimination against Catholics in employment and housing, and escalated into internal war. One of the first major demonstrations, a civil rights march in Londonderry in October 1968, was broken up by the police with what a Royal Commission headed by Lord Cameron was later to describe as "needless violence." In subsequent demonstrations, notably at Armagh and Burntollet, right-wing Protestant counter-demonstrators clashed with the civil rights marchers while the Royal Ulster Constabulary looked on (cf. Egan and McCormack, 1969). These events were followed by a series of confrontations between demonstrators and counter-demonstrators and police which continued throughout the year 1969. In the months of July and August alone, civil unrest resulted in the death of ten persons and the injury of 899 others (Northern Ireland, Tribunal of Inquiry, 1972).

The violent rioting of 1969, and the failure of the existing security forces to maintain civil order, led to the intervention of the British

Table 17
Deaths from Political Violence in Northern Ireland, 1969–77

Year	Police	Army[a]	Civilian	Total	Cumulative total
1969	–	–	13	13	13
1970	2	–	23	25	38
1971	11	48	114	173	211
1972	17	128	322	467	678
1973	13	67	171	250	928
1974	15	37	165	218	1,146
1975	11	18	220	249	1,395
1976	23	29	243	295	1,690
1977	14	29	67	110	1,800
Total	106	356	1,338	1,800	1,800

Note: The data are from "Table of casualties," 1978.
a   Includes the Ulster Defence Regiment.

army. The violence also stimulated the growth of paramilitary groups, formed for both protection and aggression. On the Catholic side, the Irish Republican Army actively engaged in a campaign of terrorist bombings and selective assassinations. On the Protestant side, the IRA was matched by more than forty armed associations, the largest being the Ulster Defence Association (UDA), but also including the Ulster Freedom Fighters (UFF), the Red Hand, the Ulster Volunteer Force (UVF), the Loyalist Defence Force, and the Orange Volunteers. Thus, beginning in 1969, the province experienced continuous waves of bombings, assassinations, rioting, and mass intimidation. By 1977, political violence had resulted in a total of 1,800 dead and more than 18,000 injured, most of whom were civilians (see Table 17). The British army had recorded more than 4,500 explosions and more than 22,000 shooting incidents. Further, following the introduction of internment, the army had searched up to 75,000 households, or just less than a fifth of households in the province (Rose, 1976, p. 25).

The Northern Ireland violence has been sufficiently extensive that it encompasses all three of the major dimensions of civil strife: turmoil, conspiracy, and internal war (cf. Gurr, 1968). It has covered the whole gamut of conflict behaviours, including demonstrations, riots, assassinations, terrorism, and guerrilla war. Ranked on the civil strife scale, Northern Ireland scores higher than any of the polities studied by Gurr and McClelland (1971), except pre-Civil War Spain and post-revolutionary Mexico. By contrast, New Brunswick's strife during the same period

Table 18

Summary Scores of Political Stability, 1965–74

Component[b]	% Deviation from Twelve-Nation Average[a]	
	New Brunswick	Northern Ireland
Durability	+122	−60
Legitimacy	+82	−348
Efficacy	+211	−278
Civil Order	+33	−508

a The twelve nations are the modern-day polities studied by Gurr and McClelland (1971) and include Canada, Columbia, France, Italy, Mexico, Netherlands, Philippines, Spain, Sweden, Tunisia, West Germany, and Yugoslavia.
b Efficacy is measured using the scale for elite conflict in government incumbency (see Gurr and McClelland, 1971, p. 61). Scores for legitimacy and civil order are obtained by reversing the signs of the measures of illegitimacy and civil strife.

(1965–74) has been largely confined to the turmoil dimension: its principal manifestation being the various demonstrations of 1968 and 1972 in Moncton, Fredericton, and Bathurst, all of which were comparatively non-violent. Since the Caraquet riots of more than a century ago, the amount of civil strife in New Brunswick has been relatively insignificant.

Study of the various components of political stability thus leads to the unequivocal conclusion that New Brunswick is stable and Northern Ireland unstable. Comparison of the two communities with the nations studied by Gurr and McClelland (1971) demonstrates clearly that New Brunswick and Northern Ireland are at opposite poles in all the components of political stability (see Table 18). In terms of constitutional durability, New Brunswick ranks particularly high, having guarded essentially the same political structures—with gradual modifications to cope with changing circumstances—for almost two centuries. This durability has been supported, as the study of modern-day New Brunswick reveals, by consistently high levels of political legitimacy, governmental efficacy, and civil order. Northern Ireland, by contrast, ranks relatively low in terms of constitutional durability, having seen the failure of three distinct political constitutions since its foundation in 1920. The first such constitutional arrangement, based on the Northern Ireland Parliament, was the most long lasting of these; but its tenuousness was underlined by consistently high levels of political illegitimacy and recurring incidents of civil strife. These, combined with the striking decrease in governmental efficacy during the 1960s, marked the collapse of the political regime in 1972.

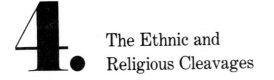

4. The Ethnic and Religious Cleavages

Historically, the process of nation-building gives rise to conflict along two primary lines of cleavage (Lipset and Rokkan, 1967, p. 14). First, conflict occurs along an ethnic cleavage as the dominant nation-building culture attempts to assimilate localized counter-cultures within its territorial boundaries. The attempt by the dominant culture to impose a standard language, a uniform law, and a central administration inevitably meets with resistance from these local cultures. Second, conflict occurs along a religious cleavage as the nation-state centralizes its control and expands its power, threatening the traditional privileges of the church. The attempts of the state to gain jurisdiction of problems relating to the family, morality, and education meet with opposition from the church, which sees its authority being usurped. Insofar as one religious denomination may be allied with the state, often as a "national church," the dispute between church and state frequently appears as an interdenominational conflict.

The long-term effects of these conflicts are determined to a significant degree by the relationship between the two cleavages. Where these cleavages are congruent, resolution of the conflicts is more difficult; the issues tend to accumulate as new disputes reinforce traditional ones. Antagonisms build up between the major subcultures making future reconciliation difficult. However, where these cleavages crosscut, resolution of the conflicts is facilitated; each issue may be settled, independently, as it arises. Current conflicts are not unduly complicated by traditional ones. Lipset (1963), in discussing the appearance of major social issues in the western nations, poses the question:

> Were these issues dealt with one by one, with each more or less solved before the next arose; or did the problems accumulate, so that traditional sources of cleavage mixed with newer ones? Resolving tensions one at a time contributes to a stable political system; carrying over issues from one historical period to another makes for a political atmosphere characterized by bitterness and frustration rather than tolerance and compromise. (p. 71)

In both New Brunswick and Northern Ireland, the ethnic and religious cleavages which developed during the early period of colonization have proved to be extremely durable. The ethnic conflict between the dominant English culture and the local culture, and the religious conflict between the state and the Roman Catholic Church, have continued to be the major sources of social division over the past century. However, while the nature of the conflicts in the two communities has been similar, the patterns they have assumed have an important difference: in one community the conflicts have been crosscutting, and in the other, congruent. The impact of this difference is visible in the varying degrees of success the two communities have experienced in resolving their respective conflicts.

THE ETHNIC CLEAVAGE

Both New Brunswick and Northern Ireland are biethnic communities. The dominant ethnic group in both is of British origin and constitutes almost two-thirds of the population. The minority ethnic group is French in New Brunswick, and Irish in Northern Ireland. Max Weber's (1968) definition of ethnic groups as "those human groups that entertain a subjective belief in their common descent because of similarities in physical type or of custom or both, or because of memories of colonization and emigration" (p. 389) aptly describes each of these groups. While many years, indeed centuries, have passed since the original colonization, the identity of each ethnic group continues to be strong. This is reflected particularly in their divergent national allegiances, and in their distinctive national symbols (see chapter 2).

The early history of ethnic conflict in the two communities is typical of the process of nation-building (and empire-building) where a dominant centralizing culture attempts to assimilate localized counter-cultures by imposing a standard language, a uniform law, and a central administration. In New Brunswick, the conflict between the two cultures began in 1713 when the French colony of Acadia was ceded to the British. Early attempts to impose the English language and British allegiance on the Acadians met with little success and the British consequently undertook a massive deportation of the local French-speaking inhabitants: between 1755 and 1763, an estimated 7,000 French Acadians were exiled (R. A. LeBlanc, 1967). Their places were taken, first, by settlers from New England and then, later, in the years following the American Revolution, by United Empire Loyalists. An estimated 14,000 Loyalists settled in the area which is now New Brunswick (MacNutt, 1963, p. 41). The British, thus, effectively, but brutally, consolidated their control over the colony.

In Northern Ireland, the conflict between the British and the Irish also has its origins in military conquest. Following their victory in the northern province of Ulster in the early seventeenth century, the British confiscated major tracts of land and deported large numbers of the native Irish inhabitants to the West Indies (Leyburn, 1962, p. 125). Between 1610 and 1640 an estimated 100,000 new colonists, largely loyal Scots, were settled on the confiscated land. The remaining Irish inhabitants, however, fiercely resisted both these new settlements and the attempts by the British to impose their government and their language on them. A massive uprising in 1641, which resulted in the massacre of thousands of Scottish settlers, was brutally suppressed several years later by the arrival of Oliver Cromwell at the head of a vengeful army. Civil war between British settlers and Irish natives broke out again near the end of the seventeenth century, culminating in 1690 with the victory of the British Protestant supporters of William of Orange at the Battle of the Boyne.

The focus of modern discord, particularly in Northern Ireland, is largely on the conflicting national allegiances and constitutional preferences of the different ethnic groups. The British-origin majority in Northern Ireland has traditionally favoured the maintenance of the union between Northern Ireland and Great Britain. "Apart altogether from their social and spiritual links with Great Britain, the Ulstermen are Unionist because, as they see it, the constitutional (and economic) links with Great Britain are the sole guarantee for the preservation of their identity" (Heslinga, 1962, p. 57). The Irish, on the other hand, have traditionally supported the breaking of ties with Britain and the establishment of an independent, united Ireland. This reflects both their shared national identity as "Irish," and a traditional perception of Britain as a foreign invader. A leading Orangeman summarizes his view of the conflict: "Ulster's antagonisms have their basis in the political attitudes and aspirations of the majority, who declare for union with Great Britain, and of the minority who want a United Ireland. It is a question of nationality" (Long, 1972, p. 23).

Prior to 1920, the conflict of national identities manifested itself primarily on the question of "Home Rule." The beginnings of the dispute were marked in 1873 by the formation by the Home Rule League, an organization whose primary goal was self-government for Ireland. This objective found instant support among the native Irish population, which looked upon the movement as a means not only to preserve Irish culture, but also to develop Irish industry and to abolish landlordism. The British-origin population of Ireland—located largely in the northern province of Ulster—rallied against the proposal, however. In their eyes the establishment of an Irish Parliament would weaken the link with Great Britain, a link which could be justified "on the grounds of racial sentiment" (Sinclair, 1912/1970, p. 172), by which was meant their continuing loyalty to Great Britain.

To the ethnic division was thus added a political dimension, dividing the Northern Ireland population into opposing camps of "unionists" and "nationalists." Conflict between these camps on the question of Home Rule frequently erupted in violence, notably in 1886 when the Home Rule Bill was first introduced, and then again in 1920 when Home Rule was granted to twenty-six of the thirty-two counties in Ireland. The creation of an independent Ireland did not reduce ethnic conflict in Northern Ireland; it simply redefined the political dimension. Henceforth the Irish minority in Northern Ireland demanded not "Home Rule" but rather a "United Ireland," in effect, an end to the partition between northern and southern counties. The British-origin population continued to demand the maintenance of the union with Great Britain, but it was a union which now excluded southern Ireland.

Since the 1920 partition of Ireland, the question of Northern Ireland's constitutional future has dominated political life. The major political parties, the Ulster Unionist Party and the Nationalist Party (largely superseded by the Social Democratic and Labour Party in 1970) have been essentially one-issue parties, and all subsequent elections have taken the guise of referendums on the status of the union with Great Britain, pitting British unionists against Irish nationalists. Political campaigning, invariably featuring militant sectarian marches and provocative displays of rival national emblems, has frequently culminated in violent confrontations between the rival blocs. The character of this polarization was vividly illustrated in 1964 when four days of rioting broke out in West Belfast after the minister of home affairs directed the police to remove an Irish flag displayed in the window of the Republican

Party headquarters. Ian Paisley, the Protestant leader who had initiated the request for the flag's removal, stated: "I don't accept that any area in Ulster is Republican and I don't want to see the Tricolour flying here. I intend to see that the Union Jack flies everywhere and that it keeps flying" (Marrinan, 1973, p. 82).

The continuing prominence of ethnic conflict was again evident in 1973 in the public reaction to the decision of the governments of Northern Ireland and the Republic of Ireland to establish a Council of Ireland. This council, with equal representation from both Irish governments, was to be a forum for economic and social cooperation. While the council's powers were extremely limited, it was widely perceived as a first step toward a united Ireland. Thus, reaction to the council conformed to the traditional ethnic division: the British majority opposed it, the Irish minority supported it. Opposition was manifested, first, in the massive electoral victory of the council's opponents in the 1974 Westminster elections, and, second, by a general strike which brought the province to a standstill. This led not only to the cancellation of the proposed Council of Ireland, but also to the prorogation of the Northern Ireland Assembly.

In New Brunswick, by contrast, the divergent national allegiances have not been the major source of ethnic conflict. This is undoubtedly due to the fact that time and distance have greatly weakened the ties between the Acadians and France and between the Loyalists and Britain. Some hostility was aroused among English New Brunswickers in the late 1960s when General de Gaulle proposed to organize the solidarity of the French community on both sides of the Atlantic and noted: "I think particularly of those 250,000 Acadians who are implanted in New Brunswick and who have also kept for France, its language and its soul, a very moving fidelity" (Wade, 1974, p. 52). Although De Gaulle's initiative did lead to closer cultural ties between the Acadians and France, the issue was soon forgotten. The relationship between the Acadians and Quebec, however, is a potentially more volatile question. The leaders of the Société des Acadiens du Nouveau-Brunswick and the Parti Acadien have both indicated that the annexation of the French-language areas of New Brunswick to the province (or independent state) of Quebec would be seriously considered if Acadian attempts to achieve greater autonomy—either within New Brunswick or as a separate Acadian province—were not successful. Nevertheless, it appears that only a minority—no more than a quarter—of the Acadians would support such a step (De la Garde, 1966) and the question has not yet been fully politicized.

The major source of ethnic conflict in New Brunswick has been over the question of language rights. English has traditionally been the prin-

Table 19

*Linguistic Character of the French-origin Population
in New Brunswick, 1921–71*

Year	% Unilingual French	% Unilingual English	% Bilingual English-French	N
1921	55	1	44	121,111
1931	52	4	43	136,999
1941	49	5	45	163,934
1951	50	7	43	197,631
1961	47	10	43	232,127
1971	42	9	49	235,025

Note: In 1921 and 1931 the census indicated the language only of those who were ten years of age and older. The percentages given here for 1921 and 1931 are estimates for the total French-origin population based on the assumption that those under the age of ten were unilingual, speaking only their mother tongue. The table is calculated from Canada, Dominion Bureau of Statistics, 1873–1971; and Canada, Statistics Canada, 1973–77.

cipal language in the province, a fact which reflects not only the political and commercial dominance of the English ethnic group, but also their overwhelming numerical superiority during the early years of New Brunswick's development. (For example, in 1871, the French-origin population of New Brunswick constituted only 16 percent of the total population, and was relatively isolated in the rural north.) Although relations with family and friends within the Acadian group are conducted in French, the contacts with the business and political world are usually in English. This has encouraged the widespread use of English among the Acadian population and a gradual process of assimilation: between 1921 and 1971, for instance, the proportion of Acadians unable to speak French increased from 1 percent to 9 percent (see Table 19). In turn, however, the numerical growth of the Acadian population has created pressure on the various segments of New Brunswick society to provide additional French-language services. These demands for the greater use of French generally have met with strong opposition from the English-speaking population who fear the loss of their previously dominant position. Since only a small proportion (amounting to about 5 percent in 1971) of the English population is bilingual, any decision to provide services in both English and French languages is perceived by them to be costly, inconvenient, and a potential threat to their own employment opportunities.

Much of the early ethnic conflict in post-Confederation New Brunswick centred on Acadian attempts to increase the use of French within the Roman Catholic Church. Up until the early twentieth century, the hierarchy of the church was strongly opposed to the use of French, believing that the development of Catholicism in Canada would be more successful if it were linked to the linguistic majority, rather than to the minority (Spigelman, 1975, p. 80). Thus, English-speaking priests were frequently appointed to Acadian parishes to encourage the use of English in religious services. And, in 1882, the Collège Saint-Louis, the major Catholic college serving Acadians, was closed as a result of opposition from the bishop of Chatham, who claimed that it unduly promoted the use of the French language (Rumilly, 1955, p. 790).

By 1912, this dispute had been largely resolved and Acadian efforts focused next on the public schools, where the texts, the instruction, and the examinations were predominantly in English. While the use of French was permitted, this was considered largely a temporary measure to give French-speaking students time to learn English. Although in 1928 the Acadian leaders were able to obtain an agreement from the government to permit the adoption of a bilingual program in Acadian schools, the agreement aroused such opposition among the province's English-speaking community that it was revoked by the government a year later (Godin, 1951, p. 188). Subsequently, in the absence of any provincial legislation specifying the language of instruction, much of the linguistic conflict shifted to the local school districts in those regions which had a mixed English-French population. The major battle occurred in Moncton when, in 1959, Acadians presented a petition to the local school board, requesting the establishment of a French-language high school. The request was initially blocked by bitter opposition from English-language associations but, four years later, after discreet negotiations, the decision was reached to build Ecole Vanier, probably the first public, non-denominational French-language secondary school in Canada.

In more recent years, the major issue of contention has been the use of the French language in public life. In 1968, Acadians demonstrated outside the Moncton City Hall in protest against the civic administration's refusal to introduce French-language services. Although some arrests were made, in general, the protests were peaceful. The conflict was partially defused in 1969 when the New Brunswick Legislature passed an Official Languages Bill, assuring the use of French (in addition to English) in the legislature, courts, municipal governments, schools, and civil service. However, the implementation of the bill has been less than enthusiastic, and the use of French in the public domain continues to be a major issue of dispute between the two ethnic groups.

In Northern Ireland, the linguistic aspects of the ethnic cleavage have been comparatively less important because the Irish population has been largely assimilated into the English language since the nineteenth century. Nevertheless, the Irish regard their language as an important part of their cultural heritage and it is commonly studied in the Catholic schools. Further, when the Republic of Ireland was established, Irish and English became the two official languages, and Irish was declared compulsory for a School Leaving Certificate and for entry into the civil service. The majority bloc in Northern Ireland, as in New Brunswick, has opposed establishment of a second official language on the grounds that it is a costly and unnecessary measure.

THE RELIGIOUS CLEAVAGE

Just as New Brunswick and Northern Ireland are biethnic communities, so too are they biconfessional communities. The religious cleavage separates each community into two groups, Protestants and Catholics. In New Brunswick, the Catholics constitute over one-half of the population and, in Northern Ireland, just over one-third. While this Protestant-Catholic division is the dominant religious cleavage, it should be noted that the Protestant segment is subdivided into additional components including, principally, Presbyterians, Anglicans, Baptists, and Methodists (see Table 20).

While increasing secularization has diminished the prominence of religious differences in many western societies, in both New Brunswick and Northern Ireland the religious cleavage continues to have an important social impact. In Northern Ireland, more than 99 percent of the population identify with a specific denomination, and 66 percent attend church at least once a week. In New Brunswick, an equally high proportion of the population identifies with a specific religious denomination, and 47 percent attend church at least once a week. Further, 77 percent of those in New Brunswick, and 75 percent of those in Northern Ireland (Independent Television Authority, 1970) describe themselves as either "fairly religious" or "very religious."

The early history of religious conflict in the two communities is typical of that stage in nation-building when the centralizing nation-state, expanding its influence and control, threatens the traditional privileges of the church. The state attempts to increase its jurisdiction in the domains of the family, morality, and education, and meets with opposition from the church, which sees its authority being usurped. The decision of Henry VIII to establish a national church in the United Kingdom

Table 20
Major Religious Denominations

New Brunswick		Northern Ireland	
Denomination	% of Total population	Denomination	% of Total population
1921		1926	
Roman Catholic	44	Roman Catholic	34
Baptist	22	Presbyterian	31
Anglican	12	Anglican	27
Presbyterian	11	Methodist	4
Methodist	9	Brethren	1
1971		1971[a]	
Roman Catholic	52	Roman Catholic	35
Baptist	14	Presbyterian	29
United[b]	13	Anglican	24
Anglican	11	Methodist	5
Pentecostal	3	Baptist	1

Note: The New Brunswick data are from Canada, Dominion Bureau of Statistics, 1873–1971; and Canada, Statistics Canada, 1973–77. The Northern Ireland data are from Northern Ireland, Information Service, 1973; and Northern Ireland, General Register Office, 1973–74.

a At the 1971 census more than 9 percent of the population refused to state their religious persuasion. The Northern Ireland figures for that year are calculated as a percentage of those who gave a religion.

b The United Church of Canada was formed in 1925 as a result of the merger of the Presbyterian, Methodist, and Congregationalist churches.

during the sixteenth century assured that this dispute between church and state would become an interdenominational conflict: the conflict between church and state became a conflict between the Church of Rome and the Church of England.

This Catholic-Anglican conflict was, for a time, transplanted into New Brunswick and Northern Ireland. The Anglican Church was the established national church in New Brunswick until 1867, and in Ireland until 1869, and Catholics were subject to important civil disabilities in both communities. For example, it was not until 1810, in New Brunswick, and 1829, in Ireland, that Catholics were permitted to vote in general elections. Anglican leadership of the Protestant churches, however, soon gave way in the face of a revival of the Nonconformist sects. In New Brunswick, this revival was fostered by the Baptist Church which succeeded in winning over, first, poorer settlers in remote communities and, later, affluent seceders from the Anglican Church (MacNutt,

1963, pp. 167–69). By mid-century, the zeal and evangelistic fervour of the Baptists had firmly established them as the backbone of Bible fundamentalism and anti-Catholicism, as well as the largest Protestant denomination, in the province. In Northern Ireland, the revival took place largely within the Presbyterian Church, where the triumph of conservative factions led by Henry Cooke, a leading opponent of Catholic emancipation, resulted in a resurgence of militant street preaching and bitter anti-Catholicism (Barkley, 1959; Boyd, 1970). Nevertheless, in spite of the divisions between the Protestant sects, the Anglicans and Nonconformists presented a relatively united front in their opposition to the authority of the Roman Catholic Church. The major religious cleavage has thus been between Protestant and Catholic.

The fundamental issue in Protestant-Catholic conflict has been, with few exceptions, the rightful jurisdiction of church and state. While Catholics have traditionally claimed the domains of education, morality, and the family for the church, Protestants have attributed responsibility in such areas either to the state or to the individual conscience. The breadth of the jurisdiction claimed by the Roman Catholic Church, combined with its authoritative position in the lives of its adherents, has sparked Protestant claims that it represents a threat to their individual liberty. Hence the General Assembly of the Presbyterian Church in Ireland has described the Roman Catholic Church as "a world-wide religious organization that seeks to gain control of the institutions of mankind and of public life generally," with the result that "the Protestant often fears the dangers of the violation of his freedom and/or ecclesiastical power in religious, political and social affairs" (Barritt and Carter, 1972, p. 29). In more virulent terms, the Protestant political leader Ian Paisley describes the Northern Ireland conflict as a battle between "Papal Tyranny and Protestant Liberty" (F. Wright, 1973, p. 224).

In New Brunswick the most contentious issue in Protestant-Catholic conflict has been, historically, the question of state-controlled versus church-controlled education. When in 1871 a Protestant government introduced the Common Schools Act, designed to create a public nonsectarian school system, the proposal was strongly opposed by the Catholic population. Later, when it became known that the government had secretly ceded parts of its authority within some of these public schools to the Roman Catholic Church, there was vehement Protestant opposition. Since that time, conflict based on Protestant fears of Catholic authority has been relatively less frequent. At the provincial level it was last a major political issue in 1935 when the Liberal Party was led by a Catholic, Allison Dysart. During the tumultuous election campaign — which included the shadowy participation of the Ku Klux Klan — it was widely implied that the election of a Catholic prime minister would result in a New Brunswick government directed from Rome (Surette, 1974). Dysart was successfully elected, however, and in the absence of any evidence that government policy was subsequently dictated by the Roman Catholic Church, religious tension abated. In more recent years, when the issue has reappeared, it has generally been at the local level — often in matters relating to the administration of hospitals and schools. Protestants and Catholics came into conflict in the early 1960s, for example, when it was alleged that the church had applied pressure on the Catholic members of the Kent County Council to finance the construction of a new hospital operated by a Catholic religious order, rather than to finance the enlargement of the existing non-sectarian community hospital (Balthazar and Despland, 1966).

In Northern Ireland, the question of church versus state schools has also proved to be a major source of dispute between Protestants and Catholics. As in New Brunswick, the passage of an act, in 1923, which established a state school system was widely opposed by Catholics, although here the situation was further complicated by stipulations permitting Protestant religious instruction only within these schools. Outside the educational domain, Protestant fears of Catholic influence have been heightened by the actions of the Catholic majority in the Republic of Ireland where, for example, church doctrine on such subjects as divorce and contraception has been incorporated into the statutes of the state. In 1950, the church successfully blocked a government bill to provide free maternity care, on the grounds that such matters were outside the state's competence (see Whyte, 1971). On a more local level in Northern Ireland, the question of church versus state control became a contentious issue in Belfast during the early 1970s, when the Protestant government refused to give financial assistance to the Catholic Mater Hospital unless its ownership was transferred to the state (see Budge and O'Leary, 1973).

Conflict along the religious cleavage has also developed on a number of less central issues, where Protestants have attempted to impose their social values on Catholics. Protestant fundamentalists have tended to support political policies which would, for example, maintain a strict observance of the Sabbath, restrict the consumption of alcohol, and prohibit gambling activities. These measures have frequently been perceived by Catholics as an undue restriction of their liberty. In Northern Ireland, the Portadown Borough Council refused to issue permits to Catholic churches to hold Sunday dances. Similarly, the Belfast Council enforced sabbatarian measures which, until 1968, included locking children's swings and play centres in public parks on Sundays. In New

Brunswick, Protestants have consistently favoured the imposition of strict controls on alcoholic consumption and gambling activities. In a turn-of-the-century plebiscite on prohibition, popular opinion in the province polarized along the Protestant-Catholic cleavage. The New Brunswick Baptist Convention subsequently referred to the issue as a contest of "moral law-abiding Christian citizens" versus "the saloon keeper, the brewer, the fallen inebriate and Rome" (Hatfield, 1975, p. 60). At the present time, bottled alcohol is sold only at government-operated retail outlets, and all advertising of alcoholic beverages is banned by law.

CLEAVAGE PATTERNS

If the nature of the conflict experienced by New Brunswick and Northern Ireland along their ethnic and religious cleavages has been very similar, the pattern of the conflict has been significantly different. With few exceptions, the cleavages in Northern Ireland have been congruent, while those in New Brunswick have been crosscutting.

The congruence of the two cleavages in Northern Ireland was deliberately constructed by the British as a means of ensuring that the new colonists would not be assimilated. Since the natives were Irish-speaking and Catholic, the new settlers were English-speaking and Protestant: it was hoped that the combination of ethnic and religious differences would create an effective barrier between the two groups. Mountjoy, the British general who successfully defeated the Irish in 1603, observed:

> Great care was thought fit to be taken that these new colonists should consist of such men as were most unlike to fall to the barbarous customs of the Irish, or the Popish superstition of Irish and English-Irish, so as no less cautions were to be observed for uniting them and keeping them from mixing with each other than if these new colonists were to be led to inhabit among the barbarous Indians. (De Paor, 1971, p. 6)

After the plantation, the linguistic difference between the two groups proved to be a formidable impediment to attempts to change the relationship between the ethnic and religious cleavages. The English intended to convert the Irish to Protestantism but they did not have, or were unwilling to send, men capable of preaching to the Irish in their own language. Thus, the Irish remained Catholics and, as O'Farrell (1971) has observed: "The Papacy won by default" (p. 21). By the eighteenth century, religious denomination had become a convenient means for distinguishing between settlers and natives. A series of acts known as the Penal Code, passed between 1695 and 1727, effectively institutionalized this religious distinction by imposing severe restrictions on those who would not take an oath against Roman Catholic doctrines. The imposition of civil disabilities on Catholics was intended, not to increase the converts to Protestantism, but rather to protect the privileged position of the British colonists.

The congruence of the religious and ethnic cleavages in Ireland was briefly threatened during the late eighteenth century when radical Ulster Presbyterians, inspired by the French Revolution, founded the Society of United Irishmen and rose in rebellion against the British Crown. However, the rebellion—opposed by most Protestants and unsupported by most Catholics—was of short duration and violently suppressed. By the time of the foundation of the Northern Ireland state, the Protestant-Catholic cleavage was again perfectly congruent with the British-Irish cleavage. Heslinga (1962) has observed: "If for an Irish Roman Catholic his nationality is hardly separable from his religion, the same is broadly true of the Ulster Protestant." And, further, "the 'most true Irishman' would be a Gaelic-speaking Roman Catholic" (p. 54).

The Northern Ireland census does not ask any questions relating to ethnicity and there is therefore little statistical evidence of the congruence between ethnic origin and religious denomination. Nevertheless, family names provide a rough guide to this congruence: in general, Protestants have British surnames, while Catholics have Irish surnames. An analysis of the surnames of the candidates in the last Northern Ireland parliamentary election, for example, shows that this rule is valid for at least 87 percent of the candidates (see Table 21). However, even this underestimates the link between the two cleavages: some Irishmen, for convenience or from compulsion, took British surnames; some British settlers on coming to Ireland adopted Irish surnames.[1]

The early years of New Brunswick history reveal a congruence between ethnicity and religion which resembles that in Northern Ireland. The eighteenth-century confrontations between Acadians and New Englanders were essentially conflicts between French-speaking Catholics and English-speaking Protestants. Thus, the 1767 census of the counties which were later to become the colony of New Brunswick shows that the population was made up predominantly (88 percent) of British-American Protestants, with a small minority (12 percent) of Acadian Catholics. When the New Brunswick colony was officially established, therefore, there was no crosscutting between the religious and ethnic cleavages.

---

1. Terence O'Neill, for example, the former Protestant prime minister of Northern Ireland, possesses one of the most famous Irish surnames, but is of English descent. The name is inherited from a great-grandfather who, during the nineteenth century, changed the family name from "Chichester" to "O'Neill" by royal licence.

Table 21
Religion and Ethnicity
Candidates in the Northern Ireland General Election, 1969

Ethnicity	% of Protestant candidates ($N = 82$)	% of Catholic candidates ($N = 37$)	% of Total candidates ($N = 119$)
British	88	14	65
Irish	11	84	34
Other	1	3	2
Total	100	101	101

Note: $\chi^2(2) = 62.3$, $p < .0001$; $V = .723$. Ethnicity was determined by classifying each candidate according to the ethnic origin of his surname. In making this classification, reference was made to Black, 1946; MacLysagt, 1969; Matheson, 1909; and Reaney, 1958.

After the American Revolution, however, a series of waves of immigration altered this dichotomy. The influx of Loyalists into New Brunswick, while in great majority made up of Protestants, also included a significant proportion of Catholics: they included English Catholics from Maryland and Scottish Catholics previously settled as tenant farmers in New York (Bradley, 1932; Brown, 1965; Metzger, 1962). In addition, several Scottish regiments, composed largely of Catholic Highlanders, chose to take their discharge in North America, and were given land grants in New Brunswick (Ganong, 1933; E. C. Wright, 1955). In the century that followed, these groups were joined by large numbers of other English-speaking immigrants from Scotland and Ireland. Many of these too were Catholics, forced to emigrate because of economic hardship and religious discrimination. By the time of the Canadian Confederation in 1867, these various immigrants to New Brunswick—New Englanders, Loyalists, English, Scots, and even Irish—had merged to form a common English-speaking, pro-British bloc.[2] But while they

2. It is significant that the leading spokesman of the period for the creation of a new "British-American nationality," D'Arcy McGee, had been a Fenian in his native Ireland (Burns, 1968). The fact that the New Brunswick Irish were, at least in some respects, pro-British, may have reflected a process of natural selection—those Irish who arrived in New Brunswick and who did not favour British rule simply moved across the border to the United States. Or it may have reflected, as Baker (1974) suggests, a "compartmentalization" of opinion: "For Ireland, the British connection was bad and ought to be ended; for the North American colonies it was useful enough and might be maintained" (176).

Table 22

Ethnicity and Religion in New Brunswick, 1871 and 1971

Ethnicity	% of Protestants	% of Catholics	% of Total
1871[a]			
English	100	53	84
French	0	47	16
Total	100	100	100
1971[b]			
English	97	32	63
French	3	68	37
Total	100	100	100

Note: The census of 1871 did not give a religious breakdown of the two ethnic groups. However, if the results of later censuses are projected back to 1871, it appears evident that the number of French Protestants was less than 0.5 percent of the total French ethnic group. The data are from Canada, Dominion Bureau of Statistics, 1873–1971; and Canada, Statistics Canada, 1973–77.
a $\chi^2(1) = 105,209$, $p < .0001$; $\phi = .607$.
b $\chi^2(2) = 288,074$, $p < .0001$; $V = .674$.

shared a common ethnicity, they were not uniformly Protestant; a substantial minority were Catholic.

For more than a century, therefore, the ethnic and religious cleavages in New Brunswick have been crosscutting rather than congruent. While this crosscutting is significant, it has only been partial; the religious cleavage cuts through the English bloc, but not, to any great extent, through the French bloc (see Table 22). The French in New Brunswick are relatively homogeneous in terms of religion, being overwhelmingly Catholic. The English, however, while predominantly Protestant, are more than one-quarter Catholic.

EFFECTS OF CONGRUENCE AND CROSSCUTTING
The effect of congruent cleavages is amply revealed by the history of unresolved conflicts in Northern Ireland. These conflicts have inevitably combined both ethnic and religious dimensions, and have thus been very difficult to resolve. Historians make repeated mention of the complex, multi-issued nature of Irish conflicts, and of their consequent severity. Regarding the first major Irish uprising, Owen Dudley Edwards (1968) observes: "Land had begun the insurrection; religion greased its wheels; cultural nationalism gave it the force of an ideal" (p. 44). Ian Colvin (1936), in explaining the violence of political quarrels in Ireland, notes:

"To drive out the invader, to punish the heretic, to spoil the possessor, these motives concentrated in one object gave to this feud a strength of which the English Liberal politician had no conception" (p. 12).

The "Home Rule" conflict has been the dominant conflict in Irish history and its traces are still visible in the issue of a "United Ireland." In its origins, the conflict was essentially ethnic, based on the differing national identities and cultural traditions of the two blocs. Along the ethnic cleavage, those of British origin favoured strong ties with Great Britain, while those of Irish origin favoured an independent Ireland, free from British influence. This conflict was further exacerbated, however, by the religious dimension. Along the religious cleavage, the Ulster Protestants feared submersion in a largely Catholic Ireland, while Irish Catholics resented their minority position in an overwhelmingly Protestant United Kingdom. Given Ireland's Catholic majority, many Protestants believed that an Irish Parliament would be controlled by the Roman Catholic Church—hence the slogan "Home Rule is Rome Rule"—and that they would lose their civil and religious liberties. Buckland (1973) sums up some of the feared consequences:

> Even if Protestants were not actually persecuted and burned, Roman Catholicism would be made supreme by placing education in the hands of priests and by compelling Protestants to attend Catholic schools: by nationalising the railways and reserving employment on them for Catholics; by excluding Protestants from every position in government and by taxing Protestant industries out of existence. (p. xxxii)

The fact that the conflict was based on both ethnic and religious differences made it doubly difficult to resolve. The dual aspects assured that the issues were more deeply felt, and that political defeat or victory would be total rather than partial. This explains the success of the Protestant political leaders in mobilizing massive numbers of Ulstermen in militant opposition to Home Rule. No individual could remain indifferent, since the conflict threatened simultaneously his national identity, religious faith, and economic well-being. Not everyone, however, attributed the same weight to each of these dimensions and this often created confusion over what the "real" issues at dispute were. Rose (1971), for example, suggests that conflict resolution has been difficult because "Catholics see discord in nationality terms whereas Protestants see it in religious terms" (p. 216).

The question of state-supported non-sectarian schools is a further example of the effects of congruent cleavages in Northern Ireland. The proposals of the new Northern Ireland government in the early 1920s to introduce a public school system met with Catholic opposition not simply for religious, but also for nationalist reasons (Akenson, 1973, p. 47). Catholic educational leaders, anticipating assistance from the Irish Free State, refused to recognize the authority of the Northern Ireland government and pursued a policy of non-cooperation with the Northern Ireland Ministry of Education. When, in 1921, the Northern Ireland government appointed a committee to advise it on reforms to the school system, the Catholic school managers refused to participate, a decision which Akenson (1973) describes as "the single most important determinant of the educational history of Northern Ireland" (p. 52). Ironically, then, the divergent national loyalties of the antagonists served as the major obstacle to the resolution of a conflict based essentially on religious differences.

The combination of religious and national antagonism thus created a formidable barrier to negotiation between the two blocs, and a wide variety of seemingly unconnected grievances was never settled, and continued to accumulate, until the outbreak of violence in the late 1960s. These grievances included the restricted franchise, electoral gerrymandering, unfair housing allocation, and discriminatory employment practices. In each case, the fear of both Roman Catholicism and Irish nationalism led Protestants to introduce practices which clearly disadvantaged the Catholic minority (see Northern Ireland, Commission appointed by the Governor of Northern Ireland, 1969). By preventing Catholics from obtaining political influence and economic advantages, Ulster Protestants apparently hoped to minimize the possibility of either domination by the Roman Catholic Church or secession to the Republic of Ireland. These measures, however, led instead to further tension and resentment, and assured that yet another major cleavage, the class cleavage, would be congruent to the line of fragmentation (see chapter 5).

The history of New Brunswick, in contrast, provides extensive evidence of the moderating effects of crosscutting cleavages. First, unlike the Northern Ireland conflicts, the major New Brunswick disputes have involved single issues. The ethnic and religious issues have been largely dissociated, and thus have not reinforced each other. Second, the parties to the conflict have been restrained by the common bonds derived from alliances along an alternate cleavage. The protagonists have had a common ground for negotiation since those opposed on the ethnic cleavage might be allied on the religious cleavage (or vice versa).

The major exception to this general pattern is the early colonization period of New Brunswick history when the major cleavages were congruent, with British Protestants opposing French Catholics. The point of contention between the British and the Acadians was not only national—specifically, loyalty to Britain versus loyalty to France—but also religious. The neighbouring colonies, especially Massachusetts, were staunchly Protestant and fiercely anti-Catholic; in their eyes it was important that the Acadian colony be Protestant as well as British. Governor Shirley of Massachusetts believed that this could be accomplished "by removing the Romish Priests out of the Province, and introducing Protestant Ministers, and due encouragement given to such of the Inhabitants as shall Conform to the Protestant Religion and send their Children to the English Schools" (Brebner, 1927, pp. 128–29). When, in 1755, it was apparent that these measures had failed, the British deported the Acadians. The dual ethnic and religious dimensions of this early confrontation have long been recognized by the Acadians, and the Acadian Bishop Robichaud has noted: "Our ancestors were persecuted for their language just as for their faith, because if they had wanted to renounce the one just like the other, they would have been spared the lot they were made to suffer" (Bernard, 1945, p. 118).

The congruent cleavages which contributed to the brutal deportation of the Acadians gave way, by the time of New Brunswick's entry into Confederation, to crosscutting cleavages. The contrasting effects of these crosscutting cleavages are particularly evident in the successful resolution of the common schools conflict in the 1870s. Unlike Northern Ireland, conflict was limited to one cleavage, that of religion. When, in 1871, the Protestant government of New Brunswick eliminated its financial support for denominational schools, French Catholics united in opposition behind a predominantly English-speaking leadership—notably, their bishop, Sweeney, and their members of Parliament, Anglin and Costigan. Thus, this dispute was simply between Catholics and Protestants; it was not between French and English. Significantly, controversy on ethnic questions, such as the use of the French language in the schools, did not arise (MacNaughton, 1947, p. 231). The absence of any such ethnic dimension greatly facilitated the attainment of a compromise settlement. Certainly, this was the view of the church hierarchy, which argued that English Protestants did not fear the Catholic Church as much as they feared a French Catholic Church (Spigelman, 1975). Further, the English-speaking Catholics, many of whom were of Irish descent, played an important mediary role between the English Protestants and the French Catholics. Henri Bourassa (1914) recognized the importance of this role in his prediction for the future of Canada: "Associated by their language with the English-speaking majority, by their faith and their common remembrances with the

French-speaking minority, the Irish, who had no part to play in the earlier life of Canada, may become the everlasting link of union between English and French" (p. 15).

Just as the common schools conflict was limited to a single cleavage (the religious cleavage), so too the subsequent language conflicts were limited to a single cleavage (the ethnic cleavage). They were English-French conflicts, but not Protestant-Catholic conflicts. In fact, much of such English-French confrontation occurred within the confines of the Roman Catholic Church. Until 1921, the hierarchy of the church in New Brunswick was completely English-speaking and largely unsympathetic to Acadian linguistic demands. English-speaking priests were appointed to Acadian parishes, Acadians were discouraged from entering the priesthood, and efforts to establish French-language newspapers were thwarted (Spigelman, 1975, p. 74). The dominance of the English Catholics provoked heated Acadian opposition, culminating in their concerted effort to obtain the appointment of a French-speaking bishop. In a direct appeal to the Pope in 1900, the Société Nationale l'Assomption protested: "Among the grievances which we raise are the scarcely disguised hostility that is demonstrated with regard to the Acadians, hostility which goes sometimes as far as extreme partiality, even in religious matters" (Rumilly, 1955, p. 839). Their efforts resulted finally in the appointment of an Acadian as bishop of Saint John in 1921, and another as bishop of Chatham in 1922. Since 1944, three of the four bishops in New Brunswick have been French-speaking.

Although this struggle was probably the most severe English-French conflict in recent New Brunswick history, the two language groups were restrained by the common allegiance which both bore to the church. Their shared faith created a bond which prevented escalation of the conflict; and it also permitted both groups to accept the church as a fair arbitrator for their grievance. René Baudry (1960) confirms the importance of this religious bond in the resolution of language conflict:

> The frictions, an astonishing enough fact, have been produced rather inside Catholicism, between the clergy and faithful of different languages. But these disputes are answerable to the religious authorities and are regulated by way of representation to the hierarchy.... The religions, and particularly Catholicism, far from being a subject of division, can help create a ground for agreement. (p. 379)

The language conflict within the church also contributed to the long-term dissociation of the issues of language and religion. This dissociation

was recognized by Jean Hubert (1963), editor of the Acadian newspaper, *L'Evangéline*, when he observed:

> Certainly, it must be admitted, the Acadian is indebted in large part
> to the French-language Catholic clergy for having preserved, until
> this day, his language and French traditions. But on the other hand,
> and this must also be admitted, a large part of the anglicization is due
> to a clergy, just as Catholic as the first, just as religious, but of the
> English language. Thus religion can also act for or against French
> with us, and history proves to us that it has effectively played this
> double role.

While the crosscutting of the ethnic and religious cleavages in New
Brunswick has occurred mainly within the Roman Catholic Church, it
should be noted that the growth of a French-language Baptist Church in
recent years has led to some crosscutting within the Protestant churches.
This has further contributed to the dissociation of religious and ethnic
issues, particularly on questions such as bilingual education. Since the
1950s, French-speaking Baptists, especially in Moncton, have performed
the important function of interpreting French aspirations for their
English-speaking colleagues. Where previously English Baptist leaders
opposed not only Catholic schools but also French schools, they now
accept the principle of French-language public schools: "The phrase
'French yes, confessionality no' could therefore be used to express the
views of most Baptist ministers" (Balthazar and Despland, 1966, p. 24).

The two cases of New Brunswick and Northern Ireland thus suggest
several means by which crosscutting cleavages might contribute to
political stability. First, crosscutting cleavages permit the dissociation
of conflict issues. The conflicts are more amenable to solution because
they focus along only one cleavage at a time. When the cleavages are
congruent, however, the conflicts involve multiple issues, each of which
reinforces the other. Second, crosscutting cleavages create a common
ground of shared interest between opposed blocs. Thus, for example, the
shared religious values of English and French Catholics have served as
the basis for negotiation between the two language groups. Conflict
along the crosscutting cleavage tends to bring the blocs together by
strengthening the (religious) alliances between them. Third, by permitting the resolution of issues as they arise, crosscutting cleavages reduce
the probability that these will accumulate over time. Congruent cleavages create a formidable barrier to negotiation, thereby ensuring that
political problems, whether related to the principal cleavages or not, will
go unsolved, leading to ever-increasing sentiments of grievance and
resentment.

5. The Class Cleavage

Beginning in the sixteenth century, the process of nation-building—or what Lipset and Rokkan (1967) describe as the *national* revolution—brought conflict along both the ethnic and the religious cleavages into prominence. Much later, in the nineteenth century, the *industrial* revolution produced a further critical cleavage—the class cleavage—characterized first by conflict between the traditional landed interests and the new industrial entrepreneurs, and then subsequently by conflict between the industrial owners and their hired workers. If the conflicts inspired by the national revolution generally took place along a territorial axis, those originating with the industrial revolution tended to occur along a functional axis. In the one case, the major criterion of alignment was "commitment to the locality and its dominant culture" while, in the other, the criterion was "commitment to a class and its collective interests" (Lipset and Rokkan, 1967, p. 14). Thus, insofar as the members of the competing ethno-religious groups shared common economic interests, there was an historical tendency for the class cleavage to cut across the ethnic and religious cleavage.

The fundamental characteristic of class division is the unequal distribution of scarce resources, and most particularly those relating to authority. Karl Marx, undoubtedly the foremost class theorist, has thus described the primary historical division in all societies as being between the "oppressing and oppressed classes" (Marx and Engels, 1848/1955). Marx proposed that in capitalist societies it was the ownership of private property, and more specifically, the means of production, which constituted the major distinction between the dominant bourgeois class and the subordinate working class. This proposition was based on the assumption that economic control meant control of other sectors of society. However, as Ralf Dahrendorf (1959) has noted, a theory of class based upon the division of society into owners and non-owners, bourgeoisie and proletariat, loses its analytical value when ownership of the means of production ceases to be the sole source of social authority. In modern western societies it would appear that the distribution of authority in a large number of sectors—whether political, economic, religious, or cultural—is partially independent. Dahl (1961), for example, has noted the transition of the United States from a situation of "cumulative inequalities" to one of "dispersed inequalities" in the distribution of political resources (p. 228). This underlines the necessity of examining the distribution of a variety of scarce resources—such as income, occupation, education, and electoral representation—in order to distinguish the lines of class division.

In both New Brunswick and Northern Ireland, the early development of the class division was largely shaped by the existing pattern of social fragmentation. Thus, in the nineteenth century, the distribution of economic, social, and political resources was to the advantage of the British-origin majority, and to the disadvantage of the ethnic minority. This congruence of the class and ethnic cleavages led Marx to predict that Ireland was likely to have a proletarian revolution before England: the abolition of the aristocracy would be easier because "in Ireland it is not merely a simple economic question but at the same time a *national* question" (Marx and Engels, 1971, p. 281). Similarly, Engels, after describing the class conflict between tenants and landlords in Ireland, observed: "To this has to be added the passionate national hatred of the Gael for the Saxon, and the Roman Catholic fanaticism, which is fanned by the clergy against Protestant-Episcopalian arrogance. Anything can be accomplished with such elements" (Marx and Engels, 1971, p. 35). Examination of the distribution of resources such as occupation, income, education, and political representation in modern-day Northern Ireland suggests that the class cleavage continues to be congruent with the other major cleavages. In contemporary New Brunswick, however, it would appear that the link between the class cleavage and the ethnic cleavage has considerably weakened, to the extent that it may be described as crosscutting.

OCCUPATIONAL STRATIFICATION
Comparison of New Brunswick and Northern Ireland reveals a striking similarity in the early patterns of occupational stratification. From the

period of colonization, the British-origin population, possessing both better educational training and greater political influence, established itself
firmly in the superior economic classes of the community. By contrast,
the minority French and Irish populations were left the less desirable
occupations, chiefly within the industries employing unskilled labour. In
spite of many improvements in the condition of the minority blocs, the
effects of this early pattern are still evident today.

In the Acadian colony, the French settlers formed a successful agricultural society, supplementing their farming activities with hunting
and fishing. The society was largely egalitarian, with little social distinction existing between its members. After the deportation of 1755, and
the resettlement in northern New Brunswick, the Acadians continued to
farm, although their land was much less fertile. The British settlers who
joined the Acadians in New Brunswick followed very different occupations. Of the eighteenth-century settlements along the north shore,
Krueger and Koegler (1975) observe: "While the French at this time
came as farmers and fishermen, the British for the most part came as
traders and merchants" (p. 12). In southern settlements such as Saint
John, the Loyalists included predominantly yeomen, merchants, and
craftsmen (carpenters, shoemakers, tailors, masons, smiths, and bakers)
but also significant numbers of such professions as "gentlemen," school-
masters, and physicians (E. C. Wright, 1951, p. 161). With these
beginnings, the Loyalists early established their dominance over the
commercial and professional life of the province, while the Acadians
remained isolated in the rural northeast, living at a subsistence level.
When, during the nineteenth century, the lumber trade expanded to
become the major New Brunswick industry, it was controlled almost
entirely by British-origin merchants.

In Northern Ireland, the pre-colonial native Irish population similarly
constituted a simple agricultural society. The British plantation of the
province largely disrupted this society, however, by depriving the Irish
peasants of their land, and forcing them to become labourers or, in some
cases, tenants. By 1641, more than 85 percent of the land in the six
counties which now constitute Northern Ireland was owned by Protestants; and by the end of the century the proportion was even greater
(E. Curtis, 1936, p. 232). The majority of Protestant settlers came as
tenants rather than landowners but, nevertheless, relative to the Catholic tenants, they were accorded superior rights which made them virtually co-proprietors. Protestant dominance was further assured by the
passage of the anti-Catholic penal codes which largely restricted education, landownership, commerce, professions, and public office to Protestants. As a result of this legislation, as Hereward Senior (1966)
observes, even the "lower orders" of Protestants became a kind of "ple-

bian aristocracy" compared with the Catholics (p. 4). With the growth
of industrialization in the nineteenth century, it was largely the Protestant population, possessing more technical experience and greater capital resources, which was the chief beneficiary (see, for example, Gill,
1925/1964). The textile and engineering industries, later to become the
mainstays of the Northern Ireland economy, were developed and dominated almost entirely by Protestants.

The general pattern which thus evolved in both New Brunswick and
Northern Ireland showed an early concentration of the minority bloc in
primary industries such as farming and fishing, while the British-origin
majority dominated the more advanced secondary and tertiary industries, particularly manufacturing and commerce. During the twentieth
century, however, this distinction between the two blocs in each community gradually diminished as technological innovations reduced the
demand for manpower in the primary sector while creating new employment opportunities in the tertiary sector. If, in 1911, 50 percent of
Ulster's male population, and 43 percent of New Brunswick's male
population, were employed in agriculture, by 1971 the proportions were
only 11 percent and 4 percent, respectively. Those members of the
Acadian and Irish minorities who sought employment outside the primary sector, however, generally lacked sufficient training in other than
the most menial secondary and tertiary occupations. Lyons (1971),
describing stratification during the early period of industrialization in
Northern Ireland, concludes:

> The landed gentry and the professions tended to be the preserve of
> the Church of Ireland [i.e., the Anglican Church], whereas Presby-
> terians dominated the world of business and were also well repre-
> sented among the more prosperous farmers. Catholics by contrast
> gravitated in industry towards the lower-paid jobs and in the coun-
> tryside took the poorer farms and supplied much of the labouring
> population. (p. 11)

And Emrys Jones (1957), describing the influx of rural Catholics seeking employment into Belfast, remarks: "Always they [the Catholics]
came in at the lowest economic levels; and the lingering effects of the old
penal code, one of which was a very high rate of illiteracy, saw to it that
few prospered enough to move from these [poor] sectors to the better
residential areas" (p. 97). The process was not too dissimilar in New
Brunswick where those Acadians who abandoned the traditional occupations of farming and fishing started at the bottom of the ladder in
business and industry. Mason Wade (1961), for example, comments:

"Gradually Acadians drifted into business, but as clerks and small shop-keepers rather than as builders of great enterprises; and into industry, but as skilled or semi-skilled workmen or white-collar workers, rather than as managers or executives" (pp. 40–41).

The extent to which this development contributed to occupational differences between the blocs in each community may be illustrated by examining the occupations having the highest proportions of each bloc (see Table 23). In New Brunswick, the occupations with the highest proportions of Acadians continue to be either in the primary sector—notably, fishing, mining, and lumbering—or in manufacturing industries very closely tied to the primary sector. Thus, for example, industries such as food processing and pulp and paper have disproportionately high numbers of Acadians, particularly at the unskilled and the labouring levels. By contrast, those occupations with the highest proportions of English New Brunswickers are largely white collar positions, often requiring advanced training and skills. Engineering and accountancy fall into this category. In other white collar occupations requiring less skill, for instance, stenography, the large proportion of English workers likely reflects the dominant position of the English language in the business world.

In Northern Ireland, similarly, the highest proportion of Catholics are found in those occupations which are often menial or, at least, less desirable in the eyes of Protestants. For example, the labouring population is disproportionately Catholic in most industries. Catholics are also found in large numbers in the various occupations of the construction industry (such as bricklayers and plasterers), an industry in which employment is often insecure and seasonal. Isles and Cuthbert (1957) described this industry as the "sump into which workmen, particularly the unskilled, tend to dift as casual workers" (p. 65). The occupations dominated by Protestants show a considerable contrast. In general, they tend to be within the non-manual sectors of business and industry; and they often imply either advanced skills or social authority. Authoritative positions as diverse as policemen and sales managers are thus characteristically Protestant, as are skilled occupations, such as engineers and draughts-men. Taken as a whole, occupations within the engineering industry, ranging from riveters to fitters, have historically been the preserve of Protestants. The industry is the largest employer and the major exporter of all the manufacturing industries; and its high pay scales and high proportion of skilled labour make it the most prestigious industry in manufacturing.

It should be noted that the occupations in which the minority blocs are concentrated are also those which have the highest levels of unemploy-

Table 23

Occupations Dominated by Each Bloc, 1971

New Brunswick

	"English" occupations				"French" occupations	
Occupation	Total employed	% English		Occupation	Total employed	% French
Engineer	1,285	87		Fish processor	3,665	67
Clerical supervisor[a]	1,410	84		Miner	1,145	62
Typist	2,315	81		Fisherman	2,750	61
Plant nursery worker	1,330	80		Food labourer	2,435	60
Accountant	2,225	80		Pulp labourer	1,070	54
Bookkeeper	4,545	79		Lumberman[a]	5,210	53

Northern Ireland

	"Protestant" occupations				"Catholic" occupations	
Occupation	Total employed	% Protestant		Occupation	Total employed	% Catholic
Riveter	1,519	95		Publican	4,406	69
Policeman	4,046	90		Woodsman	1,187	55
Sales manager	1,159	89		Building labourer[a]	12,118	55
Engineer	3,282	89		Dock labourer	1,439	54
Production manager	3,297	88		Bricklayer	4,305	51
Draughtsman	2,467	87		Plasterer	1,817	51

Note: In some cases the censuses use longer occupational titles to include additional related occupations. The descriptions in this table employ only the key words.

a In the census classification, this occupational group is a semi-residual category, including occupations not classified with a more specific designation.

Table 24

Unemployment Rates in Selected Countries, 1967–72

Country	1967	1968	1969	1970	1971	1972	average
NEW BRUNSWICK	6.9	7.2	8.5	8.0	7.4	8.4	7.7
NORTHERN IRELAND	7.4	7.1	7.1	6.9	7.8	8.2	7.4
Ireland[a]	6.7	6.7	6.4	7.2	7.2	8.1	7.1
Canada	4.1	4.8	4.7	5.9	6.4	6.3	5.4
United States	3.8	3.6	3.5	4.9	5.9	5.6	4.6
France	2.7	3.2	2.8	3.3	2.4	n.a.	2.9
United Kingdom	2.3	2.5	2.5	2.6	3.4	3.8	2.9

Note: The data for France are from Caloren, 1973, while those for New Brunswick are from Canada, Statistics Canada, 1972, and those for Northern Ireland are from Great Britain, Central Statistical Office, 1974. All other data are from International Labour Office, 1974.

a Excludes agriculture, fishing, and private domestic service.

ment. In Northern Ireland, the major employer of Protestant manual workers, the engineering industry, had only 5 percent unemployment in 1971, while the major employer of Catholic manual workers, the construction industry, had 19 percent unemployment. Among male workers as a whole, 7 percent of the Protestants and 17 percent of the Catholics were unemployed. The pattern is similar, although less marked, in New Brunswick. The largest employer of English manual workers, the transportation industry, had 9 percent unemployment, while the largest employer of French manual workers, the construction industry, had 13 percent unemployment. Both New Brunswick and Northern Ireland represent economically depressed regions with unusually high levels of unemployment (see Table 24). It seems clear, however, that the brunt of this unemployment is borne by the minority bloc, particularly in Northern Ireland.

A more precise representation of the occupational stratification of each bloc may be arrived at by calculating the proportions of each within the major occupational classes of the community. In order for these class divisions to be comparable in both communities, and to be based upon empirical rankings, the scales developed by Hall and Jones (1950) in the United Kingdom, and by Pineo and Porter (1973) in Canada, were used to construct five occupational classes. Details on the construction of these classes are contained in Appendix B. In total, 222 occupational groups in Northern Ireland, and 498 in New Brunswick— taken from the unpublished results of the 1971 censuses—were categorized according to these five classes. The results of this classification, for

Table 25

Occupational Stratification of the Blocs,
for the Male Population, 1971

Occupational strata	New Brunswick[a]		
	% of English males (N = 97,700)	% of French males (N = 51,200)	% of Total males (N = 148,910)
Professional, managerial	14	9	12
Lower grade non-manual	21	14	18
Skilled manual	21	22	22
Semi-skilled manual	20	21	21
Unskilled manual	24	34	27
Total	100	100	100

Occupational strata	Northern Ireland[b]		
	% of Protestant males (N = 227,599)	% of Catholic males (N = 102,748)	% of Total males (N = 330,347)
Professional, managerial	16	9	14
Lower grade non-manual	17	12	16
Skilled manual	27	23	26
Semi-skilled manual	24	25	24
Unskilled manual	16	32	21
Total	100	101	101

a $\chi^2(4) = 3,177$, $p < .0001$; $V = .146$.
b $\chi^2(4) = 12,591$, $p < .0001$; $V = .195$.

economically active men, confirm the observation that the British-origin majority in both communities has a higher occupational level than the minority bloc (see Table 25). In general, the majority dominates the non-manual occupations, while the minority is disproportionately represented in the manual occupations, particularly those which are unskilled. While this pattern is very similar in the two communities, it appears somewhat stronger in Northern Ireland than in New Brunswick in that the gap between the two blocs, in both the highest and the lowest strata, is smaller in New Brunswick than in Northern Ireland.

While Table 25 indicates the general tendency for the minority blocs to be disadvantaged, it greatly underestimates this tendency in Northern Ireland by concealing further stratification *within* each of the five occupational classes (see Aunger, 1975). The significance of this internal differentiation may be illustrated by examining the non-manual strata in more detail. Generally, the middle classes of the minority blocs (both the Acadians and the Irish Catholics) tend to be disproportionately composed of occupations which reflect the societal fragmentation, that is, occupations which serve exclusively the members of that bloc. For example, among the Irish Catholics and French Acadians, male school teachers make up a major portion of those in the professional-managerial class (25 percent and 21 percent, respectively); but among the Ulster Protestants and English New Brunswickers, they make up a much smaller portion of those in that class (12 percent and 13 percent). The middle classes of the majority blocs tend to be disproportionately composed of occupations which possess significant social authority and which have impact on the community as a whole—as in politics and business, for example. While this general pattern exists in both communities, it is considerably more evident in Northern Ireland. If selected non-manual occupations in the two communities are compared, it is apparent that the Irish minority in Northern Ireland possesses considerably less influence in the political and financial sectors of the community than do the Acadians in New Brunswick. Within strategic political occupations, notably at senior government levels and in the police force, the Irish Catholics are virtually blocked out, while the Acadians, although underrepresented, are present in substantial numbers (see Table 26). Similarly, within business and finance, the Irish Catholics have only token representation—especially at the managerial level—while the Acadians are a much more substantial force.

This, in fact, points to a very significant difference in the class structures of New Brunswick and Northern Ireland. In New Brunswick, there exists an important Acadian elite, possessing both political and economic influence to an extent unmatched by the minority in Northern Ireland. This elite is readily recognizable within New Brunswick society and is popularly referred to as *la patente*, a term which originally described the members of a French-Canadian secret society, the Ordre de Jacques-Cartier. The financial strength of this elite is based in the Acadian cooperative movement, the two mainstays of which are the credit unions of the Fédération des Caisses Populaires Acadiennes and an insurance company, Assomption Mutuelle-Vie. In a small and relatively underdeveloped community such as New Brunswick, these organizations have had considerable political and economic impact.[1] They have

1. In 1971, Assomption Mutuelle-Vie financed a $20 million business complex in Moncton—"La Place Assomption"—containing a twenty-storey office tower, hotel, retail stores, and the Moncton city hall. The company required that all leases in the complex, which is the business centre of Moncton, contain a

Table 26

Selected Non-Manual Occupations, 1971

Occupation	New Brunswick		Northern Ireland	
	Total employed	% French	Total employed	% Catholic
Political				
Senior government officials	450	27	1,058	13
Government officers	1,165	28	2,702	21
Policemen	875	21	4,046	10
Lawyers[a]	370	20	725	28
Economic				
Senior management[b]	360	18	347	7
Managers	1,720	31	10,312	12
Accountants	2,225	20	1,377	17
Commercial travellers	1,285	24	4,936	13
Insurance agents	740	22	256	13
Social				
School teachers	9,095	36	15,726	37
Nurses	4,130	23	12,249	43
Physicians	550	15	2,011	21
Clergymen[c]	1,120	41	2,351	37
University teachers	715	24	866	17

a Includes judges and magistrates. For Northern Ireland, barristers, advocates, and solicitors have all been classed as "lawyers."
b In the absence of any other satisfactory equivalent for Northern Ireland, the occupational group "company secretaries and registrars" was used.
c Includes members of religious orders.

created employment opportunities for Acadians in finance and business, and have provided an important source of investment capital. Further, they have provided a financial base for the Acadian elite to expand its influence; this it has done by buying ownership of other business concerns, gaining directorships in major New Brunswick corporations, and winning appointments to government commissions and advisory councils. It is noteworthy that this Acadian influence in business has been

clause guaranteeing that signs would be in both English and French. This led to a furore when the mayor of Moncton, Leonard Jones, a staunch opponent of bilingualism, refused to permit French signs in the city hall; and hence no signs at all were mounted. Four years later, however, under a new mayor, a sign bearing the dual inscription "City Hall" and "Hotel de Ville" was installed. The incident indicates the possible potential of Acadian economic influence as a counterweight to the traditional English political dominance.

matched in politics, especially between the years of 1960 and 1970 when an Acadian, Louis Robichaud, was prime minister of the province. During this period, the proportions of Acadians in the civil service increased to a level not far below the percentage of Acadians in the province as a whole.

While the New Brunswick Acadians possess an elite whose economic and political influence extends beyond the Acadian bloc, the Northern Irish Catholics have no such elite. Catholics are largely absent from both the senior levels of government and the management positions of business. Historically, the community's most prestigious industries, such as engineering and shipbuilding, were founded by Protestants and—given the tendency for each bloc to give preference to its own members—have remained Protestant. This Protestant dominance has also been aided by the uninterrupted control of the Northern Ireland government, from 1921 until 1972, by the Unionist Party. Catholics have not lacked spokesmen and self-styled leaders, but such leadership has been limited to a smattering of teachers, politicians, and priests. And since this leadership has been largely excluded from the economic and political power structure of the Northern Ireland community as a whole, it has never attained the elite status of *la patente* in New Brunswick.

SOCIO-ECONOMIC INEQUALITIES

The class cleavage is determined not only by occupation but also by a variety of additional socio-economic resources. Among the most important of these scarce resources must be included education, income, and housing. Each of these generally contributes to the economic standard of living and their unequal distribution may divide a community into opposing classes of "haves" and "have-nots."

Historically, it is evident that the minority blocs in both communities have not had equal educational opportunity. In Northern Ireland, this has resulted, at least in part, from the differing legal status of the Protestant and Catholic schools. The Protestant schools, as "county" schools, have been wholly maintained from public funds; while the Catholic schools, as "voluntary" schools, have been only partially supported by the government. Thus, a substantial portion of the capital and maintenance costs of the Catholic schools has been met by the Catholics themselves. It would not be surprising if this financial burden resulted in schooling of inferior quality and, indeed, a recent study completed for the Fair Employment Agency shows that, for the core subjects examined, Catholics consistently obtained lower grades than Protestants in their O-level examinations (Osborne and Murray, 1978). It is also likely that the higher educational costs for Catholics have contributed to unequal accessibility, particularly at the more advanced grades. This is reflected in the relatively small proportion of Catholic students (compared to Protestant students) who attend a grammar school, rather than a secondary school. Nevertheless, there is evidence that these inequalities may be diminishing. While, in 1967, only 25 percent of those students who passed three or more A-levels in their Northern Ireland examinations were Catholics, by 1975 this proportion had increased to 33 percent (Osborne and Murray, 1978).

In New Brunswick, the Acadian minority has been disadvantaged both by the financial decentralization of the educational system, and the dominant position of the English language. Until 1967, the autonomy of the local school boards in financing and administering education led to serious disparities between the rural and urban regions of the province. Since the Acadians tended to be located in rural areas more often than the English, they suffered more frequently from a lower standard of education. To this financial barrier was added a linguistic handicap. English tended to be the universal language of instruction, particularly at the secondary school level, and the texts and examinations established by the Ministry of Education were often in English only. Krueger (1970), describing the early 1960s, has observed: "The majority of the French-speaking population could not attend a junior high school or high school where they were taught in their own language, and some had to attend private church-supported schools to obtain even their elementary school education in French" (p. 106). It has also been suggested that educational attainment was greatly hampered because the Acadian culture did not highly value school attendance, viewing it as an activity reserved largely for women (Even, 1971, pp. 280–86).

The worst of these inequalities were greatly alleviated by the introduction of the Program of Equal Opportunity in 1967. In that year the government — following the recommendations of the Byrne Commission — centralized the responsibility for education with the provincial Ministry of Education, reduced the number of school districts from 422 to thirty-three, established a uniform rate of school taxation, and standardized the scale of teachers' salaries. In effect, this permitted the creation of equal standards of education throughout the province, regardless of the wealth of the region. In addition, the new Schools Act of 1967 guaranteed that all students would receive instruction in their mother language, whether English or French. To this end, a Faculty of Education for the training of French-language teachers was established at the Université de Moncton. Although these measures did not immediately eliminate the educational inequalities, they nevertheless led to significant improvements. While in 1966, only 20 percent of the students

Table 27

Educational Stratification of the Blocs

Years of schooling	New Brunswick (1971)[a]		
	% of English (N = 246,645)	% of French (N = 120,230)	% of Total (N = 366,875)
13 or more	9	6	8
9–12	52	30	45
5–8	34	44	37
0–5	5	20	10
Total	100	100	100

Years of schooling	Northern Ireland (1968)[b]		
	% of Protestants (n = 749)	% of Catholics (n = 535)	% of Total (n = 1,284)
13 or more	9	5	7
9–12	45	35	41
5–8	46	60	52
0–5	0	1	1
Total	100	101	101

Note: The New Brunswick data are from the Fédération des Francophones hors Québec, 1977, while the Northern Ireland data are from the Northern Ireland Loyalty Survey.

a $\chi^2(3) = 29{,}326$, $p < .0001$; $V = .283$.
b $\chi^2(3) = 27.7$, $p < .0001$; $V = .147$.

writing the departmental exams of the Ministry of Education were French-speaking, by 1972, 30 percent were French-speaking—in spite of the fact that the French proportion of the school-age population was diminishing during this same period (New Brunswick, Department of Education, 1971).

Comparison of the number of years of formal education, for the members of each bloc, bears out the relatively disadvantaged position of the minority in each community (see Table 27). In both New Brunswick and Northern Ireland, a member of the minority is most likely to have eight or fewer years of education, while a member of the majority will have nine or more years. The gap between the blocs is most pronounced in New Brunswick because of the low educational attainment of the Acadians. For example, 20 percent of the French minority have fewer than five years of schooling. A further striking difference between the two communities, however, is the large amount of differentiation within the Acadian bloc itself. If there is a relatively great number of Acadians with little education, there is nevertheless a larger proportion of Acadians with superior education in New Brunswick than of Catholics with the same level of education in Northern Ireland. This confirms the tendency that was observed in comparing occupational strata: the Acadian minority has a larger socio-economic elite than the Catholic minority of Northern Ireland. It is likely that this greater differentiation has served to strengthen the position of the Acadian elite and, at least in the past, to assure it of the unwavering support of the mass of the Acadian population. Alain Even (1970), after pointing to the under-education of the Acadian population, and the mediocre quality of its schools, concludes: "This lack of instruction has numerous consequences for this population which, frustrated enough, is going to have an almost blind confidence in the more educated elites and in particular the clergy, and an almost total lack of confidence in itself" (p. 118).

It might be anticipated that the income differences between the two blocs would be similar to the education differences, that is, that there would be a substantial differentiation in New Brunswick and less differentiation in Northern Ireland. However, this is not the case. In New Brunswick, there is relatively little difference between the income levels of the English and French (see Table 28). Jean Cadieux (1965), after comparing the English and French regions of the province, concluded: "Here at least is an established datum which should give those who always claim that the Acadian population is poor cause to reflect. If it is relatively poor, it is not poorer than the English population of the province. There exists therefore a certain harmony here" (p. 4). Indeed, if adjustment is made for the educational differences between the two blocs, Acadians obviously have higher incomes relative to the English. This contrasts with Northern Ireland, where the income differences between the blocs closely match the education differences. The relationship between religion and income ($V = .152$), showing Catholics with generally lower incomes, is consistent with the relationship between religion and education ($V = .147$), showing the Catholics with fewer years of schooling. Nevertheless, Richard Rose (1971) has suggested that well-educated Catholics are not as well treated as their Protestant counterparts: "Protestants who have some sort of qualification — whether a diploma, a degree or a certificate — are likely to enjoy higher wages than educated Catholics" (p. 289). This supports the earlier observation that Catholics have tended to be excluded from certain of the more prestigious (and better paying) occupations at the elite level, notably those in the financial and commercial sectors.

Table 28
Income Stratification of the Blocs

Annual income, in dollars	New Brunswick (1971)[a]		
	% of English ($N = 288,515$)	% of French ($N = 142,980$)	% of Total ($N = 431,495$)
5,000 or more	25	17	22
3,000–4,999	15	13	14
1,000–2,999	22	25	23
0–1,000	39	44	41
Total	101	99	100

Annual income, in pounds	Northern Ireland (1968)[b]		
	% of Protestants ($n = 719$)	% of Catholics ($n = 510$)	% of Total ($n = 1,229$)
1,326 or more	27	17	23
1,066–1,325	17	13	15
806–1,065	20	24	22
0–806	36	47	40
Total	100	101	100

Note: The New Brunswick data are based on individual income (male and female), while the Northern Ireland data are for total family income. Since respondents in Northern Ireland were asked to give their weekly income, this figure was multiplied by 52 in order to give an estimate of annual income. The New Brunswick data are from the Fédération des Francophones hors Québec, 1977, and the Northern Ireland data are from the Northern Ireland Loyalty Survey.

a $\chi^2(3) = 3,501, p < .0001; V = .090.$
b $\chi^2(3) = 28.3, p < .0001; V = .152.$

Where houses are privately built and owned, as in New Brunswick, it might logically be expected that the quality of housing would be closely linked to income levels. Thus, the French bloc, with a marginally lower income would likely have slightly poorer housing. Where houses are largely publicly built and allocated, as in Northern Ireland, the link with family income should be much weaker. Thus, Catholics, in spite of their lower income, need not necessarily have poorer housing. Nevertheless, it appears that the public allocation of housing in Northern Ireland has tended to exacerbate, rather than reduce, the differences between the blocs. The local governments, which had responsibility for housing until 1970, seldom utilized objective criteria for judging housing need, and were often influenced by religious and political considerations: there was a marked tendency for some councils to favour their coreligionists in the allocation of housing. Such discrimination involved not simply religious prejudice, but also derived from the fact that the franchise was restricted to ratepayers—occupancy of a house was thus linked to the right to vote. The Cameron Commission, which documented some of the worst abuses by Protestant-dominated councils, concluded that the principal criterion in the allocation of houses "was not actual need but maintenance of the current political preponderance in the local government area" (Northern Ireland, Commission appointed by the Governor, 1969, p. 61). While the Northern Ireland Housing Trust could, in principle, compensate for the partiality of the local councils, the effectiveness of the trust was greatly reduced because of local government obstruction. During the 1968–69 period, for example, a number of county councils refused to grant the trust planning permission to construct new housing for Catholics, fearing that such a measure would alter the composition of the electorate, and thereby undermine Protestant control of the local governments (Birrell, Hillyard, Murie, and Roche, 1972).

The question of housing conditions has been a much more serious issue in Northern Ireland than in New Brunswick, simply because of the much higher proportion of inadequate housing. The results of a Northern Ireland survey (Northern Ireland, Ministry of Health and Local Government, 1961) showed that 26 percent of the housing was considered "unfit"; while a New Brunswick study (New Brunswick, Office of the Economic Advisor, 1965) revealed that only 9 percent was in need of "major repairs." It is largely the minority that has suffered from inadequate housing, particularly in Northern Ireland (see Fig. 6). Estimating from the least squares line, it would appear that, in Northern Ireland, 53 percent of the Catholic population lived in unfit housing, compared with only 12 percent of the Protestant population. In New Brunswick, 21 percent of the French population lived in housing in need of major repairs, but only 6 percent of the English did so. Comparison of the valuation of the housing yields similar results. In Northern Ireland, the per capita valuation of houses in districts which are disproportionately Catholic is 34 percent lower than in Protestant districts. In New Brunswick, the valuation in French districts is 13 percent lower than in English districts.

POLITICAL INFLUENCE

Political influence constitutes an important—and often scarce—resource; and its unequal distribution contributes to the class distinctions found within a community. While such influence may be found at many dif-

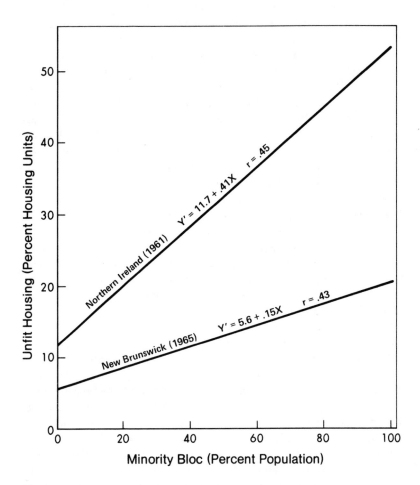

Fig. 6. Unfit housing in local districts. (The data for the least squares lines are from New Brunswick, Housing Corporation, 1968; New Brunswick, Office of the Economic Advisor, 1965; and Northern Ireland, Ministry of Health and Local Government, 1961.)

ferent levels, the focus here will be limited largely to the level of local government. (The political influence of each bloc at the provincial level is discussed in more detail in chapter 6.) The role of the local government authorities was one of the major political issues of the 1960s in both communities. The debate on this issue led to far-reaching reforms of the local government structure in New Brunswick in 1966, and in

Northern Ireland in 1973. Until these reforms, however, the local authorities possessed very considerable responsibilities in a wide range of areas (Hayes, 1967; Lawrence, 1966; Whalen, 1963). In addition to the usual services, such as sanitation, fire protection, water supply, and community planning, the local councils were also responsible for the provision of elementary and secondary education, the administration of social welfare services, and the construction of public health facilities. Further, in New Brunswick, the local governments were charged with the administration of justice while, in Northern Ireland, the local councils were heavily involved in the provision of public housing. The control of these local councils thus became a major source of contention, particularly in Northern Ireland, where the distribution of local government power was manifestly unequal.

A basic element of political influence in a democratic system is simply the right to vote, and on this dimension Catholics in Northern Ireland were clearly disadvantaged. Until the election of 1973, the local government franchise in Northern Ireland was restricted to ratepayers and their spouses. Consequently, approximately 25 percent of those possessing the vote in Northern Ireland parliamentary elections were disenfranchised in local elections. (Further, some electors—almost 2 percent of those eligible to vote—possessed more than one vote in the local elections.) Since Catholics, as was noted above, were disadvantaged in the allocation of housing, and were thus less likely to be ratepayers, they were also more likely to be disenfranchised. The extent of this disenfranchisement may be summarized by correlating the proportions of Catholics in each of the sixty-eight districts (weighted by population) with the proportions of eligible voters (see Fig. 7). Estimating from the least squares line, it would appear that while only 19 percent of the Protestant adults did not possess a vote, 30 percent of the Catholic adults could not vote. While this might be of only small consequence in relatively homogeneous districts, it had an important effect on elections in areas where the population was closely balanced. For example, a local district such as Dungannon, which possessed a small Catholic majority in population, nevertheless had a substantial majority of Protestant electors, and a Protestant-controlled local council.

In New Brunswick, the local government vote was based on universal adult suffrage and was thus not biased toward either of the two blocs. Comparison of the 105 local districts in 1967 shows that there was no difference between English and French regions. In both cases, an average of 95 percent of the adult population was listed on the electoral rolls, and therefore was eligible to vote. Although, in earlier years, New Brunswick had had a ratepayers' franchise, the possibility of its dis-

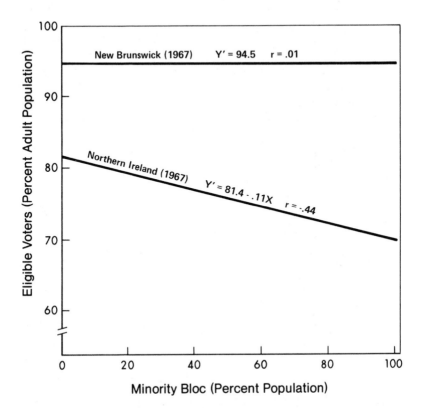

Fig. 7. Enfranchisement in local districts. (The data for the least squares lines are from New Brunswick, Chief Electoral Officer, 1967, and Northern Ireland, Ministry of Home Affairs, 1967.)

criminating effect was never a political issue. On the one hand, it is unlikely that it affected either bloc adversely; on the other hand, it would have had little effect on the election outcomes since most of the municipalities were relatively homogeneous in ethnic composition.

The distribution of political influence in Northern Ireland was further biased toward Protestants by discriminatory electoral boundaries, resulting from gerrymandering. These electoral boundaries disadvantaged Catholics in two principal ways. First, there was a marked tendency for the ward system to eliminate Catholic representation in Protestant urban districts, while assuring Protestant representation in Catholic urban districts. For example, in districts where Protestants were in the majority (such as Lurgan), the absence of wards (combined with a Prot-

Table 29

Electoral Wards in Mixed Districts of Northern Ireland, 1967

District[a]	Number of electors	Majority party	% Catholic councillors	% Catholic population[b]	Wards
Limavady U.D.	2,212	Unionist	0	37	nil
Cookstown U.D.	2,826	Unionist	0	39	nil
Lurgan M.B.	9,811	Unionist	0	48	nil
Newcastle U.D.	2,120	Independent	33	48	nil
Dungannon U.D.	3,396	Unionist	33	50	3
Enniskillen M.B.	3,060	Unionist	33	56	3
Armagh U.D.	4,778	Unionist	35	57	5
Omagh U.D.	4,128	Unionist	43	61	3

a The abbreviation U.D. indicates an urban district, and M.B. a municipal borough.
b The percentage used here is the average of the 1961 and 1971 census figures.

Table 30
Electoral Wards in Londonderry, 1967

Ward	Protestant electors	Catholic electors	Total electors	Seats
North	3,946	2,530	6,476	8
Waterside	3,697	1,852	5,549	4
South	1,138	10,047	11,185	8
Total	8,781	14,429	23,210	20

Note: The data are from Northern Ireland, Commission appointed by the Governor of Northern Ireland, 1969.

estant bloc vote) guaranteed that a completely Protestant slate of councillors would be returned. In districts where Catholics were in the majority (such as Londonderry), the existence of wards ensured some Protestant representation and, indeed, often gave Protestants control of the council. This tendency for electoral wards to exist in Catholic, but not in Protestant urban districts, is most evident in the regions where the two blocs were closely balanced (see Table 29). Second, the boundaries of the electoral wards were often drawn so that Protestant electors were overrepresented. That is, either Protestant wards were given a disproportionate number of representatives or Catholic electors were allocated to various wards in such a manner as to construct a Protestant majority. The most controversial example of such gerrymandering was (until 1968) the municipal borough of Londonderry, Northern Ireland's second largest city. Although the majority of electors were Catholic, the electoral boundaries created two wards with a Protestant majority, and only one with a Catholic majority, thereby ensuring continuous Protestant political control (see Table 30).

In New Brunswick, there is no evidence of such manipulation of local government boundaries. All six cities within the province, and a small number of the larger towns, have electoral wards, but these do not appear to distort the vote along ethnic lines alone. It should be remembered, however, that New Brunswick has a smaller proportion of mixed regions. Insofar as the municipalities tend to be relatively homogeneous in ethnic composition, there is little temptation to gerrymander a constituency in order to ensure the control of any one ethnic bloc. The cities of Campbellton (55 percent French) and Moncton (62 percent English) are the only two large districts with mixed populations, and examination of their wards shows little indication that they have operated to the disfavour of either bloc.

It is possible to summarize the extent of each bloc's political influence by comparing their proportions on the local government councils with their proportions within each local district.[2] In general, it must be anticipated that the minority bloc—by virtue of the simple fact that it is a numerical minority in a "first past the post" electoral system—will be underrepresented. Nevertheless, in ideal terms, its "expected" representation on each council should be equal to its proportion of the local population. When the actual representation is compared to the expected representation, we find that the New Brunswick Acadians have 81 percent of their expected representation, but the Northern Ireland Catholics have only 54 percent of their expected representation (see Fig. 8). Closer examination shows that in New Brunswick the French tend to be underrepresented in municipalities where they are only a small minority. As their proportion increases, however, their representation becomes equitable; and indeed in districts where they are in a clear majority, they are frequently overrepresented. By contrast, in Northern Ireland, Catholics are underrepresented, not only in districts where they are in a minority, but also in many where they constitute a majority of the population.

In some respects it may be more important to evaluate the number of cases in which the minority bloc actually exercises control of a local council, rather than simply the extent of its representation. A minority might, for example, have a level of representation equal to its proportion within the community as a whole, without ever being in the position to control a local government. Although it need not always be so, there is a strong possibility that a group which has only minority representation on a council will find its political influence highly restricted. When the local governments are compared (with each weighted according to population), we find that during the 1967–73 period the New Brunswick Acadians controlled 22 percent of the councils. The Northern Ireland Catholics, on the other hand controlled only 7 percent of the councils.

The unequal distribution of political influence in both communities has had very tangible social consequences for each bloc. In Northern Ireland, as noted above, the Catholics' lack of political influence affects the quality of social services which they receive, particularly housing

---

2   These data were based on 105 New Brunswick councils and 64 Northern Ireland councils, with each weighted according to population size. Ethnic representation in New Brunswick was established by classifying the councillors according to the ethnic origin of their names. In Northern Ireland, the classification was based on published reports and personal informants. The assistance of Denis P. Barritt, who made available some of his own Northern Ireland data on the subject, is gratefully acknowledged.

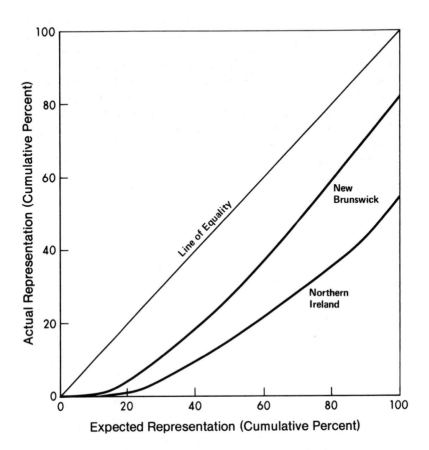

Fig. 8. Minority bloc representation on local government councils, 1967–73.

services. It also means a further limitation on job opportunities — especially jobs connected with the local governments. For example, in the city of Londonderry — which is more than two-thirds Catholic by population — only 30 percent of the government employees, and only one-tenth of the best paid employees, in 1968, were Catholic (Northern Ireland, Commission appointed by the Governor of Northern Ireland, 1969, p. 60). A study published in 1957 revealed that the predominance of Protestants in local government employment was quite general: in Northern Ireland as a whole, only 12 percent of the district council employees, and 7 percent of the county council employees were Catholics (Gallagher, 1957, pp. 209–10). In New Brunswick, English predominance has its major effect on the availability of government services in both languages—it reduces the probability that the Acadian population will be served in French. Nevertheless, even in Moncton, where the issue of bilingualism has been the most salient, the proportion of government employees from the minority bloc is much higher than in comparable cases in Northern Ireland. In Moncton, 34 percent of the civil employees in 1972 were French, a proportion not far below their strength in the city's population, which was 38 percent French (Carroll, 1972).

CONCLUSION

Class is not a nominal variable such as ethnicity or religion and thus specification of the class cleavage is more difficult. Nevertheless, examination of the distribution of scarce resources in the two communities clearly suggests that the division between those who are advantaged and those who are disadvantaged corresponds much more closely to the Protestant-Catholic division in Northern Ireland than to the English-French division in New Brunswick. First, while the minority blocs in both communities are relatively disadvantaged, it is the Irish Catholic minority in Northern Ireland that is the most severely affected. Second, while there is some differentiation within the minority blocs of both communities, it is greatest in New Brunswick where there is an important Acadian elite. Both these findings confirm that there is significantly more crosscutting in New Brunswick than in Northern Ireland.

Although the impact of the crosscutting class cleavage in New Brunswick has not been examined here, the effects would appear to be similar to those resulting from other crosscutting cleavages. Notably, conflict issues have tended to be dissociated rather than cumulative, and tensions have tended to be dispersed. In New Brunswick, it is particularly noteworthy that class conflict has occurred largely within rather than between the two blocs. Thus, for example, the demands by some Acadians for more political and economic power have been directed against their own elite, rather than against the English bloc. When, during the civil confrontations of the late 1960s, Roger Savoie (1969), an Acadian political scientist, referred to a "climate of repression and fear created by a domineering, paternalistic and ignorant elite," he was criticizing his own ethnic elite. In appraising the class confrontation within the Acadian bloc, Savoie concluded:

What is happening in New Brunswick, and particularly in Moncton, is that the French-speaking population is led by a small group of ambitious and power-hungry men, who don't hesitate to utilize methods worthy of the worst Duplessis years, in order to brush aside all those who could want to thwart their designs of domination....A self-styled "elite" holds all the powers and systematically eliminates all forms of opposition, all forms of radical social criticism, all forms of contending thought. (p. 55)

By contrast, demands for reforms in Northern Ireland pit Protestant against Catholic. Class conflict is synonymous with religious conflict because both blocs recognize that it is the Protestants who are advantaged and the Catholics disadvantaged. In spite of the original non-sectarian intentions of the civil rights movement, Hastings (1970) has observed that "it was inevitable that any reform movement should be almost exclusively Catholic based" (p. 41). Even Bernadette Devlin (1969) acknowledged this development, noting that "what started out as a generous (though vague) protest on behalf of the oppressed began turning into an all-class alliance of Catholics" (p. 155). Eamonn McCann (1974), with the advantage of hindsight, explains quite simply why the class confrontations of the late 1960s became also a religious and nation-alist confrontation: "In a situation in which Protestant workers had more than their 'fair' share of jobs, houses and voting power, the demand for an end to discrimination was a demand that Catholics should get more jobs, houses and voting power than they had at present—*and Protestants less*" (p. 241).

The finding that there is more crosscutting of class cleavage in New Brunswick than in Northern Ireland is consistent with the hypothesis that crosscutting cleavages are conducive to political stability. Such crosscutting in New Brunswick likely has facilitated the resolution of conflict and prevented its accumulation along the line of fragmentation. Further, to say that there is crosscutting is to say that there is a sub-stantial elite within each bloc. The presence of a strong elite (such as is found within the Acadian bloc, but not within the Irish Catholic bloc) is likely to be an important prerequisite for the second variable in our guiding hypotheses, elite cooperation.

6. The Political Elites: Coalescence and Competition

The major conclusion of Lijphart's (1968a) study of the Netherlands was that "overarching cooperation at the elite level can be a substitute for crosscutting affiliations at the mass level" (p. 200). Lijphart observed that the Netherlands, although severely fragmented, has nevertheless enjoyed a long history of political stability, and attributes this to the cooperative behaviour of the political elites. This cooperative behaviour covers a wide variety of political strategies and institutional arrangements, but its most important defining characteristic is "coalescence." Coalescence refers to the establishment of a governing coalition that includes the political leaders of the principal blocs in the fragmented community. Lijphart (1968b, 1969, 1975, 1977) describes such coalescence variously as "grand coalition," "broadly-based coalition," "national unity cabinet," and "government by elite cartel." The model of elite coalescence is the Dutch model, and fragmented societies that have such elites Lijphart calls "consociational" democracies.

Coalescence is distinguished from "competition" in that it implies a multi-party coalition, based on the support of the overwhelming majority, while competition implies one-party government, based on the support of a minimal minority (Lijphart, 1977, p. 25). The model of competition is the British model with its typical government-versus-opposition pattern. Fragmented societies with competitive elites are typically unstable and are classified by Lijphart as "centrifugal" democracies.

Since coalescent elites contribute to political stability, and competitive elites to political instability, Lijphart and other members of the consociational school have championed the Dutch rather than the British model of parliamentary democracy. Lijphart (1975), for example, concludes that an "especially important obstacle" to the attainment of political stability in fragmented societies is "widespread knowledge of and admiration for the British model of democracy, which is competitive rather than coalescent" (p. 99). Daalder (1974), similarly, concludes that if elites are to be successful in stabilizing a divided society "they must consciously eschew the competitive practices which underlie the norms of British-style democracy" (p. 607). These warnings take on particular importance when the cases of New Brunswick and Northern Ireland are compared, since the governments of both these communities are widely considered to be modelled on the British parliamentary system.

ESTABLISHMENT OF THE PATTERN

The early post-Confederation period in New Brunswick exhibited a pattern of competition and polarization until 1878. Successive election campaigns, fought on the issues of Confederation and then common schools, divided the electorate along religious and ethnic lines. The confederationists successfully rallied English Protestant voters to their side, winning thirty-three seats in a forty-one-member assembly in 1866, by portraying the election as a contest of the loyal against the disloyal, and Protestants against Catholics. The eight opposition members were all returned in the three counties which contained the largest concentrations of French Catholics, and were derisively referred to as the "French brigade" (MacNutt, 1963, p. 454). The division in the New Brunswick Assembly between a Protestant government and a Catholic opposition was exacerbated in 1871 by the government's introduction of the Common Schools Act to establish a non-sectarian school system financed from public funds—a measure that was supported by Protestants but opposed by Catholics. In the election of 1874, the prime minister capitalized on this division, and assured himself of a landslide majority, by fighting the campaign on the slogan "Vote for the Queen against the Pope" (Rumilly, 1955, p. 763).

Since Protestants made up 66 percent of the New Brunswick population, the policy of polarizing the electorate along religious lines assured the Protestant government of electoral victory. But the policy also led to an unexpected outbreak of violence in Caraquet, resulting in two deaths, when French Catholics, demonstrating in opposition to the Common Schools Act, clashed with English Protestant constables. The "Caraquet riots" horrified the province, and the Protestant cabinet immediately began negotiations with the Catholic members of the opposition in the hope of finding a compromise solution. The resulting compromise, known as the *Modus Vivendi* of 1875 contributed to the establishment of a new political style of cooperation rather than competition. The subsequent election campaign in 1878 was largely non-partisan: "Practically all candidates, in fact, sought to take an independent stand in the campaign by disassociating themselves from any combinations" (Woodward, 1976, p. 15). Of even greater significance, however, is the fact that the new cabinet that was formed after the election was primarily a coalition of the leaders of the major parties to the dispute. While previously ministerial portfolios had been awarded only to Protestants, the 1878 cabinet included, for the first time, two Catholics.

The Fraser Ministry of 1878 is of particular interest because it established the pattern for future governments in New Brunswick. The cabinet was a coalition of Protestants and Catholics, Conservatives and Liberals, and most important, supporters and opponents of the Common Schools Act: it included the leading protagonists, representing all shades of opinion, in the dispute on state-supported schools (see Table 31). The two Catholics appointed to the cabinet, Pierre Landry and Michael Adams, had been outspoken opponents of the act, and had been defeated on that issue in the 1874 election. Indeed, Landry, the leading Acadian of his day, had acted as a defence lawyer for the Acadian demonstrators charged with murder following the Caraquet riots. He subsequently founded and was elected first president of the major association representing Acadians, the Société Nationale l'Assomption. While Adams assumed the position of surveyor-general, Landry was appointed to the strategic post of chief commissioner of public works, the department chiefly responsible for government patronage.

The remaining ministers represented the various shades of Protestant opinion. Robert Young, the president of the Executive Council, had been a leading participant in the Caraquet disturbances. His active support for the Common Schools Act, and his summoning of constables (described as "Young's Army" by the Acadians) to arrest the protesters, had been the instigating cause of the outburst of violence (Stanley, 1972, p. 29). Also included in the cabinet were the leading members of the major Protestant sectarian society, the Freemasons. William Wedderburn, a former newspaper editor and grand master of the New Brunswick Freemasons, became the provincial secretary. Another Freemason—the grand master of the day—was also appointed to the cabinet, but without portfolio.

Although the government was defeated in the 1882 election, the new prime minister, A. G. Blair, imitated his predecessor by welding together

Table 31

The Fraser Ministry in New Brunswick, 1878–82

Minister	Ministry	Party	Position on the School Law
John Fraser	Prime Minister and Attorney-General	Conservative[a]	"In favour of the free non-sectarian school system."
Wm. Wedderburn	Provincial Secretary	Liberal	"Stands pledged to uphold the non-sectarian school law."
Michael Adams	Surveyor-General	Conservative[a]	In favour of separate schools.
Pierre Landry	Chief Commissioner of Public Works	Conservative[a]	In favour of separate schools.
Robert Young	President of the Council	Conservative[a]	In favour of the free non-sectarian school system.
Herbert Crawford	Solicitor-General	Liberal	"In favour of the free non-sectarian school system."
William Perley	Without Portfolio	Liberal	"Supports the free non-sectarian school system."
Daniel Hanington	Without Portfolio	Liberal[a]	Advocated "Bible and religious instruction in common schools."
Robert Marshall	Without Portfolio	Conservative[a]	"Modifications might be made which, while doing no wrong to Protestants would lead Catholics to accept it without further trouble."

Note: The table is compiled from the *Canadian Parliamentary Companion*, 1862–97.
a A supporter of the Liberal-Conservative Party in national politics.

a cabinet which included both Protestants and Catholics, Liberals and Conservatives. This new government coalition continued in power without serious challenge for the next twenty-five years. During this period, opposition to the government was greatly weakened by the fact that it was an all-party coalition presenting a non-partisan program. Further, the inclusion of French-Acadian, Irish-Catholic, and Orange-Protestant leaders among the members of the government benches assured electoral support from throughout the province. Woodward (1976), in describing the strength of the government when it faced the electorate in 1895, observes: "The inclusiveness of the Blair Government made it a prodigious and almost unbeatable electoral force. Defections from the Opposition had brought to the Government the leading political notables of almost all areas in the province" (p. 28). Blair was greatly aided in the construction of these omnibus government coalitions by what Woodward (1976) has described as "highly individuated politics" (p. 2). Candidates were reluctant to commit themselves to possible alignments prior to election, leaving themselves free to negotiate later in the interests of their constituency. Thus, as one prominent Liberal complained during the 1908 election, Conservative candidates who were elected to represent the largely Acadian county of Gloucester always ended up on the government benches, whether or not the Conservatives were the majority party: "These men desired only to have power at their disposal. Thus, after an election it was easy for them to line up on the government side. Such was the political spirit of the time" (Turgeon, 1928, p. 118).

During his long tenure in office, Blair succeeded in establishing the enduring model of the omnibus government party, including the leaders of all sectional interests within the province. Examination of the first half-century after Confederation shows that most cabinets included not only a leading Acadian—usually drawn from the senior ranks of the Acadians national association, the Société Nationale l'Assomption—but also leading representatives of the English Protestant sectarian associations, such as the Freemasons and the Orange Order (see Table 32). Blair, himself, was closely associated with the Liberal Party and that party, in New Brunswick politics, became identified as the government party, *par excellence*. It was not until 1917 that New Brunswick experienced a one-party government; but even after this date, the leaders continued to appeal for non-partisan support, describing themselves simply as either members of the "government party" or the "opposition party." By this time, the tradition of a "coalescent" government, bringing together the political elite of each bloc had been well established.

In direct contrast to the coalescent behaviour of the elites in New Brunswick, the early years of government in Northern Ireland reveal

Table 32

Selected Cabinet Ministers in New Brunswick, 1867–1925

Minister	Ministry	Leadership Role
French-Acadian Cabinet Ministers		
Pierre Landry (Conservative)	Public Works (1878–82) Provincial Secretary (1882–83)	President, Société Nationale l'Assomption.
Oliver LeBlanc (Conservative)	Without Portfolio (1889–91) Solicitor-General (1892)	Vice-President, Société Nationale l'Assomption. Secretary, Société Nationale l'Assomption.
Ambroise Richard (Conservative)	Without Portfolio (1897–1900)	
Charles LaBillois (Conservative)	Agriculture (1897–1900) Public Works (1900–8)	Executive Member, Société Nationale l'Assomption.
David Landry (Conservative)	Agriculture (1908–14) Secretary-Treasurer (1914–17)	President, Société Mutuelle l'Assomption.
Peter Veniot (Liberal)	Public Works (1917–23) Prime Minister (1923–25)	Publisher, *Courrier des Provinces Maritimes*.
Leading Masonic and Orange Cabinet Ministers		
Wm. Flewelling	Without Portfolio (1867–69)	Senior Grand Warden, Freemasons. Grand Worthy Chief, Templars.
Ben. Stevenson (Liberal)	Surveyor-General (1871–78)	Grand Master, Freemasons.
Edward Willis (Liberal)	Surveyor-General (1871–78) Without Portfolio (1873–76)	Deputy Grand Master, Freemasons. Master, Orange Order.
Wm. Wedderburn (Liberal)	Provincial Secretary (1878–82)	Grand Master, Freemasons. Grand Worthy Patron, Sons of Temperance.
Robert Marshall (Conservative)	Without Portfolio (1879–82)	Grand Master, Freemasons. Lt. Grand Commander, Scottish Rite.
Harry McLeod (Conservative)	Solicitor-General (1908–11) Provincial Secretary (1911–17)	Grand Master, Orange Order.

Note: The table is derived from the *Canadian Parliamentary Companion*, 1862–97; *Canadian Parliamentary Guide*, 1895–1975; Robidoux, 1907; and Walker, 1924.

an unambiguous pattern of competition. The first Northern Ireland cabinet, formed in 1921, included members of only the Unionist Party, the party representing the Protestant majority. From the earliest days of "self-government," the government was Protestant and the opposition, Catholic. During the life of the Northern Ireland Parliament, from 1921 until 1972, there was never a governmental coalition between the parties representing the two blocs.

The absence of any coalescent behaviour in the first Northern Ireland cabinet was a natural continuation of the political polarization that had developed during the nineteenth century. If the major political division in New Brunswick had been the question of common schools, in Northern Ireland the predominant issue was the establishment of Home Rule; and in both communities, opinion was polarized along the Protestant-Catholic divide. In Northern Ireland, Protestants organized the Ulster Loyalist Anti-Repeal Union in 1886, and then subsequently the Ulster Unionist Council in 1905, to oppose the Catholic-supported Home Rule Party (see Savage, 1961). The conversion of Gladstone to Home Rule cemented the alliances between the Irish and British parties: the Nationalists became closely linked with the Liberal Party, while the Unionists remained tightly aligned with the Conservative Party. The differences between the Irish parties were exploited by their British allies who capitalized on the Home Rule issue for electoral gain. The Conservatives in particular hoped, by exacerbating the tensions, to rally sufficient Protestant support to defeat the incumbent Liberal government. The model for the future Northern Ireland Parliament, therefore, was the competitive politics of the United Kingdom Parliament, where the unionist Conservatives confronted the nationalist Liberals, and where governments were formed by the majority party.

The formation of the Craig Ministry in Northern Ireland in 1921 established the model that was to dominate Northern Ireland politics (see Table 33). All the members of the cabinet were Protestants and Unionists. Further, all but one of the ministers were members of the Orange Order, a militant sectarian organization dedicated to the preservation of the Protestant religion and the union with Britain. Three of the ministers, including the prime minister, held leading positions in the Order, two subsequently becoming grand masters of the Orange Order in Ireland. In addition, the cabinet could claim the leading members of the Protestant political organization, the Ulster Unionist Council, and its working man's affiliate, the Ulster Unionist Labour Association. The only two ministers without formal roles in Protestant sectarian organizations were, nevertheless, leading representatives of the Protestant community. Hugh Pollock, a former president of the Belfast Chamber of

Table 33

The Craig Ministry in Northern Ireland, 1921–25

Minister	Ministry	Leadership Role
James Craig (Unionist)	Prime Minister (1921–40)	Grand Master, Orange Order (Co. Down). President, Ulster Unionist Council.
Hugh Pollock (Unionist)	Finance (1921–37)	President, Belfast Chamber of Commerce.
Dawson Bates (Unionist)	Home Affairs (1921–43)	Vice-President, Ulster Unionist Council.
John M. Andrews (Unionist)	Labour (1921–37) Finance (1937–40) Prime Minister (1940–43)	Grand Master, Orange Order (Ireland). President, Ulster Unionist Labour Association.
Marquess of Londonderry (Unionist)	Education (1921–26)	Leader of the Senate. Chancellor, Queen's University, Belfast.
Edward Archdale (Unionist)	Commerce (1921–25) Agriculture (1921–33)	Grand Master, Orange Order (Ireland).

Note: The table is derived from Dewar, Brown, and Long, 1967; Harbinson, 1973; and *Who Was Who, 1897–1970.*

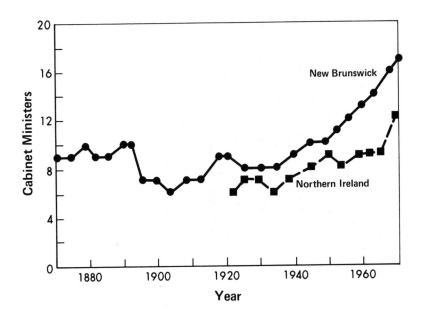

Fig. 9. Number of cabinet ministers, 1870–1970. (The data for election years are from *Canadian Parliamentary Companion*, 1862–97; *Canadian Parliamentary Guide*, 1898–1975; and Whitaker, 1869–1976.)

Commerce represented the business community, while the Marquess of Londonderry, the leader of the Northern Ireland Senate and a future leader of the House of Lords, represented the landed aristocracy.

The early pattern of elite behaviour in New Brunswick and Northern Ireland thus reveals striking contrasts. In New Brunswick, the cabinets were unmistakably coalescent in style. They constituted a coalition of the major political leaders, drawn from both political parties and, most important, both conflict groups. In Northern Ireland, on the other hand, the early cabinets were clearly competitive in style. They were composed only of members of the majority party, a party that was homogeneous in religion and in politics. The basic difference may be partially illustrated by a comparison of the size of the cabinets in each community. New Brunswick, with a much smaller population than Northern Ireland, has nevertheless possessed comparatively large cabinets (Fig. 9). The size of the New Brunswick cabinets was not necessitated by the administrative load, but rather by the need to include the representatives of as many sectional interests as possible in the government. Between 1867 and 1900, the cabinets averaged approximately nine

members, of whom at least three were usually ministers without portfolio. Commenting on the appointment of ministers without portfolio in
the Canadian provinces generally, J. R. Mallory (1957) notes: "It is to
be assumed that when such are created the purpose is to secure balanced
representation in the Cabinet" (p. 198).

MODERN COMPOSITION OF THE CABINETS

Although the influence of the early patterns of elite behaviour is still
clearly visible in the governments of the two communities, important
modifications have also taken place. First, in both communities, the role
of the political elite has become more specialized. The volume of governmental work has increased to the point where membership in the cabinet
is a demanding full-time occupation. Since the same might be said for
certain of the major bloc organizations, the instances where cabinet
ministers simultaneously occupy formalized leadership positions in the
institutions of their bloc have been reduced. Second, in the New Brunswick context, party lines have been imposed on the cabinet system in
accordance with the British model of majority government. Political
party divisions—for many years weakened by the tradition of coalition
cabinets—have become a dominant feature of New Brunswick politics
largely because of the influence of the Canadian national parties. Since
1917, all New Brunswick governments have been one-party governments; and the division between government and opposition has thus
corresponded to the division between Liberals and Conservatives.

The advent of one-party governments in New Brunswick did not fully
eliminate the earlier traditions, however. As late as 1935 the Conservative government conducted its electoral campaign, not in the name of the
Conservative Party, but rather in the name of the "Tilley Government
Party." According to Woodward (1976), formalized association of the
government with the Conservative Party was discouraged by "the need
of the provincial party to obtain Acadian support" (p. 4). It was not
until 1944 that both parties faced the electorate with formal partisan
labels, those of the Liberal Party and the Progressive Conservative
Party. This delay—in spite of the pressures of the Canadian national
parties—may be attributed in large measure to the need for each party
to present itself as a potential government party capable of representing
all sectional interests. Thus, while all-party coalitions were replaced by
one-party cabinets, the traditional belief that the government should be
representative of the community's divergent ethnic and religious interests still remained.

The representativeness of modern-day New Brunswick cabinets may
be illustrated by examining their composition over a twenty-five year

Table 34

Ethno-Religious Composition of the Cabinet and Legislature in New Brunswick, 1948–72

Ethnic group	Protestant	Catholic	Total
% of the Cabinet[a]			
English	50 (+3)	14 (−1)	64 (+2)
French	1 (0)	35 (−2)	36 (−2)
Total	51 (+3)	49 (−3)	100 (0)
% of the Legislature[b]			
English	57 (+10)	15 (0)	72 (+10)
French	1 (0)	27 (−10)	28 (−10)
Total	58 (+10)	42 (−10)	100 (0)

Note: The calculations of the proportions of each ethnic and religious group in the cabinet and the Legislature are based only on election years. The numbers in parentheses represent the deviations from the proportions in the society as a whole.

a Corrected $\chi^2(1) = 2.35$, $p < .2$; $\phi = .085$. In calculating the expected values for the null hypothesis, the proportions in the society as a whole were used.

b $\chi^2(1) = 67.0$, $p < .0001$; $\phi = .224$. In calculating the expected values for the null hypothesis, the proportions in the society as a whole were used.

period, from 1948 until 1972. During these years the ethnic and religious composition of the cabinets has closely reflected that of the community as a whole—in spite of the fact that English Protestants have been overrepresented, and French Catholics underrepresented, in the Legislative Assembly (see Table 34). The pressure to construct fully representative cabinets—even when such representativeness does not exist in the assembly—is illustrated by the results of recent provincial elections. At the 1974 election, the Conservative Party returned thirty-three members, of whom only five were Acadians. Nevertheless, all five were offered positions in the seventeen-member Conservative cabinet.[1] The role of these Acadian cabinet ministers was explicitly to represent the interests of their bloc. This was underlined by one Acadian minister, Jean-Pierre Ouellet, when the government began consideration of the

---

1. One of the five, the former minister of finance, refused an immediate appointment to the cabinet for personal reasons and, thus, he was not added to the cabinet until two years after the election. The appointments immediately following the 1974 election were: Omer Leger, provincial secretary and minister of fisheries; Roland Boudreau, minister of natural resources; Jean-Pierre Ouellet, minister of youth; and Fernand Dubé, minister of tourism and minister of the environment.

Table 35

*Ethno-Religious Composition of the Cabinet and Commons
in Northern Ireland, 1948–72*

National orientation	Protestant	Catholic	Total
% of the Cabinet[a]			
British	100 (+35)	0 (−15)	100 (+20)
Irish	0 (0)	0 (−20)	0 (−20)
Total	100 (+35)	0 (−35)	100 (0)
% of the House of Commons[b]			
British	78 (+13)	1 (−14)	79 (−2)
Irish	1 (0)	21 (+1)	22 (+2)
Total	79 (+13)	22 (−13)	100 (0)

Note: The calculations of the proportions of each national and religious group in the cabinet and the Commons are based only on election years. The numbers in parentheses represent the deviations from the proportions in the society as a whole. National orientation was defined according to political party support. Parties which favour the British connection (e.g., Unionist Party, Northern Ireland Labour Party) are judged to have a British orientation, while those which advocated a united Ireland (e.g., Nationalist Party, Republican Labour Party) are deemed to have an Irish orientation.

a Corrected $\chi^2(1) = 229$, $p < .0001$; $\phi = .308$. In calculating the expected values for the null hypothesis, the proportions in the society as a whole were used.

b $\chi^2(1) = 115$, $p < .0001$; $\phi = .298$. In calculating the expected values for the null hypothesis, the proportions in the society as a whole were used.

recommendations of the LeBel Commission on Higher Education. In a public statement, Ouellet noted: "I can assure the French-speaking population of New Brunswick that I will defend its interests in the decisions of the Cabinet on this report" ("Ouellet défendra les droits des Francophones," 1975).

The Northern Ireland cabinet, however, shows a complete contrast to that in New Brunswick. The underrepresentation of the Catholic minority in the House of Commons is even further amplified in the cabinet (see Table 35). From the foundation of the Northern Ireland Parliament until its prorogation, a period of some fifty-two years, there was only one Catholic cabinet minister. This was G. B. Newe, who, in what must be considered a token appointment, was named minister of state in October 1971. Newe was not a member of Parliament and could not, by virtue of any official position in the Catholic bloc, claim to represent the Catholic minority. He admitted at the time of his appointment that "he didn't represent anybody, that he wouldn't try and claim to do so and

Table 36

Associational Memberships of Cabinet Ministers, 1968

Proportion of cabinet	New Brunswick	Northern Ireland
one-half or more		Orange Order
one-third or more	Chamber of Commerce Board of Trade	
one-fourth or more	Barristers' Society Royal Canadian Legion Chevaliers de Colomb	Ulster Reform Club Ulster Club
one-fifth or more	Freemasons Société l'Assomption Rotary Club	Guards' Club Royal North of Ireland Yacht Club

Note: The table is derived from *Canadian Parliamentary Guide*, 1898–1975; *Canadian Who's Who*, 1969; Harbinson, 1973; New Brunswick Liberal Party; *Who's Who*, 1969.

that he was in effect joining the cabinet to try and cooperate with the government in bringing about reconciliation in the community" (H. Kelly, 1972, p. 104). Newe's tenure lasted only five months, ending in March 1972, when the Northern Ireland Parliament was suspended. In the perspective of fifty, or even twenty-five years, the five-month appointment did nothing to modify the character of the Northern Ireland cabinet as an exclusively Protestant institution. The triumph of competitive politics in Northern Ireland had led to exclusive Protestant control in government.

This distinction between the New Brunswick and Northern Ireland cabinets is apparent not only in the ethno-religious character of the ministers, but also in their associational memberships. A salient characteristic of the associational membership of New Brunswick cabinet ministers is the prominence of "functional" associations, that is, associations in which people "associate only in terms of a specific economic or social purpose," without regard for the ethno-religious divisions in the society (Lorwin, 1971, p. 141). These include the Chamber of Commerce, the Barristers' Society, and the Royal Canadian Legion (see Table 36). The Chamber of Commerce and the Board of Trade, together, account for ten of the fifteen members of the 1968 cabinet. While all of these organizations tend to be English-dominated, the regional segregation of the population permits the membership of both subcultures, without necessarily leading to contact between the blocs. Thus, for example, in Acadian regions, the members of the Chamber of Commerce or the Legion are likely to be overwhelmingly French; while in English areas, the membership is overwhelmingly English.

In spite of the prominence of membership in functional associations, it is nevertheless significant that the great majority of cabinet ministers are also members of "segmented" associations. Twelve of the fifteen ministers acknowledged membership in an organization which drew its members exclusively from one of the ethno-religious subcultures. Among Acadian ministers, this included a leadership role in two Acadian economic institutions, the Société Mutuelle l'Assomption and the Fédération des Caisses Populaires Acadiennes (FCPA), and membership in a fraternal society, the Chevaliers de Colomb. The Société Mutuelle l'Assomption—now known as Assomption Mutuelle-Vie—was originally founded in 1903 to preserve the French language, to defend the Catholic religion, and to provide financial assistance to its members. The FCPA brings together the more than ninety individual *caisses populaires* which provide banking service to the French-speaking population of the province.[2] Together, the Société Mutuelle l'Assomption and the FCPA are responsible for the publication of the province's only French-language daily newspaper, *L'Evangéline*, and for the foundation of the Société Nationale des Acadiens (SNA)—successor to the Société Nationale l'Assomption—the national association representing Acadian interests. The Chevaliers de Colomb (or Knights of Columbus), a Catholic fraternal society, is of American origin, but it has a predominantly Acadian membership in New Brunswick. It competes for members with a native Canadian secret society, the Ordre de Jacques-Cartier (and its offshoot, the Chevaliers de Champlain), an association which was formed in 1926 to defend the French-Canadian culture and the Roman Catholic religion, and to combat the influence of the Freemasons.[3]

Among the English members of the cabinet, the major segmented associations are social clubs such as the Rotary or the Lions, and a secret society, the Freemasons. The latter, although not explicitly restricted to

2. The FCPA, originally founded in 1945, had more than 107,000 members by 1972 (New Brunswick, Department of Agriculture, 1973). This number is equal to more than three-quarters of the adult French population, although some of these members may be business members and multi-members.
3. The foundation of the Ordre de Jacques-Cartier was particularly motivated by a desire to increase the employment of French Canadians in the civil service, but the keynote of its policy became the "control of patriotic societies, governments and public administration of all kinds" (Cyr, 1964, p. 35). While it is known that prominent members of the Acadian political and economic elite also occupy leading roles in the Ordre de Jacques-Cartier, the extreme secrecy of the society makes positive identification difficult. Cyr names Martin Légère, general manager of the FCPA, and Gilbert Finn, general manager of Assomption Mutuelle-Vie, as *chanceliers* of the society.

any one religious group by its constitution, has been the exclusive preserve of Protestants in the New Brunswick context. The first masonic lodges in the province were founded in the late eighteenth and early nineteenth centuries by Loyalists and "citizens of distinction," with the primary goal of providing mutual assistance to their members (Bunting, 1895, p. 19). The society's New Brunswick membership is extensive and its political influence pervasive although, because of its secret character, reliable information about its activities is rarely available.[4] Much of its influence in government likely stems from the fraternal tradition of giving preference to fellow Freemasons in decisions regarding employment and contracts. It is significant, therefore, that many of the English Protestant members of New Brunswick cabinets are Freemasons, and that a long tradition assures the appointment of at least one senior member of the society. The 1968 Liberal cabinet, for example, included a master of the Scottish Rite, an elite branch of Freemasonry; while the 1970 Conservative cabinet included the grand master of the New Brunswick Grand Lodge.

While the New Brunswick cabinet is pluralist in its membership, the Northern Ireland cabinet is essentially homogeneous. The associational memberships of its cabinet ministers are not only limited to largely segmented associations but, obviously, they are restricted to associations within the Protestant bloc. Some of these associations, such as the Ulster Reform Club—an affiliate of the Ulster Unionist Council, limited to leading members of the business community—have a narrow class base; others, notably the Orange Order, are much more broadly based. Without question, the dominant organization is the Orange Order, a secret society formed during the eighteenth century to defend the Protestant religion. In 1968, all members of the cabinet were also members of the Order, a fact that is not surprising when it is considered that, between 1921 and 1969, 138 of the 149 Unionist members of Parliament belonged to the Order at the time of their election (Harbinson, 1973, p. 91).

Historically, the Unionist Party and the Orange Order have been closely allied, a consequence, in part, of the role which the Order played in the founding of that party. In 1970, 138 of the 1,000 delegates to the Ulster Unionist Council (UUC) were the direct representatives of the Orange Institution—including related organizations such as the Appren-

---

4. During the 1920s as much as 10 percent of the adult male Protestant population were members of the masonic lodges (see Walker, 1924, p. 115) and there is little evidence that their popularity has diminished. Acadians have frequently criticized the upper ranks of the civil service as being *franc-maçon, anglais* (Leslie, 1969).

tice Boys of Derry and the Association of Loyal Orange Women ("Central power of Ulster Unionism," 1970). In addition, the local Orange lodges participated in the nomination of delegates from the local Unionist associations who made up the majority of the UUC members. Further, although the heads of the Orange Order were not members of the 1968 cabinet, they nevertheless occupied important posts within the Unionist Party. The grand master of the Orange Council of the World was the leader of the Unionist Party in the British House of Commons. The grand master of the Royal Black Institution, an elite of the Order, was the Speaker of the Northern Ireland House of Commons from 1946 until 1969.

It is likely that the competitive style of the Northern Ireland cabinet has owed much to the pervasive influence of the Orange Order. The Order has consistently opposed any cooperation with Catholics, thereby blocking the potential entry of Catholics into the cabinet. When in 1959, for example, some leading Unionists suggested that Catholics should be admitted into the party, both as members and as parliamentary candidates, the proposal was effectively vetoed by the Order. The grand master of the Order responded: "It is difficult to see how a Catholic, with the vast difference in our religious outlook, could be either acceptable within the Unionist Party as a member or, for that matter, bring himself unconditionally to support its ideals. Further to this, an Orangeman is pledged to resist by all lawful means the ascendancy of the Church of Rome" (Harbinson, 1973, p. 44). The prime minister and the Executive Committee of the Unionist Council subsequently reiterated the grand master's position and, as Harbinson (1973) comments: "There seems little doubt that in closing the doors to Roman Catholic members, the party, on this occasion, was following the advice of the Orange Institution" (p. 45).

The comparison of the Northern Ireland and New Brunswick elites provides new insight into the structure of elite competition and coalescence. The Northern Ireland elites have clearly been competitive in their behaviour. Until its prorogation in 1972, the Northern Ireland Parliament was consistently divided between a one-party Protestant government and a Catholic opposition. The New Brunswick elites have a long tradition of coalescence; but this coalescence has often differed considerably from Lijphart's definition. New Brunswick cabinets have been representative of the two blocs in the community, but there have been no multi-party coalitions since 1917. In modern times, the assembly has seen one-party governments, opposed by one-party oppositions. Nevertheless, the tradition of representative cabinets has evidently been an adequate functional alternative to the grand coalitions thought essential by Lijphart. This suggests that the term coalescence, if it is to be applied to the New Brunswick elites, must be interpreted in a broader sense to include any government—even a one-party cabinet—which succeeds in bringing together the representatives of the principal blocs.

THE CIVIL SERVICE

Not unexpectedly, the contrasting patterns of coalescence and competition in the cabinets are reflected in the composition of the civil services in the two communities: the administrative elites tend to share the same ethnic and religious attributes as the political elites who were instrumental in their appointment. In New Brunswick, the appointment of substantial numbers of Acadians to the senior ranks of the civil service was most evident during the 1960s, when as many as half of the cabinet ministers were, themselves, Acadians. Hugh Thorburn (1966), in his study of ethnic participation in the New Brunswick civil service, concluded that the presence of a French-speaking minister had a significant effect on the character of a department since he "normally seeks to see his group represented in the department in an equitable manner. Therefore as vacancies occur he is bound to have this in mind" (p. 31). Additional pressure to construct a civil service which might fairly represent the population of the province came with the passage of the New Brunswick Official Languages Act in 1969. The act, by requiring the government to provide public services in French as well as English, led inevitably to an increase in the number of Acadian employees.

In Northern Ireland, there has been no such pressure to increase the representation of the minority bloc in the civil service. In fact, the homogeneous Protestant character of the cabinet has worked against the employment of Catholics in government. Many of the early cabinet ministers vigorously defended themselves against suggestions that they employed significant numbers of Catholics in their ministries. Edward Archdale, for example, announced in Parliament: "I have 109 officials and so far as I know, four of them are Roman Catholics, three of whom were civil servants turned over to me, whom I had to take on when we began" (*Sunday Times* Insight Team, 1972, p. 30). The government encouraged, at least unofficially, all efforts to hire Protestants rather than Catholics, in both the private and public sectors. Basil Brooke, while minister of agriculture, advised "those people who are Loyalists not to employ Roman Catholics, ninety-nine per cent of whom are disloyal" (Campaign for Social Justice in Northern Ireland, 1969). In giving preference to Protestants, the government was largely supported by the Orange Order although, in the view of the latter, the government did not always go far enough. One resolution passed by the Order, and made

Table 37
Composition of the Provincial Civil Services

	New Brunswick (1966)[a]		
Occupational grade	% English ($N = 3,375$)	% French ($N = 1,186$)	% Total ($N = 4,561$)
Professional	79	22	101
Managerial, supervisory	71	29	100
Clerical	78	22	100
Labour	69	31	100
Total	74	26	100

	Northern Ireland (1969)[b]		
Occupational grade	% Protestant ($N = 492$)	% Catholic ($N = 36$)	% Total ($N = 528$)
Senior administrative	93	7	100
Professional, technical	94	6	100
Total	93	7	100

Note: The data are adapted from Thorburn, 1966, and Campaign for Social Justice in Northern Ireland, 1969. As in previous tables, the English category for New Brunswick includes a small number of persons of neither British nor French origin (in addition to those of British origin).

a $\chi^2(4) = 269$, $p < .0001$; $V = .243$. In calculating the expected values for the null hypothesis, the proportions of each bloc in the society as a whole were used.

b $\chi^2(1) = 185$, $p < .0001$; $\phi = .592$. In calculating the expected values for the null hypothesis, the proportions of each bloc in the society as a whole were used.

public in 1970, demanded a reduction in the number of Catholics employed, on the grounds that they constituted a security risk: "We ask that the Government be called upon to cease employment of Roman Catholics by an early date (Date and conditions as fixed by the Grand Lodge), and that, where possible, without causing obvious discrimination which might act adversely on the Government and the Orange Order, dismiss as many as possible of those already in their employment" (J. Kelly, 1970).

A comparison of the proportions in the civil services of the two communities shows that while the minority is underrepresented in both communities, this underrepresentation is the most severe in Northern Ireland. In 1969, Catholics made up only 7 percent of those in the senior ranks of the Northern Ireland civil service (see Table 37). It is unlikely that this pro-

Table 38

Composition of the Senior Administrative Positions

| | New Brunswick (1976)[a] | | |
Position	English	French	Total
Deputy ministers	15	6	21
Assistant deputy ministers	12	2	14
Directors	166	24	190
Total	193	32	225

| | Northern Ireland (1969)[b] | | |
Position	Protestant	Catholic	Total
Assistant secretaries	52	1	53
Principal officers	91	11	102
Deputy principal officers	153	11	164
Total	296	23	319

Note: The data are from Losier, 1977, and Campaign for Social Justice in Northern Ireland, 1969.

a Corrected $\chi^2(2) = 52.2$, $p < .0001$; $V = .481$. In calculating the expected values for the null hypothesis, the proportions of each bloc in the society as a whole were used. Otherwise, $\chi^2(2) = 3.94$, $p < .14$; $V = .132$.

b Corrected $\chi^2(2) = 111$, $p < .0001$; $V = .591$. In calculating the expected values for the null hypothesis, the proportions of each bloc in the society as a whole were used. Otherwise, $\chi^2 = 4.25$, $p < .12$; $V = .115$.

portion was ever exceeded. Barritt and Carter (1972) calculate the proportion of Catholics in senior positions as 6 percent for the years 1929 and 1959, while an evaluation by Donnison (1973) puts it at 5 percent for 1972. Possible explanations given to account for these low numbers have included both the possible lack of educational qualifications and the political disaffection of the Catholic minority. However, these explanations seem dubious in light of the fact that the proportion of Catholics in the "Imperial" civil service, under the jurisdiction of the British government (for instance, the Post Office, Inland Revenue, National Defence), varies between 33 percent and 55 percent (Barritt and Carter, 1972, p. 97).

The New Brunswick Acadians are also underrepresented—although not to the same extent as the Northern Ireland Catholics. In the civil service as a whole, Acadians accounted for 26 percent in 1966. Their proportions, however, tended to be much lower in the senior ranks. In 1976, only 14 percent of those in the top administrative positions were Acadian (see Table 38). Socio-economic explanations for this underrepresentation would appear to be more plausible here than in Northern

Table 39
Composition of the Judicial Positions

Position	New Brunswick (1974)[a]		
	English	French	Total
Supreme court judges	7	3	10
County court judges	4	3	7
Provincial court judges	13	3	16
Judges of probate	10	2	12
Crown prosecutors	13	8	21
Sheriffs	7	2	9
Clerks of the peace	8	2	10
Total	62	23	85

Position	Northern Ireland (1969)[b]		
	Protestant	Catholic	Total
High court judges	6	1	7
County court judges	4	1	5
Resident magistrates	9	3	12
Crown solicitors	8	0	8
Under sheriffs	6	0	6
Clerks of the peace	6	0	6
Total	39	5	44

Note: The data are calculated from Wharton, 1975; and Campaign for Social Justice in Northern Ireland, 1969. The classification of the judicial positions in New Brunswick was based on the ethnic origin of the individual's name.

a $\chi^2(6) = 8.03$, $p < .3$; $V = .307$. In calculating the expected values for the null hypothesis, the proportions of each bloc in the society as a whole were used.

b   Corrected $\chi^2(6) = 15.7$, $p < .02$, $V = .597$. In calculating the expected values for the null hypothesis, the proportions of each bloc in the society as a whole were used.

Ireland. The inferior educational attainment of the Acadians has likely been an important factor. Further, according to Thorburn (1971), the Acadians have been disadvantaged by their greater tendency to live in rural areas.

A comparison of the major judicial positions in the two communities reveals a similar situation. While 27 percent of those occupying important positions in the judicial sector in New Brunswick are French, only 11 percent of those in Northern Ireland are Catholics (see Table 39). In both New Brunswick and Northern Ireland, political patronage plays a significant role in the allocation of judicial appointments—a judgeship is often a favoured reward for retiring cabinet ministers with a training in law. Thus, here again, there is a tendency for the judiciary to possess the same social and political attributes as the cabinet. The political link is particularly evident in Northern Ireland, as Boyle, Hadden, and Hillyard (1975) have observed:

> Of twenty High Court judges appointed since the independent Northern Ireland courts were established, fifteen had been openly associated with the Unionist Party; of twenty-three County Court appointments, fourteen had been visibly connected with the Unionist administration. At the height of the civil rights campaign in the late 1960s two of the three judges in the Northern Ireland Court of Appeal were ex-Attorney-Generals in Unionist governments; one of the four High Court judges was likewise an ex-Attorney-General, and another the son of an Attorney-General; two of the five County Court judges were ex-Unionist M.P.s and another the son of a Unionist M.P.; and among the twelve Resident Magistrates there was an ex-Unionist M.P., and ex-Unionist Senator, a defeated Unionist candidate and a former legal advisor to the Ministry of Home Affairs. (p. 12)

Political patronage has played a less obvious role in judicial appointments in New Brunswick; but it is also true that such patronage as there is has not worked against the French minority, because of their participation in both the national and the provincial cabinets.

THE NORTHERN IRELAND COALITION EXECUTIVE, 1974

If the behaviour of the political elite is a major variable explaining the maintenance of stability in a fragmented community, then the formation of a coalition government in Northern Ireland in 1974 must be considered an event with important theoretical implications. It permits, at the very least, a more precise evaluation of the conditions in which elite coalescence is likely to be effective.

Since the suspension of the Northern Ireland Parliament in 1972, both the major British parties—the Conservative Party and the Labour Party—whether in opposition or in government, have agreed that the most likely solution to the "problem" would be a new political arrangement that would give Catholics increased opportunity for participation in the government of Northern Ireland. In short, it was believed that political stability could be established through a coalition of the leaders of the Protestant and Catholic blocs. In 1973, the Conservative government indicated that it would permit the devolution of political power only if an executive could be formed that would command the support of both segments of the community. A year later, a Labour government reiterated the Conservative stand, and Harold Wilson, the British prime minister, gave assurances that any settlement of the Northern Ireland question would have to allow for the sharing of power with Catholics. Wilson noted: "There must be some form of power-sharing and partnership because no political system will survive or be supported unless there is widespread acceptance of it within the community. There must be genuine participation by both communities in the direction of affairs" (Holohan, 1974).

The British desire to create a coalition government in Northern Ireland took concrete form in 1973 with the passing of the Northern Ireland Assembly Act and the Northern Ireland Constitution Act. These acts provided for the establishment of a new assembly containing seventy-eight members, to be elected by means of the single transferable vote. However, the actual devolution of legislative and executive power to this assembly was to be permitted only if the Secretary of State could be assured that "a Northern Ireland Executive can be formed which, having regard to the support it commands in the Assembly and to the electorate on which that support is based, is likely to be widely accepted throughout the community" ("Power-sharing executive agreed," 1973). The intent of this clause was to make the devolution of power to a Northern Ireland government dependent upon the formation of a coalition between the political parties representing both Protestant and Catholic opinion.

The British proposals, as contained in the White Paper entitled *Constitutional Proposals*, became the primary issue in the 1973 Northern Ireland election. The White Paper was supported by the Catholic Social Democratic and Labour Party (SDLP) but the Protestant Loyalist and Unionist parties were divided on the issue. The election was followed by six weeks of interparty talks, at the end of which the Secretary of State for Northern Ireland, William Whitelaw, announced the formation of a coalition government composed of three parties, the Unionist Party, the SDLP, and the Alliance Party. In stark contrast to the comparatively small cabinets of the former Northern Ireland Parliament, the new administration contained fifteen members, four of whom were nonvoting. The government was carefully balanced to give the Unionist Party a majority among the voting members, although in a minority in the administration as a whole (see Table 40). The former Unionist prime minister became the chief executive, while the former SDLP leader of the opposition took the post of deputy-chief executive. Northern Ireland's first and only coalition government was of short duration, how-

Table 40

Northern Ireland Coalition Executive, 1974

Minister	Department	Religion	Party
Brian Faulkner	Chief Minister	Protestant	Unionist Party
Gerard Fitt	Deputy-Chief Minister	Catholic	SDLP
Oliver Napier	Law Reform	Catholic	Alliance Party
Herbert Kirk	Finance	Protestant	Unionist Party
John Hume	Commerce	Catholic	SDLP
Patrick Devlin	Health/Social Services	Catholic	SDLP
Austin Currie	Local Government/Housing	Catholic	SDLP
Roy Bradford	Environment	Protestant	Unionist Party
Basil McIvor	Education	Protestant	Unionist Party
Leslie Morrell	Agriculture	Protestant	Unionist Party
John Baxter	Information Services	Protestant	Unionist Party
Lloyd Hall-Thompson[a]	Chief Whip	Protestant	Unionist Party
Robert Cooper[a]	Manpower Services	Protestant	Alliance Party
Ivan Cooper[a]	Community Relations	Protestant	SDLP
Edward McGrady[a]	Planning/Coordination	Catholic	SDLP

a A non-voting member.

Table 41
Northern Ireland Assembly Election, 1973

Party	First preference votes		Seats in Assembly	
	N	%	N	%
Loyalists[a]	255,200	35.4	27	34.6
Official Unionists	182,700	25.3	22	28.2
SDLP	159,700	22.1	19	24.3
Alliance	66,700	9.2	8	10.3
NILP	18,800	2.6	1	1.3
Other	39,100	5.4	1	1.3
Total	722,200	100.0	78	100.0

Note: The data are calculated from Knight, 1974.

a Includes the Loyalist coalition (Vanguard Unionists and Democratic Unionists) and the anti-White Paper Unionists.

ever. In April 1974, a massive general strike brought about its collapse, less than four months after it had taken office.

The failure of the coalition to establish political stability in Northern Ireland—or even to assure its own feasibility—may be found in its artificial origins: the power-sharing executive was largely imposed on Northern Ireland by the British government and was never supported by the dominant Protestant bloc. The majority of Protestant votes in the 1973 election went to "Loyalist" parties which were unequivocally opposed to the White Paper proposal of a coalition between Protestants and Catholics (see Table 41). A large number of Protestant votes also went to the Official Unionist Party, but the policy of that party on the question of power-sharing was extremely ambiguous: "While not insisting on one-party government, the party did declare that it would not participate in an Executive with those whose primary aim was to break the union with Great Britain" (Lawrence, Elliott, and Laver, 1975, p. 59). In fact, four days after the coalition government took office, the Unionist Council voted against the arrangement and their leader, Brian Faulkner, was forced to resign from the party, although he continued to hold the parliamentary office of chief executive in the assembly. The new leader, Harry West, brought the Unionists into an alliance with the Loyalist parties in the assembly. West was unhesitating in his opposition to sharing power with the Catholic SDLP, declaring later in the year that "we are not prepared to share power with those who are the enemies of Ulster and who give allegiance to another country" (Ellis, 1974). William Craig, leader of the Vanguard Unionist Party and a

Table 42

Preferred Political Alternative in Northern Ireland, 1974

Alternative	% of Protestants	% of Catholics	% of Total
Power-sharing executive	18	55	29
United Ireland outside U.K.[a]	1	23	8
Integration with U.K.	33	6	24
Return of N.I. Parliament	33	1	23
Direct rule by U.K.	8	8	8
Other	8	8	8
Total	101	101	100

Note: $\chi^2(5) = 405$, $p < .0001$; $V = .645$. The data are from National Opinion Polls, 1974.

a Includes the alternative of an amalgamated Ireland.

former cabinet minister, also made the Loyalist position clear: "There are many changes that can be made in the whole apparatus of the Government that will make the minorities feel assured that they are getting fair and equal treatment with all citizens and have an effective voice in the Government and administration of the country. But it does not mean participation at the Cabinet or on Executive level" (O'Connor, 1974).

A general election for the United Kingdom Parliament held in February 1974 provided further evidence that the great majority of Protestants were opposed to the policy permitting Catholics to share political power. In the election, which became largely a poll on the new executive, Loyalist candidates opposing the coalition won eleven of the twelve parliamentary seats, the twelfth being won by the leader of the Catholic SDLP. Unionist candidates supporting the coalition obtained only 13 percent of the vote. A month later, a survey of public opinion in Northern Ireland revealed that support for the principle of power-sharing was largely restricted to the Catholic population (see Table 42). While 55 percent of the Catholic population gave the coalition as the preferred alternative, the majority of Protestants desired either a return to the previous Protestant-dominated Northern Ireland Parliament or full integration of the province with the United Kingdom. The full extent of Protestant opposition to the power-sharing executive became even more apparent, however, with the outbreak of a general strike by Protestant workers in April 1974. The chief executive, Brian Faulkner, in announcing the resignation of his government, concluded: "We believe that Northern Ireland can only be maintained as a part of the United Kingdom on the basis of cooperation between Protestants and Roman

Catholics, and that is why I and my party have taken part in the Executive....It is, however, apparent to us, from the extent of support for the present stoppage, that the degree of consent needed to sustain the Executive does not exist" (Fisk and Tendler, 1974).

The failure of the 1974 power-sharing executive indicates clearly that the imposition of a coalition structure is not an instant remedy for instability. In the Northern Ireland case, certain important ingredients were lacking. First, the coalition was not created at the initiative of the political leaders of the major blocs, but rather was imposed from the outside. Second, the principle of coalition with religious opponents lacked widespread popular support, particularly within the Protestant bloc. Third, the principal political leaders of the Protestant bloc—the Loyalists—were not included in the coalition. It is evident that successful coalescence is a function not simply of the coalition structure *per se*, but of community support for elite cooperation.

The New Brunswick example provides pervasive evidence that coalescence is compatible with the government-versus-opposition style of the "British" model: a representative cabinet in a one-party government is a satisfactory substitute for a grand coalition in a multi-party government. The Northern Ireland experience of 1974, on the other hand, demonstrates that the coalescence is not automatically obtained by imposing a coalition styled after the "Dutch" model. Clearly, the structural means of attaining elite coalescence are secondary. The essential is that the political elites are willing to share political power with their opponents, and that the interests of each bloc are seen to be represented within the government.

7.

Elite Political Culture:
Cooperation and Confrontation

The political process in a homogeneous community has been aptly described by Almond (1956) as a game where the outcome is in doubt but "the stakes are not too high." Since there is a high degree of consensus in the community, the triumph of one party rather than another is unlikely to result in far-reaching change. Thus, while confrontation between opposing players may add to the excitement, it is rarely threatening: victory and defeat can be accepted with equal equanimity. The political process in a fragmented community, however, is a much more serious matter, fraught with danger. Because of the profound differences between the blocs, victory and defeat are objects of widespread concern. The stakes are high. Thus, confrontation politics exacerbates the ever-present tensions and antagonisms and contributes to the development of political instability.

If the political leaders are to maintain stability in a fragmented community, they must reduce the occasions for conflict and lower the stakes. In short, they must adopt a policy of cooperation. Coalescence is the most important element of such a policy, but there are several others: the principle of proportionality, the mutual veto, and purposive depoliticization. These are described variously as "cooperative strategies" (Lehmbruch, 1975), "rules of the consociational game" (Lijphart, 1968), and "conflict-regulating practices" (Nordlinger, 1972). Such practices cannot be plucked from a vacuum, however; they must be part of a larger political culture. The importance of this elite culture for the stabilization of a fragmented community is evident in the contrasting experiences of New Brunswick and Northern Ireland.

THE TRADITIONS OF COOPERATION AND CONFRONTATION
Political relations between the two major blocs in New Brunswick have been largely distinguished by a tradition of cooperation—a tradition commonly referred to within the province as *bonne entente*. Public dispute on the sensitive issues of religion and language is avoided. Instead, such questions are resolved by discreet negotiation between the political leaders of each bloc. Or, if the questions do become the subject of partisan debate, they are redefined by the leaders in order to minimize their religious and ethnic implications. In short, they are depoliticized. By contrast, political relations in Northern Ireland have largely followed a course of confrontation. Instead of avoiding sensitive issues, the political leaders have mobilized sectarian loyalties and exploited religious fears. Nicholas Mansergh (1936), in an assessment of Northern Ireland political behaviour—which is as valid today as it was several decades ago—concluded that "parties in Ulster emphasize traditional religious and racial antagonisms" and that they "subordinate every vital issue, whether of social or economic policy, to the dead hand of sectarian strife" (pp. 224, 225).

The development of a tradition of cooperation in New Brunswick political life dates from the Caraquet riots of 1875. Until that time, election campaigns appealed directly to sectarian feeling: MacNutt (1963) observes that "demagogues kept gentleman out of politics" and the model politician was one "whose crusade of Protestant and Saxon against Catholic and Celt, couched in coarse, insulting language, fostered religious bigotry and a war of sects" (p. 403). However, the deaths resulting from the unexpected clash between French Catholics and English Protestants at Caraquet led the political leaders to adopt a new tack. Henceforth the government—rather than appealing to the religious prejudices of the majority—would attempt to achieve accommodation by negotiating with the leaders of each subculture. Stanley (1972) describes the aftermath of the Caraquet troubles: "The impact they made was deep enough in 1875, and lasting. Neither English nor French, Catholic or Protestant wanted to see any repetition of what had occurred on the North Shore. That is why they all welcomed the news that a group of Roman Catholic members of the Legislature, encouraged if not actively assisted by Bishop Sweeney, had resumed talks with the provincial cabinet" (p. 37). The settlement that came out of these negotiations, known generally as "The Compromise" or *Modus Vivendi* of 1875, stands as a model of conflict management in New Brunswick.

The result of the negotiations between the cabinet and the political leaders of the Catholic community was a series of concessions which, in fact, permitted "separate" Catholic schools *within* the public school system.[1] Although the concessions fell short of the demands which had been made by Catholic leaders, they were accepted as the best that could be arranged. The major characteristics of the compromise are worthy of note. First, the focus of the negotiations was at the highest level, involving the leaders of the Catholic minority and the cabinet. Second, important concessions were made by the Protestant government to the minority group, and these were accepted by the latter as being satisfactory. Third, all the negotiations were secret and, perhaps most important, the resulting agreement was *not* made public. It is highly likely that announcement of the concessions would have aroused vehement opposition from the Protestant supporters of the government. Thus, there was no official declaration of the concessions and no formal modification of existing regulations. Rather, the compromise has been rather aptly called "a gentleman's agreement" (Canada, Royal Commission on Bilingualism and Biculturalism, 1967, p. 43).

One of the principal long-term consequences of the Caraquet riots and the subsequent compromise was a tendency to depoliticize religious and ethnic issues. Political leaders subsequently avoided public appeals likely to aggravate the ethno-religious divisions, reserving such questions for private negotiation. Stanley (1972) comments on the "surprising thing" that the members of the assembly avoided raising the issue of the Caraquet disturbances because "without any formal agreement, they decided that a discussion of Caraquet would only serve to exacerbate racial and religious feelings in the province" (p. 36). In the first election that followed the settlement of the issue, little reference was made to the religious antagonisms of previous election campaigns. Instead, candidates emphasized local issues and personal qualities: "Most simply indicated the need for honest and economical administration and pledged themselves, if elected, to conduct in support of good government and the interest of their constituents" (Woodward, 1976, p. 22). New Brunswick politics thus moved toward a restrained partisanship, which removed the appeal to ethnic and religious loyalties from the public arena.

The crucial test, and ultimately the confirmation, of New Brunswick's politics of cooperation did not come until the 1890s, when confrontation

---

1. The specific terms of the agreement permitted the grouping of Catholic students together in separate schools, recognition of teaching certificates issued by the church, revision of school texts to meet the objections of the church, and the renting of church-owned buildings to be used as "public" schools (see MacNaughton, 1947, pp. 220–21).

politics was temporarily, but unsuccessfully, reintroduced by the opposition. Tension was aroused when it became publicly known for the first time that the government had made secret concessions to the Catholic minority on the question of separate schools eighteen years earlier. The disclosure was sparked by the imprudent decision of the Bathurst school board, first, to transfer Catholic students to a convent school and, second, to assign teachers from a Catholic teaching order to instruct Protestant children (Hatfield, 1975, p. 50). Bathurst Protestants petitioned the Legislative Assembly, but the Blair coalition government refused to debate the question publicly.[2] The matter became a major political issue in 1892, however, when the grand master of the New Brunswick Orange Order, Herman Pitts, ran against the prime minister in his own constituency, campaigning against the government's granting of "special favours" to Catholics and the "open catering to the Roman Catholic vote." According to Hatfield (1975), Pitts' goal was "the exclusion of French Canadians and Roman Catholics from political power and the creation of a militant English Protestant majority which would enact the measures he advocated and bring cultural homogeneity to New Brunswick and Canada" (p. 60). When Pitts succeeded in defeating the prime minister, the opposition promptly adopted his platform.

The subsequent 1895 election thus represented an explicit contest between two opposing strategies: the government party advocated a policy of cooperation, permitting both Protestants and Catholics to share in government, while the opposition party pursued a policy of confrontation that would assure only the dominant Protestant majority of political power. The choice was between Blair, who would avoid politicizing the province's ethno-religious differences, in order to maintain his omnibus government party, and Pitts, who would exacerbate the ethno-religious tensions in order to establish the dominance of the majority bloc. The results of the election decisively established the politics of cooperation and accommodation, by returning Blair with an overwhelming majority of thirty-seven of the forty-six seats. In the new Legislature, the government numbered among its supporters all the French-Catholic members and two-thirds of the English-Protestant members, including a former grand master of the Orange Order, George

---

2. The refusal has been attributed to the fact that the government depended upon the support of both Protestants and Catholics and was thus anxious to avoid questions likely to create a religious division. According to Little (1972): "Under normal conditions, Blair was able to maintain power by keeping his efficient patronage machine running smoothly, but a religious or language controversy could have caused a party split, or presented the opposition with a real campaign issue" (p. 47).

Fowler, elected on the government ticket in the Protestant constituency of Kings. The Blair victory was constructed out of the bloc vote of the Catholic minority, plus the votes of moderate Protestants; the latter were wooed both by the government's policy of accommodation, and by its astute application of patronage. Hatfield (1975) concludes: "The politics of accommodation had defeated and discredited the politics of confrontation. New Brunswickers had demonstrated that they had no desire to see a renewal of the sectarian conflict of the 1870s" (p. 57).

In the century since Pitts' defeat, the most striking example of the political elite's conscious effort to depoliticize ethnic and religious differences in the province has been the debate concerning the "Equal Opportunity Program," introduced by the Liberal government in 1967. The program implemented a radical restructuring of municipal government, taxation, and education, with the goal of reducing regional economic disparities. However, since the poorer French regions benefited more than the wealthier English regions, popular opinion believed that the program would "rob Peter to pay Pierre." One observer noted: "Some English-speaking New Brunswickers were sure that what they had feared from an Acadian Premier was finally coming to pass, that their capital endeavours were going to be taxed to support an indigent French population" ("Happy Birthday, 'tit Louis," 1970). Nevertheless, the political leaders deliberately pursued a strategy of avoiding any confrontation between the two subcultures on the new program. First, the responsibility for preparing the outline of the program was given to a Royal Commission on Finance and Municipal Taxation, composed of respected representatives of the major ethno-religious groups. The commission — composed of two English Protestants, two French Catholics, and one English Catholic — presented unanimous and detailed recommendations after an exhaustive study of the whole provincial-municipal system (see Krueger, 1970). Second, the Liberal government emphasized that the program would reform existing injustices and inequalities, but carefully avoided placing it in an English-French context. This was often a difficult problem since many of the inequalities chiefly affected the Acadians. J. C. LeBlanc (1972) comments: "All the reformers were mindful of this problem and deemphasized the French-English differences to the point that when they gave examples of areas needing reforms they often cited an English municipality when there was a better example in an Acadian area" (p. 137). The Conservative opposition, in turn, responded by objecting that the program centralized too much power, that it was too expensive, and that it would reduce educational standards overall. Further, the opponents of the program, while almost entirely English, organized an advertising campaign in both languages and elected an Acadian businessman as chairman of their coordinating committee. Thus, while the program sparked the most acrimonious debate in recent New Brunswick history, the decision of the political leaders to treat it as a non-communal issue was probably crucial in preventing the outbreak of violence. As one political scientist observed: "It would probably be fair to say that almost all those who concerned themselves with the Program, whether in supporting or in attacking it, have recognized that it has presented the province with an issue which has terribly important ethnic implications. Nevertheless, the public debate has been conducted almost entirely on the basis of the non-ethnic aspects of the issue" (Leslie, 1969, p. 426).

In Northern Ireland, the development of a tradition of confrontation in political life predates partition. In many instances, it was directly encouraged by the street preaching of militant religious leaders, such as Henry Cooke, a leading Orangeman and Conservative, who has been described as "the framer of sectarianism in the politics of Ulster" (Boyd, 1970, p. 9). Cooke and his disciples became renowned for their vitriolic attacks against the Catholic Church and its adherents; and many of these attacks led directly to rioting and violent religious clashes. In 1857, a sermon by George Drew, a Presbyterian minister and deputy grand chaplain of the Orange Order, was followed by illegal Orange demonstrations and two months of rioting. A subsequent commission appointed by the lord lieutenant to investigate the rioting placed the blame on the provocation of Orange leaders and the open-air preaching which had led "to violence, outrage, religious animosities, hatred between classes, and, too often, bloodshed and loss of life" (Boyd, 1970, p. 44).

In other instances, confrontation was encouraged by British political leaders for their own electoral gain. The leaders of the Conservative Party, for example, played on Protestant fears and antagonism in order to rally opposition to the Home Rule Bill introduced by the Liberal government. In 1886, the Conservatives organized a series of meetings in Ulster "to stir up the protestants and unionists of Ulster and to impress the people of Britain with Ulster's determination to stand free of an Irish parliament" (Savage, 1961, p. 157). These culminated in a "monster meeting of Conservatives and Orangemen," addressed by Lord Randolph Churchill who, in a speech which bordered on sedition, urged Ulster Protestants to use whatever means necessary to resist Home Rule, promising them the support of "those of position and influence in England." Later, in a public letter, he repeated with emphasis the famous slogan he had first used in his Northern Ireland speech: "Ulster at the proper moment will resort to the supreme arbitrament of force;

Ulster will fight, and Ulster will be right" (Stewart, 1967, p. 22). The inflammatory oratory of Churchill and other political leaders aroused emotion to a fever pitch which, with the news that the Home Rule Bill had been defeated, resulted in four months of serious rioting and thirty-two deaths. In the report of the Belfast Riot Commissioners, testimony placed much of the blame on "respectable people" who had put forward the idea of an appeal to force: "It was unwise to use such words, as they were likely to cause the poorer classes to carry out what they only talked about and threatened" (Boyd, 1970, p. 173).

The encouragement by the Conservative leaders of forceful Protestant resistance to Home Rule continued right up until the decision to partition Ireland. In 1911, the leader of the Conservative Party, Bonar Law, assured Ulster Protestants: "I can imagine no length of resistance to which Ulster can go in which I should not be prepared to support them, and which, in my belief, they would not be supported by the overwhelming majority of the British people" (Stewart, 1967, p. 57). Law, himself, was of Northern Ireland parentage but, ironically, had been born in New Brunswick. An effort was made by the King, in 1914, and by Liberal Prime Minister Lloyd George, in 1917, to bring together the political leaders of the opposing factions in the hope of negotiating a compromise. But this came much too late. Passions had been aroused to such a point that the Irish leaders were reluctant to back down; and both sides stood poised with their private armies in anticipation of the civil war which shortly erupted. Of the Home Rule dispute generally, Buckland (1973) concludes: "There was no dialogue between unionists and nationalists, only mutual recrimination in slanging matches undertaken with a view to influencing opinion in Great Britain. So concerned were both sides to hurl accusation of intolerance at each other, that it never occurred to them to see how problems of mutual suspicion could be overcome" (p. xxxv).

While in New Brunswick the politics of confrontation had ultimately met with a resounding electoral defeat, in Northern Ireland it was reaffirmed by the evidence of its political success. For the British Conservatives, the appeal to Protestant fears was the key to the defeat of the Liberal government in the 1886 general election. For the Irish Protestants, the appeals of "No Surrender" and "Not an Inch" had ensured that Northern Ireland would remain within the United Kingdom. It is not surprising, therefore, that with the establishment of the new Northern Ireland state, the tried and proven strategy of confrontation politics continued unchallenged. The new government resolved to fight all elections on the question of maintaining the border and the union with Great Britain, a policy which reduced politics to a contest between Protestants and Catholics. Following partition, the government "noted that the simplest and surest way to rally Unionist voters was by identifying Catholicism with Nationalism and Nationalism with disloyalty. The slogan 'Not an Inch' proved to be the equilibrant of all the forces tending to disrupt the Unionist vote" (Kennedy, 1967, p. 144).

All general elections subsequent to the 1920 partition became essentially referendums on the union with Great Britain, demanding the unified expression of Protestant opposition to Irish Catholic nationalism. Harbinson (1973), in his study of the Ulster Unionist Party, concludes that the leaders who attained a position of dominance in the party were "those who sought Party advantage and quick and easy electoral success by emphasizing those things which divide Ulstermen. They tended to simplify the division and present it in religious terms, although the problem was much more complex." In sum, "the strategy they followed was short-term, based on banging the big drum and waving the flag" (p. 165). This strategy was not without its dangers, and the frequent outbreaks of violent rioting could often be attributed to the inflammatory speeches of the political leaders. Among the worst of those disturbances that occurred in the decades following the 1921 "troubles" were the 1935 riots which left eleven dead and hundreds injured. The Belfast city coroner, in reporting his findings on the causes of death, warned: "The poor people who commit these riots are easily led and influenced almost entirely by the public speeches of men in high and responsible positions. There would be less bigotry if there was less public speech-making of a kind by the so-called leaders of public opinion" (McCann, 1974, p. 199).

In the late 1960s, Northern Ireland's politics of confrontation became fully evident in the government's response to the civil rights movement, a movement which attempted to draw attention to a wide range of social grievances, including a restricted franchise, discrimination in housing, unfair employment practices, and local government gerrymandering. Although, as a subsequent Royal Commission confirmed, the Civil Rights Association was both non-sectarian and non-violent in its policies and its purpose, Protestant political leaders succeeded in arousing Protestant opposition to the movement by placing it in the context of traditional Protestant-Catholic confrontation. William Craig, who occupied the strategic position of minister of home affairs, portrayed the civil rights movement as a Catholic subterfuge which would undermine Protestant control in Northern Ireland: "There is all this nonsense about civil rights. These are our old traditional enemies exploiting the situation. The civil rights movement is bogus and is made up of ill-informed radicals and people who see in unrest a chance to renew the campaign of violence" (Rose, 1971, p. 225). Craig's hardline position extended beyond his verbal attacks to the use of strong-arm police tactics. The Royal Commission appointed to investigate the subsequent disturbances concluded that the actions of Craig, and the "unnecessary and ill controlled force" used by the police under his direction, had greatly exacerbated the tensions between the blocs (Northern Ireland, Commission appointed by the Governor, 1969, pp. 72–93).

While Craig was later removed from office, the escalation into violence had already begun, bringing with it the involvement of sectarian paramilitary organizations such as the Irish Republican Army and the Ulster Volunteer Force. In 1972, Craig formed a new political party, the Vanguard Unionist Party, with the support of the leading Protestant organizations, including the Grand Orange Lodge, the Young Unionist Council, and the paramilitary Ulster Defence Association, and canvassed the province in a series of rallies at which he attacked the "revolutionary force" in the community and assured Protestants that the Vanguard supporters "were going to beat this conspiracy into the ground... and make no accommodation with the enemies of this country, the enemies of democracy" (Boyd, 1972, p. 99).

Ian Paisley—the founder of several militant religious and political organizations, including the Free Presbyterian Church, the paramilitary Ulster Protestant Volunteers, the Ulster Constitution Defence Committee, and the Democratic Unionist Party—also led an active campaign in opposition to political concessions to the Catholic minority. Paisley, however, unlike Craig, was in the tradition of militant religious preachers (such as Henry Cooke) who focused their attacks on the Roman Catholic Church. According to one English observer of the troubles which began in the late 1960s, Paisley did more than any man "to arouse the feelings of fury, bigotry, ignorant fear and lust for blood" (Hastings, 1970, p. 69). The Royal Commission, headed by Lord Cameron (Northern Ireland, Commission appointed by the Governor, 1969) concluded that the likelihood of "clashes and disorder was heightened by the inflammatory speeches" made by Paisley, and that he was heavily responsible "for the disorders in Armagh and Burntollet Bridge and also for inflaming passions and engineering opposition to lawful, and what would in all probability have been peaceful, demonstrations" (pp. 89–90). Like Craig, Paisley attacked the civil rights movement as a threat to Protestants and, in a speech to a Protestant rally, he warned that "the Civil Rights Association was an I.R.A. front organization which was out to destroy Northern Ireland and they as Protestants would not tolerate any appeasement of such an organization" (Marrinan, 1973, p. 182). The effect of Paisley's tactics was to contribute to the politicizing of religious differences on an issue which might otherwise have been non-sectarian.

At the 1969 general election, in an action reminiscent of the contest between Pitts and Blair in New Brunswick, Paisley opposed the prime minister, O'Neill, in his own constituency, accusing the government of appeasing Catholics. Paisley's attitude is aptly illustrated by his earlier retort when faced with O'Neill's avowed aim to build bridges between Protestants and Catholics: "A traitor and a bridge are very much alike, for both go over to the other side" (Rose, 1971, p. 101). Although O'Neill was re-elected in his constituency by a narrow margin, the opposition of Protestants to his moderate policies forced his resignation as prime minister shortly afterwards. In 1970, Paisley was elected to represent the constituency in the Northern Ireland Parliament and in the United Kingdom Parliament. During the 1973 assembly election, Craig and Paisley joined their respective parties in an alliance to create the Loyalist coalition—an alliance which was later joined by the Official Unionists. This alliance, which was the largest political grouping in terms of electoral support, effectively established its dominance as the political spokesman for the Protestant bloc, and as the successor of the traditional Unionist Party.

Although, on various occasions, some political leaders indicated a willingness to pursue a policy of cooperation, the dominant pattern of behaviour among the political leadership of Northern Ireland has been that of confrontation. Under the leadership of Ian Paisley, Unionism has continued its traditional style of political campaigning, pitting Protestant against Catholic. This political style is aptly summarized by the two traditional Protestant slogans "No Surrender" and "Not an Inch." These contrast considerably with the commonly used New Brunswick expression: *bonne entente*.

ELECTION SLATES

The respective importance of cooperation and confrontation in the political culture of the two communities is particularly evident in the election slates constructed by the leading political parties. The composition of a party's slate of candidates often influences the extent to which ethnic and religious issues become the basis for partisan conflict. For example, if political contests are between candidates who differ not only in political affiliation but also in national origin and religious denomination, there is a strong incentive to politicize these differences. Elections take on the visible character of a conflict between the major blocs. On the other hand, if political contests are between candidates who, while differing in political affiliation, share the same religious and ethnic attributes, the confrontation between the blocs is reduced. Sensitive issues between blocs are less likely to become politicized; no matter which candidate wins, the bloc is assured its representation. If the electoral slates in the two communities are compared, it is evident that Northern Ireland tends to fit the former example more closely, and New Brunswick the latter.

In New Brunswick both parties have consistently attempted to select candidates who reflect the ethno-religious character of the constituency in which they run. Until the 1974 election, most members of the Legislative Assembly (MLAs) in New Brunswick were elected from constituencies which returned from two to five members. In these multi-member constituencies the parties invariably presented carefully balanced slates, likely to appeal to the various ethnic and religious denominations. In homogeneous regions this was not difficult, but in mixed areas ingenious combinations were often necessary. In the city of Moncton, which, until 1967, was a two-member constituency, each political party nominated one French Catholic and one English Protestant candidate. When a third seat was added to the constituency in 1967, both parties nominated an English Catholic as the third member of their slate—English Catholics have long been favoured as compromise candidates likely to appeal to the English by language and to the French by religion. In Northumberland, the Liberals successfully returned a slate composed of two English Protestants, one English Catholic, and one French Catholic for many years; in 1967, a further French Catholic was added when the constituency gained a fifth seat. In Westmorland, both parties generally put forth two French Catholics and two English Protestants as candidates.

A comparison of the 1970 and the 1974 general elections reveals that it is rare for English and French candidates to confront each other directly in an electoral contest (see Table 43). Under the 1970 multi-member system, a large proportion of the contests involved mixed English-French party slates, except in the south of the province where the slates of both parties contained only English candidates. Under the 1974 single-member system, mixed slates of candidates were no longer possible, and both parties tended to present French candidates in French constituencies, and English candidates in English constituencies. While, in both elections, there were very few English versus French contests, closer examination of these reveals a certain paradox. Although the Liberals are largely French-supported, and the Conservatives largely English-supported, in virtually all instances such contests were between an *English* Liberal and a *French* Conservative. Thus, as a consequence, in the 1974 election, the "English" Conservative Party presented a larger number of French-speaking candidates than did the

Table 43
*Ethnicity and Political Party of Election Candidates
in New Brunswick, 1970 and 1974*

Political party of contestants	Ethnicity of contestants			
	Opposed	Same	Mixed	Total
Multi-member constituencies, 1970				
Opposed	1	32	25	58
Single-member constituencies, 1974				
Opposed	5	53	n.a.	58

Note: The table includes only the candidates of the two parties which received the largest number of votes in the constituency. In classifying the ethnic character of the contest, "opposed" means English against French, "same" means English against English or French against French, and "mixed" means English and French against English or French. In both elections, the Liberals and the Conservatives were the leading parties in each constituency. In the case of the 1970 election, where multi-member constituencies were in use, the weight given to each constituency corresponds to the number of MLA's elected from the constituency.

"French" Liberal Party. This paradox reflects the use of a rather pragmatic electoral strategy in a mixed constituency: both parties, anticipating reliable support from within their own bloc, attempt to attract support from their opponents by nominating a candidate drawn from the other ethnic group.

In Northern Ireland, the leading political parties have traditionally selected candidates only from their own religious blocs. From 1929 until the suspension of the Stormont Parliament, most members of Parliament were elected in single-member constituencies. In some of these, where the population was mixed, the parties simply chose candidates likely to appeal to their own coreligionists: in Mourne, for example, the Nationalists consistently nominated a Catholic, and the Unionists a Protestant. The electoral contest was thus a confrontation between the two religious blocs. In many other constituencies, where one religious bloc was in a clear majority, there was often only one candidate—the Unionists seldom nominated a candidate in a largely Catholic constituency, and the Nationalists rarely put forward a candidate in a strongly Protestant constituency. Thus, in Mid-Down and Central Armagh, the Unionist candidate was unopposed in nine different elections during the 1929–65 period; while in Mid-Londonderry and South Fermanagh the Nationalist candidate was elected by acclamation eight times during the

Table 44

*Religion and Political Party of Election Candidates
in Northern Ireland, 1969 and 1973*

	Religion of contestants			
Political party of contestants	Opposed	Same	Mixed	Total
Single-member constituencies, 1969				
Opposed	11	1	n.a.	11
Same	0	33	n.a.	33
Multi-member constituencies, 1973				
Opposed	38	0	6	44
Same	0	34	0	34

Note: The table includes only the candidates of the two parties which received
the largest number of votes in the constituency. In classifying the religious
character of the contest, "opposed" means Protestant against Catholic, "same"
means Protestant against Protestant or Catholic against Catholic, and "mixed"
means Protestant and Catholic against Protestant or Catholic. In classifying the
political party of the contestants, candidates were classed as either unionist or
nationalist according to their position on the question of a united Ireland. In the
case of the 1973 election, where multi-member constituencies were in use, the
weight given to each constituency corresponds to the number of MPs elected
from the constituency.

same period. In Northern Ireland as a whole, the proportion of uncontested seats during the nine general elections between 1929 and 1965
varied from a low of 39 percent to a high of 64 percent.

The number of contested constituencies increased significantly after
the 1965 election because of the splintering of the major political
parties: there were an increased number of constituencies being contested by candidates representing different political factions of the same
religious bloc. Nevertheless, the confrontation of Protestant and Catholic candidates in the same constituency continued to be commonplace.
Although the multi-member system was introduced in 1973, the leading
parties did not attempt to achieve any sort of religious balance in their
slates. In most constituencies, the contest was between a Protestant and
a Catholic slate (Table 44). One party, the Alliance Party, did present
some mixed slates, but finished no higher than third in any constituency.

The comparison of electoral slates in New Brunswick and Northern
Ireland suggests two principal differences. First, in constituencies with
a mixed population, Northern Ireland elections have represented a
direct conflict between Protestants and Catholics. The elections tend to

exacerbate tensions as candidates attempt to rally the united support of their own bloc, often by stimulating the feelings of antagonism toward their religious opponents. Since the opposing candidates differ not only in party allegiance but also in religious persuasion, there are few constraints on their behaviour. In New Brunswick, however, the electoral contests in such constituencies have traditionally been between mixed slates. Thus, the candidate's behaviour has been considerably moderated by the fact that some of his colleagues were from a different ethnic group, and some of his opponents from his own group. Thorburn (1961) has noted, for example, that it was common in Moncton for both the English and French candidates of a party to canvass as a team in order to "emphasize the goodwill between both of them and toward both English-speaking and French-speaking groups in the electorate" (p. 135).

Second, in constituencies with a relatively homogeneous population, Northern Ireland elections are either uncontested or, as in recent years, disputed by candidates representing different factions of the same bloc. It might be thought that a contest between coreligionists would effectively reduce tension by removing the question of religious differences from the campaign. This has not been the case, however. The candidates have tended to pursue a strategy of one-upmanship by portraying themselves as the only truly faithful representatives of their religious bloc, and by giving proof of this through harsh sectarian attacks on their religious opponents. In this way Republican Catholics have attempted to show themselves to be more "nationalist" than Nationalist Catholics, and Loyalist Protestants as more "unionist" than Unionist Protestants. This one-upmanship is possible because of the relative homogeneity of the political parties' candidates—unlike New Brunswick where, at least on a province-wide basis, the parties present candidates chosen from both ethnic blocs. In New Brunswick, while the opposing candidates in a constituency may be both English, or both French, competition is considerably moderated by the fact that many of their colleagues belong to the other ethnic bloc.

CLIENTELISM IN NEW BRUNSWICK POLITICS

One factor in the success of New Brunswick's political leaders in avoiding a politics based on ethnic and religious confrontation is the province's long tradition of clientelism in politics—the tradition of political relationships corresponding to those between patron and client. Such politics is based on a mutually beneficial exchange: the patron bestows certain material advantages on the client in return for his political loyalty and support (see Noel, 1976). This is typical of New Brunswick politics, where traditionally electors have granted their loyal support to a candidate in exchange for political "favours," including personal gifts, jobs, or government contracts. Fitzpatrick (1972), for example, has described the relationship between the New Brunswick elector and his party as "one of intimate reciprocity, a mutual loyalty sustained by, among other things, a wide distribution of honest patronage" (p. 119). It is partly because of this clientelist tradition that politics in New Brunswick has often appeared to be largely devoid of either sectarian or ideological issues.

The roots of present-day clientelism are to be seen in the politics of the nineteenth century, when the power to allocate government revenues rested exclusively with the elected members of the assembly. Government revenues were divided among the various constituencies where each elected representative simply decided upon their allocation. The result was the development of an extensive network of political patronage, which was described by one lieutenant-governor as a "highly organized system of corruption" (MacNutt, 1963, p. 274). The coming of responsible government, and the vesting of budget-making authority in the executive, modified the structure but not the style of government. In the Legislative Assembly, members readily bartered their political support in return for specific favours. This was typical of all the provinces of Canada, and Noel (1976) suggests that political leadership became "a matter of creating and holding together supra-local groupings of notabilities in a legislature where loyalties were notoriously unstable but where control of the government (or the prospect of control) acted as a powerful inducement to coalition-building" (p. 12). A skilled politician, such as A. G. Blair, whose coalition government lasted twenty-five years, was able to sustain his government through the shrewd management of patronage, and the efficient use of brokerage politics. It was this masterly exploitation of patronage politics that ensured Blair's success during the 1890s, when the government was threatened by the appeals of Pitts to race and religion.

With little variation, certain characteristics of political clientelism have continued to exist in New Brunswick politics for over a century. First, in certain areas of the province, support for a political candidate has been assured on election day by gifts to the electors, the most favoured being a cash envelope, a bottle of rum, or a box of chocolates. Where local patrons have been sufficiently affluent, the necessary gratuity has often come from their own supplies: in the nineteenth century, the "Lumber Lord," Kennedy Burns, ensured his repeated re-election in Gloucester by giving credit on the purchase of provisions from his stores (Turgeon, 1928, pp. 51–52), while in the twentieth century, the Ganong family brought out the Conservative vote by the judicious distribution of wares from their chocolate factory (Doyle, 1976, pp. 150–51). The modern payment for voting is usually more subtle, taking the form of a reimbursement for specific services, such as providing a car on the day of the election. But a comparison of Doyle's description of elections in the 1920s, where electors attended picnics and rallies and later were "bribed with chocolates, rum, and two dollar bills" (p. 20), with Fitzpatrick's description of the 1960s, where rural elections were "often vitalized by inducements such as two-dollar bills, mickeys of rum, or boxes of chocolates" (p. 132), suggests that some things have remained unchanged.

Second, loyal political support has often been rewarded by the offer of a job from the government. At the local level, the government candidate, whether elected or defeated, has traditionally had responsibility for distributing patronage within the constituency, including the awarding of government employment to the party faithful. This function is especially important in a province with a high level of unemployment, and in which the government is one of the largest employers. In previous decades, a change of government often meant a wholesale firing and hiring of government employees. When the Liberals defeated the Conservatives in 1917, for example, 575 of a total of 700 "permanent" government employees, and many hundreds of casual employees, were summarily dismissed and replaced by supporters of the new government (Doyle, 1976, p. 142). The creation of the Civil Service Commission in 1943, which increased the security of employment for government workers, reduced the opportunities for applying such patronage methods, except in the case of "casual" employees. A more severe setback for the practice of patronage appointments, however, was the introduction of collective bargaining in 1967. This measure greatly weakened the power of the patronage committees by severely restricting the dismissal of employees, even those "casuals" who had previously been hired for political reasons.

Finally, government expenditures have tended to be directed largely toward the supporters of the party in power. Since many contracts for construction work, supplies, or services, are given without public tender, the government has a free rein to make purchases from members of the government party and, in return, to expect financial contribution to the party's war chest. The tradition is appropriately summed up in the ringing warning of one Conservative MLA to his government, at the time of the First World War: "Don't buy no Liberal potatoes!"[3] This behaviour

3. During the First World War, the government decided to supply potatoes as a gift to Great Britain. The potatoes destined for this "Patriotic Potato Gift" were purchased only from Conservative suppliers. Because of subsequent mismanagement, many of the potatoes rotted in their containers and were never delivered (Camp, 1970, p. 45; Doyle, 1976, p. 89).

is sufficiently commonplace that many examples are available in current government practice. The government purchases its insurance coverage only from agencies headed by prominent members of the government party, and "commissions" are distributed by a patronage committee to insurance agents throughout the province, in proportion to their contribution to party work (Chambers, 1975a, 1975b). All advertising and publicity work for the government is given to the company of a leading member of the government party (Camp, 1970, p. 95; "Dubé's expenses under microscope," 1976). Similarly, the stocking of the government-controlled liquor outlets, and the granting of contracts for services such as haulage, give preference to those brewers, distillers, or truckers who have contributed to party funds (Chambers, 1975c; Richard, 1975).

The conception of government expenditure as a "favour" in return for political support applies not only to the faithful party workers, but also to the electorate as a whole. Government spending is frequently applied to entire constituencies in an effort to purchase their vote. Forthcoming provincial elections are generally heralded by a flurry of government expenditures on road building, sewer construction, and industrial development. During the 1974 election campaign, for example, extra maintenance work was carried out on the highways and roads—including in some cases the gravelling of private driveways—and special warrants were issued to maximize industrial activity, by keeping various bankrupt companies operating until after the election (DeMerchant, 1976b; "Financial critic charges reckless public spending," 1975). This style of campaigning is aptly illustrated by the 1975 federal by-election in Restigouche which saw a contest between the national Liberal government and the provincial Conservative government on the question of who had most assisted the constituency. The Liberal candidate distributed a pamphlet detailing all the benefits the constituency had received through the efforts of its elected Liberal representative, Jean-Eudes Dubé, and one astonished observer from outside the province noted: "It itemizes every dime Mr. Dubé ever won for Restigouche—$52,915,200 for highways, $18 million for a hydro plant, $3 million for an air strip, $8,675,000 for wharves, $3,387,089 in Local Initiative grants. Why go on? You get the idea" (Stevens, 1975). The reminder of past favours, and the promise of future benefits, demands that the client reciprocate these good deeds by giving his vote to the appropriate party on election day.

Added to the promissory character of New Brunswick campaigns, most elections also feature charges of political corruption. In a province where traditional moral values coexist with rife political patronage, the opposition is continuously on the outlook for either dishonesty or mismanagement. While the government's favouring of its own supporters is widely accepted as "honest" behaviour, evidence that such favouritism has resulted in increased costs, poor workmanship, or theft from the public purse, are taken as evidence of corruption and mismanagement.[4] While accusations of corruption continue to be a feature of almost all elections, few can compare with those of the first few decades of this century when successive royal commissions found the prime minister and his government flagrantly guilty of accepting bribes and kickbacks. In 1927, an American Senate committee, in its hearings on the links which a new senator had in New Brunswick politics, was told that the "wildest statements" in regard to any of the largest American states "would not be anything in comparison to the campaign contributions that were ordinarily handled and used down there in New Brunswick, and the tactics which they employed would make the wildest stories about Tammany Hall sink into insignificance" (Doyle, 1976, p. 272).

One of the major effects of this political tradition has been to depoliticize the ethnic and religious divisions within the province. The importance of this development is most evident in the 1967 election which followed the introduction of the Equal Opportunities Program. Because this program was widely believed to benefit Acadian regions at the expense of English ones, its ethnic implications were potentially explosive. Nevertheless, this issue was rarely mentioned and instead the campaign—as is traditional—was dominated by promises of new expenditures and by accusations of corruption and irresponsibility. The opposition leader presented a long list containing 113 promises, leading the prime minister to liken him to Santa Claus, while observing that his "package resembles a rummage sale more than a political platform" (Woodward, 1976, p. 81). The tenor of the campaign issues is reflected in this pre-election summary:

> The Premier began his campaign with dull statistics about new pulp mills and schools, then came out fighting in the final week. He charged that Mr. Van Horne's promises would bankrupt the province and that big capitalists are backing the Conservatives because they want to control the provincial government.... Mr. Van Horne, who has been

---

4. This attitude is evident in an editorial by Paul-Emile Richard (1975) which originally appeared in *L'Evangéline*: "Political patronage has always existed and probably will always exist to a greater or lesser degree, but that in itself does not justify it. Political patronage becomes more objectionable, however, when the government accepts without any scruples to pay inflated prices for renting a building, for example, or for other contracts because a party supporter is involved."

campaigning full-time for a year, struck early with charges that the Government is rife with patronage, kickback systems and dictatorial methods. (Lebel, 1967)

While traditional campaigns, often the major social events of the community, featured political picnics, social teas, and party dinners, the 1967 election introduced more modern versions of these practices. P. J. Fitzpatrick (1972), who called Van Horne the "ultimate wheeler-dealer, non-issue-oriented politician" (p. 126), described his election campaign: "It was characterized by a total lack of policy discussion and an emphasis on bread and circuses—dances, socials, Ski-doo parties, white cowboy hats, ball point pens, cigars, gimmicks galore—even George Hees riding on a fire engine with Van Horne" (p. 128).

The case of New Brunswick thus stands as instructive evidence that, contrary to traditional expectations, politics may take on the features of a game even in a fragmented community. When the elite political culture dictates that the partisan debate of sensitive ethnic issues will be avoided, politics may come to have the non-ideological and non-sectarian character often attributed to homogeneous societies.

COOPERATIVE STRATEGIES

The nature of elite political culture in New Brunswick is aptly summed up in one traditional expression: *bonne entente*. The relations between the political leaders of each bloc have involved, with few exceptions, friendly understanding and good faith. From the period of Confederation, the Acadians (who in 1871 composed only 15 percent of the population) presented their demands with courtesy, trusting in the fairness of the English majority. Katherine MacNaughton (1947), describing ethnic relations in the Legislative Assembly during the nineteenth century, notes: "For the most part a spirit of 'See how well we get along together' prevailed in the Legislature. It was perhaps not difficult for a majority group to exhibit such a spirit toward a relatively small minority sensible to display a pleasing combination of dignity and modesty" (p. 84). When in 1897 an Acadian member of the Legislature announced that "his nationality was not as largely represented as it should be," he nevertheless added that he believed "that the government would be just enough to grant to every nationality and to every class in the province due justice at the proper time and place" (MacNaughton, 1947, p. 229). In 1913 when the Speaker requested an Acadian MLA to address his remarks in English, this request was overridden by a motion presented by English members, who defended the use of French in the assembly as "a courtesy from English-speaking gentlemen to French-speaking gentlemen" (Doyle, 1976, pp. 40–41). While such examples are largely representative of the tradition of *bonne entente* which continues to exist in New Brunswick, the pattern is not without its exceptions. The inevitable weakness of such a tradition is the ever-present possibility that, since the English have always constituted a majority, they have always possessed the ultimate power to refuse Acadian requests, no matter how reasonable.

Although the term *bonne entente* sums up the general character of New Brunswick's politics of cooperation, it is possible to isolate several specific strategies which have been employed by the elite to reduce the possibilities of conflict between the two blocs. Although these strategies are an integral part of the elite's political culture, they in no way represent iron-clad rules. Rather, they are devices which have been so regularly employed that their use is largely accepted without discussion. Needless to say, the cooperative strategies employed in New Brunswick could be matched with the corresponding confrontation strategies used by the elites in Northern Ireland.

1. *Depoliticization.* Both Lijphart (1968a) and Nordlinger (1972) have suggested that political leaders can effectively limit tension between subcultures by depoliticizing communal issues, that is, by removing them from the arena of political debate. This can be accomplished, as in Lebanon and Malaysia, by the general acceptance that the public discussion of such sensitive issues, particularly at election time, is to be avoided. Or it can be accomplished, as in Holland, by transforming the issue by means of an appeal to principles not linked to sectarian loyalties. Both of these methods are employed in New Brunswick, although the former is the most evident.

First, the political leaders have carefully avoided debating issues which have significant ethnic or religious implications. These are readily accepted as being too explosive to be included in a political platform. Traditionally, the principal taboo subject was that of religious teaching in the schools, an emotive question which tended to aggravate tensions between the blocs. Hugh Thorburn (1961) has observed: "The politicians of all parties have been extremely anxious to avoid this issue as it could cause serious division in the electorate and make their task of governing extremely difficult. Their reaction has been to pass over the question as far as policy is concerned and to remain aloof from the discussion of the issue even in principle" (p. 34). Similarly, Sissons (1959) has noted that the question of religion in the schools "is never discussed in the Legislature, but is reserved for argument in board rooms and for cynical comment on street corners or over tea-cups" (p. 247). In more recent years, it is the question of bilingualism that has become the primary taboo subject. In 1974, a survey conducted shortly before the election found that subject to be the problem of major concern to the electorate; or in the words of one party official who summarized the results of the poll: "Bricklin and the nuclear plant were not issues, but bilingualism is dynamite" (Jennings, 1974). However, both political leaders prudently avoided the dynamite, focusing debate instead on the government's decision to finance the construction of the Bricklin sports car. The ability of the political leadership to avoid such sensitive issues is greatly facilitated by the well-established custom of fighting elections on promises and scandals.

Second, where a public policy has important communal implications, the political leaders have attempted to transform it into a "neutral" issue. A prime example of this was the Equal Opportunity Program which was debated only according to general principles, such as efficiency, centralization, economy, and justice. As Leslie (1969) concluded: "It is precisely the fact that the government has been able to present the Program for Equal Opportunity as a non-ethnic issue that has made sponsorship of it politically feasible" (p. 426). This strategy may be contrasted with the typical response in Northern Ireland, where every attempt has been made to portray issues, no matter how innocuous, as subjects of intercommunal dispute. Thus, the subcultural differences have become politicized, most particularly at election time.

2. *Secrecy.* Cooperation between the blocs can also be fostered if the political elite of each subculture conduct their negotiations in secrecy, or as Lijphart (1968a) proposes: the process of accommodation must be "shielded from publicity" (p. 131). Critical public scrutiny of the leaders' moves during such negotiations not only restricts the flexibility necessary to reach a compromise, it also inhibits the granting of concessions which, if publicly known, might arouse widespread communal opposition. Such secrecy is a common feature of politics in New Brunswick, where the government seldom feels obliged to make public the details of its operations or its negotiations. This behaviour finds support in the public acceptance of government secrecy, and in the relatively closed, static character of the community.

Secret negotiation has been most effectively used in New Brunswick in the shaping of the religious and linguistic character of the educational system. Opposition to the Common Schools Act of 1871, for example, was successfully reconciled by the series of secret agreements which restructured the school system without the need to make legislative changes. The fact that no public announcement of the compromise was made permitted the granting of concessions which would have been vociferously opposed by English Protestants, had they been known.[5] The province's success in avoiding confrontation on the question of French-language instruction in the schools may also be attributed to the policy of private negotiation. In the few cases where linguistic demands have been presented publicly, tensions have been heightened and no agreement reached. In 1928, for example, the Acadian leaders successfully persuaded the government to permit French-language instruction; however, when the decision became known, English opposition led by the Orange Order was so vehement that the government subsequently rescinded its decision (Baudry, 1966; Godin, 1951). The resolution of the schools issue was only accomplished over a period of many years as a result of discreet representations by Acadian leaders to local school boards. While the introduction of French-language schools met little resistance in districts where the Acadians were in a large majority, problems were sometimes encountered in mixed regions, such as Moncton. The decision to build a French high school in Moncton was, according to Leslie (1969), the result of "private requests from a few Acadian leaders, who took special care to see that their initiative received no publicity" (p. 429). He rightly concludes: "The most important achievements of the Acadian people in obtaining confessional and French-language schools have been made by private representations rather than by public clamour" (p. 430).

Secrecy has played an important role in government in Northern Ireland but, needless to say, it has involved only negotiation *within* blocs. There is little evidence that the major leaders have ever used private talks as a means of settling interbloc differences.

3. *Proportionality.* Tension between the subcultures may also be reduced by the policy of distributing scarce resources and positions of influence proportionately between the blocs. Where each subculture is assured that it will receive a just share of these resources, the anxiety that would result from a competitive allocation may be avoided. Lijphart (1968b) has thus described proportionality as "the most prevalent rule of the game in consociational democracies" (p. 23). While New Brunswick has no institutionalized rule providing for such a proportional distribution, the principle is widely accepted by both groups. Nevertheless, its flexibility, within the constraints of ability and circumstance, has

5. Significantly, the government met strong opposition from English Protestants in 1966 when it proposed omitting the clause in the Schools Act requiring all publicly supported schools to be "non-sectarian." The clause was therefore maintained, although discreet *de facto* separation of the schools continued.

often led to a somewhat less than proportional share for the Acadians. This must be considered a significant weakness in the application of the principle, although, in spite of this weakness, New Brunswick still provides a striking contrast to Northern Ireland, where the principle has little, if any, application.

Among the elective offices, the cabinet is the primary domain where the principle of proportionality is applied: custom dictates that each segment should receive a fair share of the government portfolios, although such representation is constrained by the need to limit the cabinet to elected members of the government party. Neither of the parties has yet developed the tradition of alternating parliamentary leaders, although the Conservatives alternate between English and French party presidents, and the Liberals have achieved a respectable balance between English-Protestant, English-Catholic, and French-Catholic leaders.[6] The custom of alternating leaders is, perhaps, better established in municipal politics. The city of Bathurst, for example, with a mixed population, has had a tradition of mayoral succession since its incorporation in 1912, moving from an English Protestant to a French Catholic to an English Catholic, and then repeating the sequence (Poulin, 1969; Thorburn, 1965). Among the elected members of the Legislative Assembly, the principle is at least indirectly applied by each party's general practice of nominating candidates who reflect the ethnic character of their constituency.

While the leaders of both political parties accept the principle that proportionality should be achieved in the public service, the current government has refused Acadian proposals that a quota system be established. A study for the Royal Commission on Bilingualism and Biculturalism (Thorburn, 1966) concluded, however: "On a straight proportional basis...there appears to be a sufficient number of civil servants who are capable of dealing with the French-speaking and English-speaking segments of the general public in the language appropriate to their own location" (p. 97). There is no specific measure to ensure that the English and French blocs *per se* receive equal considera-

---

6. Since the First World War, the provincial Liberal leadership has included three English Protestants, two English Catholics, and three French Catholics. One of the English Catholics, Allison Dysart, leader of the party for fourteen years, represented the predominantly French constituency of Kent. The increasingly prominent role played by Acadians in politics since the election of Louis Robichaud as premier in 1960 makes the establishment of a tradition of alternation between English and French leaders extremely probable. This is confirmed by the election of Joseph Daigle, an Acadian, as Liberal leader in 1978.

tion in government spending, but this is largely unnecessary because of the tendency for expenditures to be based on per capita calculations. For example, the money received by the local school boards, whether English or French, is largely a fixed per capita allocation. Discretionary spending, such as that for highways, is frequently based on patronage considerations which tend to cut across the ethnic division.

The principle of proportionality is accepted as just in New Brunswick, and the practice of the principle does not fall too far short. This contrasts with Northern Ireland where the Protestant majority has reserved for itself a privileged position. Among the positions of influence, whether in the cabinet or civil service, Protestants have maintained virtually exclusive control (see chapter 6). Similarly, in public spending Protestants have been given preference; Protestant schools, for example, receive full governmental financial support, and Catholic schools only partial support.

4. *Consensus.* Political leaders can further reduce the level of competition between blocs by reaching a consensus, whether formal or informal, on contentious communal issues. When the party leaders take up similar stances on potentially divisive questions, the probability of a severe polarization of the community because of partisan debate is greatly minimized. One of the consequences of such a consensus, however, may be to shift the conflict from an interparty to an intraparty level.

The practice of consensus has been effectively employed in New Brunswick, in a largely informal manner, on the major divisive questions relating to religion and ethnicity. In recent years, its most frequent use has been on the sensitive question of bilingualism. Because of the ethnic alignment of the two political parties, the Liberals have been the natural vehicle for the expression of Acadian demands of equal rights for the French language. Given the substantial opposition to such demands among the English bloc, the Conservative Party could realistically have been expected to oppose any such concession. However, the issue was substantially defused by the early decision of the Conservative leadership to give its support, in principle, to official recognition for the French language. The commitment was made in 1967 when the Conservative leader of the opposition, Charles Van Horne, introduced a motion in the Legislature to establish English and French as the official languages of the province. By so doing, the Conservative leader "made a contribution to the lessening of racial tensions" within the province and "created a climate of acceptability for the government's Official Languages Act when it was ultimately introduced" (Fitzpatrick, 1972, pp. 129–30). The following year, the Liberal government successfully introduced an Official Languages Act, giving equal status to the use of French in the schools, courts, Legislature, and civil service. However, because of the bipartisan consensus on the principle of bilingualism, political debate — which potentially could have polarized the community — was restricted to technical details.

While both parties have continued to present a largely united front on the issue of bilingualism, this has not been without its internal costs for the Conservatives. The Conservative government's stand has been criticized by certain of its backbenchers, although the leadership is sufficiently strong that the dissent has been restrained. A more formidable threat to the interparty consensus has come from a leading Conservative, Leonard Jones, who as mayor of Moncton had established a reputation as an outspoken opponent of French-language rights. The leadership of the New Brunswick party opposed Jones' entry as a Conservative candidate into either provincial or federal politics, fearing that it would undermine the party's position on bilingualism. Although he later attempted to contest the national leadership of the party, Jones was refused accreditation as a member of the New Brunswick Progressive Conservative Association when he tried to attend their annual meeting in September 1975.

In Northern Ireland, it goes without saying, there has been no attempt by the principal leaders of each bloc to establish a consensus on the major religious and national issues — with the possible exception being the negotiations at the time of the 1974 coalition. Interestingly enough, however, a consensus to Northern Ireland problems has been established at various times by the leaders of the Labour Party and the Conservative Party, in order to reduce the politicization of the issue in Great Britain.

The comparison of the elite political cultures in the two communities confirms that New Brunswick has been characterized by norms of cooperation and Northern Ireland by those of confrontation. In Northern Ireland, the political leaders have generally attempted to exploit the divisions between the subcultures, and to politicize the religious and national differences, for their own electoral gain. In New Brunswick, the political leaders have attempted to remove the subcultural division from the arena of partisan debate and to depoliticize the religious and ethnic differences, in order to avoid the threat of instability. But while these leaders have successfully resolved sensitive issues through a policy of cooperation, this does not mean that New Brunswick politics has ceased to be competitive. Political competition and confrontation have continued to exist, but not on communal issues. Competition has been largely limited to questions of good administration, with the issues of public spending and political honesty in the forefront. The application of cooperative strategies on one dimension has thus permitted political confrontation on another. New Brunswick politics, at least in some of its aspects, appears therefore to have the characteristics of a "game," as in homogeneous communities. In direct contrast, confrontation between rival political elites exists on all dimensions of Northern Ireland politics, even in the sensitive—and dangerous—domain of interbloc relations. Politics is not a fun-filled game here, but a deadly serious struggle.

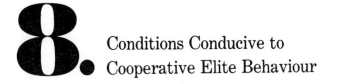

8. Conditions Conducive to Cooperative Elite Behaviour

The contrasting behaviour of the political elites in New Brunswick and Northern Ireland provides considerable insight into the origins of political instability in a fragmented community. Most notably, it suggests a close link between confrontation and instability, and between cooperation and stability. But it also raises a new question: why is it that the elites in New Brunswick are cooperative, while those in Northern Ireland are confrontative? Since elite behaviour has been crucial to the stability (or instability) of the communities, it is important that the conditions that have influenced this behaviour be defined.

One such condition has been the pattern of social cleavages. In New Brunswick, crosscutting cleavages have assured that the various ethnic and religious conflicts would be largely independent from each other. Because of this independence, the conflict issues have been more limited and the antagonisms more restrained. Hence, elite cooperation is a strategy which holds hope for success. In Northern Ireland, however, congruent cleavages have made the task of the elites extremely difficult. The consequence of congruent cleavages is multi-issued conflicts which feature high levels of tension and hostility. Inevitably, this means greater risk to elites who attempt to introduce cooperative practices. Thus, the conflict-managing effect of crosscutting cleavages is a factor contributing to successful elite cooperation.

Apart from the cleavage patterns, there are four other significant differences between the communities of New Brunswick and Northern

Ireland which likely have affected the behaviour of the elites. Two of these may be said to have increased the *capacity* of the elites to pursue cooperative strategies, by increasing their autonomy of action. These are the dominance of the elites and the distinctness of the lines of fragmentation. The other two conditions may be said to have increased the *predisposition* of the elites to pursue cooperative strategies by strengthening their commitment to the political system as a whole rather than to the narrow interests of a particular political subculture. These are the overlapping pattern of partisanship and the overarching national solidarity. Each of these warrants more detailed examination in order to demonstrate the extent to which the two communities differ, and to shed light on the responses of the respective elites.

ELITE DOMINANCE

The success of the elites in stabilizing a fragmented community presumes not only that they are willing to pursue a strategy of cooperation, but also that they are able to retain the support of their followers. This implies either widespread popular support for the specific cooperative policies, or sufficient autonomy for the elites to let them act independently. In this latter case, the strength of the elites must be such that they can pursue the potentially unpopular strategies of cooperation without undue threat. Where the elites are not strongly entrenched there is the risk, first, that they will not be able to carry their followers with them and, second, that they will be replaced by militant leaders more congenial to mass sentiments. Lijphart (1968b) observes: "Successful accommodation presumes that the elites are sufficiently secure in their position that they are able to negotiate and compromise, relatively free from the fear that their moderation will undermine their leadership" (p. 26).

There are considerable differences when the strength of the political leaders in New Brunswick and Northern Ireland is compared. In New Brunswick, the authority within each political party is centralized in the parliamentary leader. It is he who has the final word in the determination of policy and the selection of candidates. This is a result not simply of the party's structural organization, but of the prevalent cultural norms regarding leadership. Fitzpatrick (1972) notes: "Neither party is receptive to the idea, so fashionable elsewhere, of popular participation in government: Party leadership is firmly of the opinion that it should lead" (p. 116). Similarly, Thorburn (1961) observes: "The leader is given every opportunity to control his party—and all his supporters who have the interests of the party at heart hope that he will use his authority. He alone makes all important policy pronouncements. He is the personification of his party in the election campaign and is in complete executive control" (p. 108). As long as the party continues to win elections, the dominance of the parliamentary leader is assured. It is significant, for example, that only two of the twenty-four premiers since 1867 resigned as a result of pressure from their own party. Both of these were leaders of governments which had become tainted with scandal following charges of corruption. Nevertheless, even in these cases—even when, for example, a royal commission found Premier J. K. Flemming party to extortion—it proved extremely difficult to force his resignation.

The authority of the parliamentary leader over the party as a whole is mirrored in the control of the parliamentary representative over the local association. At the constituency level the party organization is controlled by a small group of local leaders, the most prominent being the elected member of the Legislative Assembly. These leaders are generally elected by acclamation to the executive positions and replenish their numbers by cooptation. The outward form of the party organization is democratic, but this merely disguises the dominance of the leadership. Fitzpatrick (1972), for example, notes: "Both parties hold annual provincial constituency meetings, but usually all the decisions have been made in advance. The leadership decides if it will remain in office; if not, it chooses its successor. At the actual meeting, those present merely concur in the leadership decision" (p. 121).

By comparison, party leaders in Northern Ireland have had relatively little independent power. Within the Unionist Party, for example, the authority of the parliamentary leader has been kept in close check by the close scrutiny of both party militants and parliamentary colleagues. The Standing Committee of the party elects a thirty-six-member Executive Committee, whose role is to instruct the leader on the wishes of the party membership. In addition, the leader must pay close attention to the views of his parliamentary caucus, since its loyalty cannot be depended upon. Four of the six prime ministers of Northern Ireland suffered opposition within their caucus and were forced to resign after relatively short terms of office. Such was the case with Terence O'Neill, whose attempts to heal the Protestant-Catholic rift by "bridge-building" alienated a large sector of the parliamentary party. These restrictions on the autonomy of the leader have severely limited his ability to implement cooperative strategies. Harbinson (1973) aptly summarizes the problem: "A Unionist leader can only remain leader so long as he, the Orange Institution and the Unionist Party at large are in accord. He may, as did O'Neill and Chichester-Clark, introduce legislation designed to promote better community relations, but unless his policies are acceptable to Unionism at large he cannot survive long. A reforming leader, to survive, would have to reform his own Party first" (p. 165).

The limitations imposed by the party on the leader's authority were strikingly illustrated during the 1969 elections. Northern Ireland parties, unlike New Brunswick, have not granted their leaders a veto over the choice of parliamentary candidates. This led to a difficult situation for Terence O'Neill, who found himself confronted by a large number of Official Unionist Party candidates openly opposed to his leadership and to his policies. O'Neill retaliated by supporting independent candidates running against his party's own official nominees. In total, fifteen "anti-O'Neill" Unionist candidates were opposed by fifteen "pro-O'Neill" independent candidates. Since only three of the fifteen independents were successful, the strategy did not give the leader the personal authority he needed to implement his program.

The relatively weak position of the parliamentary leader finds its parallel at the constituency level where the locally elected representative has long shared a similar predicament. Incumbent MPs, far from enjoying autonomy, depended greatly upon their local constituency association. Indeed their nomination was far from a formality: before each general election the association advertised for potential candidates who were then invited to compete against the sitting member. While the incumbent was always a strong favourite, the procedure forced him to pay close attention to the demands of the local association. In many cases this meant desisting from conciliatory policies which conflicted with the sentiments of his constituents. Thus, one Unionist MP, Richard Ferguson, who supported the reform proposals of Prime Minister O'Neill—and consequently resigned from the Orange Order—received a vote of non-confidence from his association and was subjected to relentless pressure until he finally resigned from the House of Commons.

The insecurity of the Unionist leaders in Northern Ireland has been further increased by the competition of other "unionist" parties for the Protestant vote. This competition has continuously threatened to undermine the Official Unionist Party's claim to be the exclusive political spokesman for Protestants. Between 1921 and 1969, for example, independent unionists were elected to the House of Commons in eight of twelve general elections. However, the main competitors have been various splinter parties which have attacked the Unionist Party as insufficiently militant. The support for these factions reached a peak in 1973 when parties such as the Democratic Unionist Party and the Vanguard Unionist Party received almost a third of the total vote (see Table 45). Additional competition has been faced from the left, notably from the Northern Ireland Labour Party which has attacked the Unionist Party as being unsympathetic to the working class. The consequence is that the two traditional parties, the Unionists and the Nationalists, received a combined vote which averaged less than 66 percent between

Table 45

Splintering of the Unionist Vote, 1921–73

Year	% Official Unionist	% Other Unionist	% N.I. Labour[a]	Total
1921	66.9	0.0	0.2	67.1
1925	55.0	9.0	4.7	68.7
1929	50.6	14.3	8.9	73.8
1933	43.1	21.4	8.6	73.1
1938	56.4	29.1	7.4	92.9
1945	50.4	5.0	30.4	85.8
1949	62.8	5.8	9.3	77.9
1953	47.5	12.9	13.6	74.0
1958	43.8	9.0	21.2	74.0
1962	48.6	0.0	29.1	77.7
1965	59.1	0.0	21.8	80.9
1969	48.2	19.5	8.1	75.8
1973	29.3	32.6	2.6	64.5

Note: Compiled from Elliott, 1973.
a Includes other labour parties which supported the union with Great Britain,
   e.g., Commonwealth Labour Party, Federation of Labour.

1921 and 1969. In the 1973 assembly election, when the vote was fragmented even further, a total of eight parties gained seats, and the two traditional parties won a combined vote of only 30 percent.

The splintering of the vote in Northern Ireland must be compared with the continuous domination of the two major parties in New Brunswick. With the exception of the 1920 election, when the United Farmers elected eight MLAs, no representatives from any party other than the Conservatives and the Liberals have been returned to power. In six of the thirteen elections since 1920, these two parties have received a combined vote of more than 99 percent. The overall average for the two parties over the last fifty years has been a combined vote in excess of 97 percent. Historically, then, competition from splinter parties has posed little, if any, threat to the leadership of the two parties.

The relative strength of the party leaders in New Brunswick as compared to those in Northern Ireland is firmly rooted in cultural norms which favour deference to social and political elites.[1] Most New Bruns-

1. Various explanations may be given for these norms. First, the conservative influence of the Loyalists favoured the maintenance of hierarchical distinctions and class privileges. Second, the relative economic underdevelopment of the region was conducive to a sense of dependence upon an affluent elite. Third, the durability of patron-client relationships in political life has tended to institutionalize the dependence of the electors on their government.

Table 46
Dimensions of Political Activity for Selected Countries

Country	Year	Awareness		Efficacy	
		% Communicant	% Informed	% Competent	% Influential
United States	1960	76	49	66	28
Great Britain	1959	70	43	56	15
Germany	1959	60	53	33	15
NORTHERN IRELAND	1968	49	31	n.a.	14
Mexico	1959	38	31	33	5
Italy	1959	32	16	27	9
NEW BRUNSWICK	1974	26	27	29	n.a.

Note: In classifying the dimensions of political activity, "communicant" refers to those who discuss politics with others; "informed" to those who usually read about politics in the newspapers; "competent" to those who think that they could do something about an unjust law; and "influential" to those who have attempted to influence a local government decision. The New Brunswick data are from the National Election Study and the Northern Ireland data from the Northern Ireland Loyalty Survey. All other data are from Almond and Verba, 1965.

wick citizens have very little confidence in their own political efficacy, that is, in their ability to have an impact on the political process and on the government. They therefore leave decision-making to their leaders. For example, 79 percent of the New Brunswick respondents in the National Election Study believed that politics was so complicated that they could not understand what was going on. Similar sentiments, expressed on other questions dealing with political efficacy and awareness, give New Brunswick a low score, comparable to that of Italy (see Table 46). This low efficacy, combined with high mistrust, has led Simeon and Elkins (1974) to conclude that New Brunswick is a "disaffected" society: "Disaffection from government and politics is very widespread, but this is not translated into political action. Neither the disaffected nor the deferentials pose much threat to existing elites" (p. 436). By comparison, Northern Ireland citizens are less likely to defer to their leaders, and more likely to believe in their own efficacy. Significantly, the proportion of "influentials"—those who have attempted to influence a local government decision—in Northern Ireland is comparable to that in Great Britain or West Germany.

DISTINCT LINES OF FRAGMENTATION
Arend Lijphart (1968b), in comparing fragmented communities, has observed that those that are stable (the consociational democracies), are even more fragmented than those classed by Almond as unstable. This

observation contributes to Lijphart's paradoxical conclusion that in some cases political stability might, contrary to expectations, actually increase with higher levels of social fragmentation. First, severe fragmentation reduces contact between the subcultures at the mass level, and thereby reduces the opportunities for conflict. Quincy Wright, writing in 1951, concluded: "If the groups with inconsistent ideologies are in close contact, that is, if the society is closely integrated, the tension will be great" (p. 196). Similarly, Karl Deutsch (1954) has claimed that "the number of opportunities for possible violent conflicts will increase with the volume and range of transactions" (p. 39). Second, the separation of the major subcultures puts the onus on the elites to resolve the differences between these subcultures. The elite level becomes the sole point of contact between the blocs, a factor which facilitates elite accommodation.

Both New Brunswick and Northern Ireland are communities which suffer from serious fragmentation, but the lines of fragmentation in New Brunswick appear to be more distinct. This is a consequence of two primary factors: geography and language. In geographic terms, the New Brunswick population is more segregated than that of Northern Ireland. This results both from the greater regional dispersion and the greater ethnic concentration of New Brunswick's population. Northern Ireland, with more than double the population of New Brunswick, is less than a fifth as large in terms of land area: the population density of Northern Ireland is 280 persons per square mile, and that of New Brunswick only twenty-two persons per square mile. To this must be added the ethnic homogeneity of the various regions of the province. In New Brunswick, 78 percent of the population live in districts that are homogeneous in terms of ethnic composition; in Northern Ireland, only 37 percent of the population live in homogeneous districts. Thus, if segregation curves for each community are compared (see Fig. 10) and a Gini index of segregation is calculated, Northern Ireland is seen to have a medium (.43) level of segregation and New Brunswick a high (.85) level. Modern means of transportation and communication have not reduced regional isolation in New Brunswick as much as might be expected. It is revealing, for example, that whereas MPs in Northern Ireland could continue to live in their constituency and commute easily to the capital, many New Brunswick MLAs must maintain a second residence in Fredericton. Not only are the distances longer, but the New Brunswick roads, barely adequate in summer, are frequently impassable in winter.

In linguistic terms there is also greater segregation in New Brunswick than in Northern Ireland. The language division in New Brunswick, non-

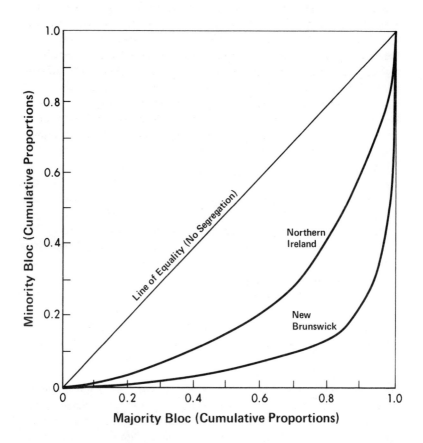

Fig. 10. Geographic segregation of the major blocs, 1971. (The data for the segregation curves are from Canada, Statistics Canada, 1973–77, and Northern Ireland, General Register Office, 1973–74.)

existent in Northern Ireland, creates a formidable barrier between the blocs. In 1971, only 21 percent of the population could speak both English and French. This has aided Acadians in preserving their distinct cultural and religious heritage; hence the traditional phrase, *la langue gardienne de la foi*. In addition, it has fostered a fragmentation which extends beyond that found in Northern Ireland, into the financial world and into the electronic media. The language division has limited not only physical contact but also intellectual contact—thus, the celebrated "two solitudes." The English majority, which is almost entirely unilingual, is often totally unaware of Acadian life, and must rely largely upon its elite to interpret Acadian demands.

A consequence of the distinct lines of fragmentation in New Brunswick has been not only less contact but also greater autonomy for each bloc. MacNutt (1963) has observed that in the nineteenth century the Acadians were considered by the government to be "a race apart," and "by mutual agreement the Acadians managed their own affairs" (p. 170). In the twentieth century, they continue to manage their own affairs, at least at the local level, by their control of regional governments and school boards in Acadian districts. Thus, the regional concentration of each ethnic group, by contributing to its local autonomy, limits English-French competition. (It is significant that the one major exception to this pattern in New Brunswick, the city of Moncton—composed of large numbers of both English and French—has also been the main site for clashes between the two groups.) In Northern Ireland, the higher religious mix of the population has meant that Catholics are less likely to constitute a majority of the local population. Not only are the occasions for competition and conflict increased, but the likelihood of the Catholics gaining political control in local affairs is reduced.

Geography and language, by restricting the opportunities for contact at the mass level in New Brunswick, have placed the onus on the leadership. The relative isolation of the two blocs has left the political and economic elites with the sole responsibility for resolving differences. The focus for contact is thus the board room, the Legislature, and the cabinet.

OVERARCHING NATIONAL SOLIDARITY

The successful implementation of cooperative strategies in a fragmented community must presume a commitment to the maintenance of the existing political system, both on the part of the elites and of the masses. Such a commitment is most likely to exist where there is a significant level of shared national feeling. There are two principal elements involved here. First, there should be an overarching national solidarity. That is, some elements of national identification should be accepted and shared by both blocs. Second, nationalistic feeling should be relatively moderate—and most especially that nationalistic feeling which is exclusive to each communal group. Since in a deeply divided community attachment to the subculture is usually very strong, nationalistic sentiments often have a divisive rather than a unifying effect.

Northern Ireland provides a fitting negative example of the need for overarching solidarity. National sentiment is strong, but exclusive to each subculture. The Protestant bloc sees itself as linked to Great Britain by religion and heritage, and identifies itself most frequently as British (see Table 47). The Catholic bloc, on the other hand, sees itself as allied to the Republic of Ireland by religion and tradition, and identifies itself overwhelmingly as "Irish." The symbols of such nationalism,

Table 47
National Identity in Northern Ireland, 1968

National identity	% of Protestants ($n = 751$)	% of Catholics ($n = 532$)	% of Total ($n = 1,283$)
Irish	20	76	43
British	39	15	29
Ulsterman	33	5	21
British & Irish	6	3	5
Other	2	1	2
Total	100	100	100

Note: $\chi^2(4) = 404$, $p < .0001$; $V = .561$. The data are from the Northern Ireland Loyalty Survey.

whether anthems, flags, or heroes, are not only different for both groups, they are in opposition: the expression of nationalism is an expression of disrespect for the opposing bloc. It is possible that the development of an "Ulster" nationalism might provide a unifying link in the future but, until now, the "Ulster" identity has been largely appropriated by the Protestant bloc. The conflicting national identities of the two groups have meant that, historically, there has been no consensus among the elites on which political system should be preserved. For Protestant elites, the commitment has been to the preservation of the British Empire, and the integrity of the United Kingdom. Their goal has been to defend the inclusion of Ireland, and later Northern Ireland, as an integral part of the British union. For Catholic elites, the commitment is to Ireland, and its integrity as an autonomous and unified country. Their aim is to separate Ireland from the influence of the United Kingdom. The incompatibility of these positions has meant, in practice, that the elites lack the shared commitment necessary to inspire a common effort of cooperation.

In marked contrast to the mutually exclusive loyalties in Northern Ireland, the particular identities of each bloc in New Brunswick are not inconsistent with a common, shared identity. The French-speaking New Brunswickers are most likely to identify themselves as "Acadians," although there are regional variations, notably in the northwest where the designation "French Canadian" is most common (see De la Garde, 1966). The English-speaking New Brunswickers are likely to describe themselves as "English Canadians." But all New Brunswickers, whether English or French, share a common identity as Canadians. While each bloc has its own particular communal symbols, including an anthem and

Table 48
National Sentiment Scores in New Brunswick, 1974

Country	English (n = 77)	French (n = 51)	F	Significance level
Canada	81	82	.00	.96
New Brunswick	68	74	1.35	.25
England	55	51	1.01	.32
United States	49	54	1.89	.17
France	44	52	3.88	.05

Note: The scores in this table are the mean "thermometer" scores on a scale from 0 to 100. The data are from the National Election Study.

a flag, both also give allegiance to the Canadian Maple Leaf flag and the Canadian anthem, "O Canada."

The development of this overarching national identity in New Brunswick, but not in Northern Ireland, may be traced to contrasting historical circumstances. Unlike Northern Ireland, where geographic location ensures continuous contact with Ireland and Scotland, New Brunswick has been relatively cut off from its founding nations. After Acadia was founded in the seventeenth century, there was remarkably little contact between the new colony and the motherland. The French settlers adopted North America as their homeland and became "Acadians" rather than "French." The allegiance of the later English settlers—and particularly of the Loyalists—to the mother country proved more durable but, nevertheless, centuries of life in North America have succeeded in fostering a more localized identity. In this regard, it should be noted that New Brunswick dates from 1784 and Canada from 1867. This must be compared with the relatively recent creation of the Northern Ireland state in 1920. The strength of this overarching identification, in comparison with the historical links which traditionally joined each subculture to nations outside of New Brunswick, is illustrated by the thermometer scores of respondents to the 1974 National Election Study (see Table 48). Both French and English, when asked to indicate their feelings toward various nations on a scale from 0 to 100, show a high degree of consensus. Canada and New Brunswick rank highest among both subcultures, outdistancing the traditional national allegiances. Although, comparatively, the English Canadians show a moderate preference for England, and the French Canadians for the United States, the only significant difference between the blocs is in their attitude to France. The relative absence of significant differences between the blocs, particularly in terms of their sentiments toward Canada, is the most striking feature of these results.

The two New Brunswick subcultures, while maintaining their individuality, are thus united by a common identity. The Acadian premier, Louis Robichaud (1961), noted: "In a sense we are separate, and yet we are one" (p. 24); and "we are united in our pride of being New Brunswickers" (p. 25). The Acadian leader, Adélard Savoie (1961), has similarly observed: "All in all, Acadian nationalism is not all-embracing, but it is subordinate to many other loyalties, it is mindful of the rights of others and it is conscious of its duties and obligations" (p. 85). This overarching solidarity between the two blocs provides the necessary incentive for the elites to work together toward a common goal, the maintenance of political stability in New Brunswick. This must be contrasted with Northern Ireland, where the lack of a common national identity has undermined the legitimacy of the existing state. Catholics have no wish to work with Protestants to preserve a Northern Ireland state which they oppose, just as Protestants do not desire to cooperate with Catholics to create an autonomous Ireland, which they fear. Without a shared allegiance, there can be no cooperation.

MODERATE PARTISANSHIP

The willingness of the elites to engage in consociational practices is likely to be strongest where partisanship is weak, or at least, very moderate. This applies most particularly to the political attachment of the elite itself, although often—as in New Brunswick and Northern Ireland—both elites and masses share similar partisan feeling. Di Palma (1973) has referred to the need for the elites to accept the "norm of restrained partisanship," a norm which "requires that the contestants see themselves as more than partisans pursuing their own demands" (p. 11). Lijphart (1968a), in his study of Holland, finds that while there exists "ideological polarization" at the mass level, there is a "high degree of pragmatism and moderation at the top" (p. 148). Even if the Dutch masses are strongly ideological, this is tempered by their "strong belief that the leaders should serve the general interest rather than the special interest of their own bloc" (p. 148). These conditions are crucial if the elite is to adopt a policy of cooperation; strong parochial and partisan sentiments tend to create a barrier to interparty cooperation and compromise.

In New Brunswick, the development of political parties occurred very slowly, and was frequently resisted by the provincial legislators. As in other parts of Canada, many candidates preferred to remain uncommitted to any party until after an election, thereby leaving themselves free to negotiate with the strongest party in the Legislature. The historian MacNutt (1963) observes: "Freedom to bargain, to support or to oppose, to form compacts according to the urgency of the hour, was the most dearly prized possession of provincial politicians. To many, a party system implied bondage" (p. 291). While many individuals adopted the labels of "Liberal" or "Conservative," these often indicated only a general political orientation rather than a binding party affiliation. This greatly facilitated the creation of the omnibus government party, made up of both Liberals and Conservatives, which was a common feature of New Brunswick politics until 1917. Undoubtedly the government's adoption of cooperative politics was also itself an important factor in weakening the political organization of Liberals and Conservatives.

Political partisanship has been further moderated by the fact that political allegiances cut across the ethnic division. While each of the two New Brunswick parties tends to be associated with one of the ethnic blocs, the association is weakened by the fact that it has not been consistent. During the nineteenth century, Acadian support was given to the Conservatives, largely because of the opposition of the Roman Catholic Church to Liberalism in any form. However, in 1887, a French Canadian, Wilfrid Laurier, was elected leader of the national Liberal Party, and he succeeded in recruiting a significant number of prominent Acadians into the party. One of these, Peter Veniot, subsequently became a cabinet minister in a provincial Liberal government formed in 1917. When, in 1923, Veniot was selected by the Liberals as their party leader, becoming therefore the first Acadian premier of the province, Acadian support for the Liberal Party was largely assured. The Acadians have continued to be predominantly identified with the Liberals since that time, although the heritage of their historical association with the Conservatives is still evident. The Conservatives represent a viable alternative for Acadian electors, and can claim a substantial number of Acadian supporters who have inherited their political affiliation from their fathers.[2] It should be noted also that both parties have long traditions of support from the English bloc, although it is the Conservatives who have been most closely identified as the English party.

In Northern Ireland, partisan labels have been anchored in strong party organizations from an early date, in fact long before the founda-

2. One prominent Acadian member of the Conservative Party, for example, while conceding "the basically English character of the Tories and the basically French character of the Liberals," explains his own party choice by noting that "of my two grandfathers, one was a staunch Liberal and the other a staunch Conservative, and that sort of left me free to float from one side to the other" ("A Conversation with Fred Arsenault," 1971, p. 16).

tion of the Northern Irish state. At first, the division was between Liberals and Conservatives, but these soon gave way to distinctive Irish parties. The origins of the Nationalist Party lie in the foundation of the Home Rule League in 1873. The Unionist Party on the other hand owes its existence to the creation of the Ulster Loyalist Anti-Repeal Union in 1886 (see Savage, 1961). Both of these parties were highly organized, with strong roots in existing religious and political associations. Unlike the early Liberals and Conservatives of New Brunswick, the Unionists and Nationalists were not simply loose labels, but were rather highly structured political movements. Further, these political parties became inseparably associated with one or the other of the major subcultures. From 1886, "Unionist" was largely synonymous with Protestant, and "Nationalist" with Catholic. There was no overlapping partisanship. Mansergh, writing in 1936, noted: "A Protestant who is a Nationalist, or a Catholic who is a Unionist, is reckoned by his co-religionists in their kinder moods as a phenomenon, and on more ordinary occasions as one who has betrayed his faith" (p. 243).

A comparison of political identification in recent years in New Brunswick and Northern Ireland confirms the continuing existence of these contrasting patterns of partisanship (see Table 49). In New Brunswick, there is a clear pattern of overlapping, in spite of the association between the Liberals and the French, and between the Conservatives and the English. Both parties—and most especially the Liberals—are able to attract both English and French support. Although only 19 percent of the Acadians indicate that they identify with the Conservative Party, this has not inhibited a much larger proportion from voting for that party. This was evident in the 1974 election, when the Conservatives were able to elect candidates in six of the twenty-three constituencies which had a French majority. Ecological analysis indicates that 39 percent of the Acadian voters supported the Conservative Party in that election.[3]

In Northern Ireland, however, the major political parties have attracted support almost exclusively from one religious bloc. Protestants have given overwhelming support to the Unionist Party; the Catholics have supported both the Nationalist Party and the Labour parties. In the period following the 1969 election, the traditional political parties splintered but, nevertheless, the pattern of congruence between

---

3. This estimate was made by correlating the proportion of French-origin voters in each constituency with the proportion of votes cast for the Conservatives. Each constituency was weighted according to its number of voters. The calculation of the proportion of French-origin voters was based on the French-origin population of voting age as at the 1971 census, adjusted to account for the higher turnout among French voters.

Table 49
Political Identification

Political party	New Brunswick (1974)[a]		
	% of English (n = 63)	% of French (n = 43)	% of Total (n = 106)
Conservative	48	19	36
Liberal	44	77	58
New Democratic	2	2	2
Independent	6	2	5
Total	100	100	101

Political party	Northern Ireland (1968)[b]		
	% of Protestants (n = 691)	% of Catholics (n = 454)	% of Total (n = 1,145)
Unionist	86	6	54
Nationalist	0	49	20
Labour[c]	11	37	22
Other	2	8	4
Total	99	100	100

Note: Those who did not indicate a political preference are not included in these results. In New Brunswick, 15 percent did not respond; in Northern Ireland, the corresponding figure was 11 percent. The data are from the National Election Study and the Northern Ireland Loyalty Survey.
a $\chi^2(3) = 11.6$, $p < .009$; $V = .331$.
b $\chi^2(3) = 767$, $p < .0001$; $V = .816$.
c Within this category, 82 percent specified simply "Labour," 12 percent, "Republican Labour," and 6 percent, "Northern Ireland Labour."

political and religious identities remained. The Social Democratic and Labour Party became the political spokesman for Catholics by consolidating the electoral support which had previously gone to the Nationalist Party and Labour parties. The Unionist Party broke down into several splinter parties, all of which continued to describe themselves as "unionist" and which catered exclusively to the Protestant community. Only one new party, the Alliance Party, could claim to overlap the religious cleavage, but it received only 9 percent of the vote in the 1973 assembly election.

The absence of a floating vote in Northern Ireland is clearly evident in the results of the Northern Ireland Loyalty Survey, which shows that less than 5 percent of the population were willing to even consider the possibility of voting for the political party commonly associated with the opposing religious bloc. It is further confirmed by Northern Ireland's experience with the "single transferable vote" during the 1973 elections. In the local government elections, where the votes could be transferred up to a maximum of seven times, only one-half of one percent of the transferred votes crossed the politico-religious divide. In the assembly elections of the same year, the number of such votes was even smaller, amounting to only one-quarter of one percent of all the transferred votes (Lawrence, Elliott, and Laver, 1975, pp. 48, 76). In New Brunswick, on the other hand, 25 percent of those who voted in the 1970 election indicated that they had voted for a different political party in a previous election.

The relatively moderate partisan sentiment found in New Brunswick is reflected in the absence of either strong likes or dislikes about the two major parties. When New Brunswickers are asked to cite what they dislike about either of the political parties, more than half reply simply "nothing" (see Table 50). Of the minority that do dislike something, very few have "strong" dislikes: 7 percent have strong dislikes for the Liberals, and 8 percent for the Conservatives. It is also significant that, where specific dislikes are mentioned, these are largely unconnected with the ethnic division. Further, the proportion of negative comments given to each political party is about the same for both ethnic blocs.[4] By contrast, in Northern Ireland reaction to the two parties is much stronger. In Belfast, when asked to cite what they dislike about either of the major parties, only 3 percent reply "nothing" (Budge and O'Leary, 1973). Curiously, however, most refuse to comment on their specific dislikes—and most especially those of their own party. But those criticisms which are made are directed almost entirely at political opponents and reveal the close association between religion and politics. For example, both Protestants and Catholics dislike their opponents for either their rigid position on politico-religious questions or their attitude to religious discrimination. Budge and O'Leary (1973) conclude: "Much of the unfavourable comment stemmed from frustration at the rigid mould forced on politics by partition and religious hostility" (p. 205).

It is likely that there is a direct link between the behaviour of the elites in the two communities, and the degree to which political loyalties overlap the ethnic or religious division. In New Brunswick, actions by a political leader which exacerbated ethnic tensions would not only threaten

---

4. There were some exceptions to this general pattern. For example, two-thirds of those who felt that the Conservatives neglected their region were French. Further, those who *liked* "nothing" about the Liberals tended to be disproportionately English.

Table 50
Disliked Qualities of the Major Political Parties

New Brunswick (1974) (n = 134)		Northern Ireland (1966) (n = 229)	
Disliked Quality	%	Disliked Quality	%
Conservative Party		Unionist Party	
Nothing	49	Unspecified[a]	47
Unspecified[a]	13	Attitude on discrimination	20
Region neglected	10	Politico-religious stand	18
Leadership	9	Leadership	16
Local candidate	3	Intolerance of opposition	6
Liberal Party		Nationalist Party	
Nothing	64	Unspecified[a]	47
Unspecified[a]	14	Politico-religious stand	33
Leadership	6	Attitude on discrimination	13
Road building	2	Leadership	8
Local candidate	1	General philosophy	5

Note: In Northern Ireland multiple responses were counted and, for this reason, the percentages may total more than 100. The data for New Brunswick are from the National Election Study. The data for Northern Ireland include only the city of Belfast and are calculated from Budge and O'Leary, 1973.
a   Includes responses which were generally unascertainable, e.g., "don't know," "no comment."

the stability of the province, but might also undermine his party's electoral support. Since the leaders have not wished to risk alienating a substantial bloc of their supporters, they have also avoided politicizing the ethnic division. Peter Leslie (1969), for example, has proposed that the New Brunswick Conservatives did not try to turn the controversy surrounding the Equal Opportunity Program into an ethnic issue because they were, even if only marginally, dependent upon Acadian electoral support. On the basis of his study of New Brunswick, Leslie (1969) concludes:

> The *less* the support which an opposition party has from a given ethnic minority, the *greater* the temptation that party has to angle for votes by emphasizing the political cleavage between the minority group and the rest of the population and then to present itself as the champion of the majority. Conversely, if a party is even marginally dependent upon support from an ethnic minority, ostentatious rejection of its demands will incur an electoral penalty. (p. 426)

This proposition is certainly applicable to Northern Ireland. Just as the biethnic support for each party in New Brunswick encourages the moderation of the political leaders, so too the homogeneity of each party in Northern Ireland fosters the extremism of its leaders. These leaders, unrestrained by any dependence on support from outside their bloc, have been concerned solely with consolidating the loyalty of their coreligionists.

OTHER CONTRIBUTING CONDITIONS
On the basis of comparisons between countries such as Belgium, Holland, Austria, and Switzerland, various other conditions have been cited, particularly by Lijphart, as having contributed to consociationalism. In some cases, the conditions have been absent in New Brunswick without deterring the development of cooperative behaviour. In other cases, they have existed in Northern Ireland but have been insufficient to stimulate the adoption of cooperative strategies. It would appear therefore that these conditions have not been essential in determining elite behaviour in these two communities. Nevertheless, they warrant evaluation because of their importance in other fragmented communities.

1. *Multiple Balance of Power.* Persuasive evidence has been given to support the proposition that a multiple balance of power among the subcultures is essential in convincing elites of the importance of cooperation. Where one bloc is in a clear majority, it is able to dominate and suppress the rival minority. Where no bloc is in a majority, however, it becomes necessary for the blocs to form a coalition in order to govern. Lehmbruch (1975) proposes this as an "internal genetic condition" of elite behaviour: "No group exists which is able to govern by a zero-sum strategy. Therefore majorities can be formed by bargaining only" (p. 381). Arend Lijphart (1975), in his review of the Northern Ireland situation, comments: "The least favourable situation is the one exemplified by Northern Ireland: a dual division into political subcultures without equilibriums and with one subculture capable of exercising hegemonic power" (p. 100).

Without denying that such a multiple balance of power may facilitate consociationalism, the New Brunswick case demonstrates that such a condition is not essential. New Brunswick, like Northern Ireland, is characterized by dual subcultures, one of which has been a permanent majority and the other a permanent minority. At the 1971 census, the English bloc constituted 63 percent of the New Brunswick population, and the Protestant bloc 65 percent of the Northern Ireland population. During the 1870s, when consociational practices first began in New Brunswick, the English bloc was even larger, making up 83 percent of the population. Thus New Brunswick provides strong evidence that cooperation is feasible even in a majority-minority situation. Indeed, it may be suggested that such a situation also has certain elements in its favour. Where a subculture is in a strong position of numerical dominance, it can afford to be more generous to its minorities. Insofar as it is largely unthreatened by the possibility of losing political power, concessions and compromises may be made which, while satisfying the minority, pose little danger to the majority. During the nineteenth century, the Acadians in New Brunswick were so small in number and so isolated regionally that they were not perceived as an opponent to be feared or mistrusted.

2. *External Threats.* Lijphart (1968b) observes that "in the five principal consociational systems, the crucial steps toward this type of democracy were usually taken during times of international crises or specific threats to the nation's existence" (p. 28). This has led Lijphart (1969) to conclude that the presence of an external threat is "the most striking" factor leading to the establishment of cooperation among the elites (p. 217). This proposition, for which support may be found in Simmel's writing, is based on the principle that conflict with an outgroup is likely to increase internal cohesion. Simmel (1908/1964) makes two important qualifications, however. First, the external opponent must be perceived as the same for each of the elements of the group. Second, if the internal antagonisms are great, the pressure to unite may also lead to a breakdown of the group. Simmel concludes that "war with the outside is sometimes the last chance for a state ridden with inner antagonisms to overcome these antagonisms, or else to break up definitely" (p. 93).

Both New Brunswick and Northern Ireland have been subjected to external threats but these have often had a negative, rather than a positive, effect on internal cooperation, underlining the importance that threats be commonly perceived as such by both subcultures. The massing of the Fenians along the New Brunswick border in the 1860s tended simply to further divide the population on religious lines. The attack of these Irish Catholic invaders stirred up anti-Catholic feeling among the population, a sentiment that was exploited by the proponents of Confederation who accused the New Brunswick Catholics of disloyalty. A similar phenomenon has occurred in Northern Ireland where the attacks of the Irish Republican Army on Northern Ireland tended to exacerbate tensions, by inflaming the antagonism of the Protestant majority toward the Catholic minority. The two world wars likewise tended to have a divisive rather than a unifying effect. The British-origin majorities in New Brunswick and Northern Ireland responded quickly to these wars:

the wars were perceived as endangering Great Britain and by extension, therefore, their own community. The minority subcultures, however, responded more reluctantly, fearing involvement in a foreign war in which they were not bound by sentiment to any of the protagonists. Thus, Northern Ireland was the only part of the United Kingdom in which conscription was not introduced during World War II. In Canada, conscription was applied throughout the country, but its introduction was delayed almost to the end of the war because of French-Canadian opposition. The difficulty in both communities has been that the perception of external threat has not been shared equally by both blocs. Further, in some cases, the external opponent has been perceived as linked to one of the subcultures.

3. *Small Population.* Consociationalism has often been considered the prerogative of small states. This derives partially from the fact that each of the five nations considered to be consociational democracies have relatively small populations, the largest having a population of only 13 million. There are also logical explanations which suggest that smallness may be a factor conducive to elite cooperation. Lehmbruch (1975) proposes that, in smaller states, the elites are less numerous and the communication channels are shorter. Lijphart (1969) claims that smaller countries are likely to have smaller loads on their decision-making apparatus—particularly with regard to foreign affairs. This enables the political leaders to devote more time to rectifying the problems created by internal divisions.

Both New Brunswick and Northern Ireland clearly qualify as small, both in terms of absolute population and in proportion to the states of which they are a part (see Table 51). Further, they have the advantage of being autonomous, or semi-autonomous, provinces of much larger states: the decision-making responsibility for a wide range of problems, such as foreign affairs, national defence, international trade, banking, and communications, has rested with the central governments. This has traditionally permitted the New Brunswick and Northern Ireland governments to concentrate on more local questions, such as education, law enforcement, and public works, which are often more sensitive in terms of the communal divisions. Further, it should be noted that both communities benefit from substantial transfers of funds from the central government to relieve the strains caused by economic underdevelopment and high unemployment. Both are able to furnish their citizens with a wide range of benefits, including unemployment insurance, national medical care, and old age pensions, which probably could not be afforded without financial assistance from the larger national government.

Table 51
Population, 1871–1971

Year	New Brunswick		Northern Ireland	
	N	% of Canada	N	% of U.K.[a]
1871	285,505	8.2	1,359,190	4.9
1901	331,120	6.2	1,236,952	3.2
1931	408,219	3.9	1,279,745	2.7
1951	515,697	3.7	1,370,021	2.8
1971	634,555	2.9	1,519,640	2.8

Note: The data are from Canada, Dominion Bureau of Statistics, 1873–1971; Canada, Statistics Canada, 1973–77; Northern Ireland, Information Service, 1973; and Rose, 1971.

a In order to maintain a consistent unit of comparison, the United Kingdom was defined as Great Britain and Northern Ireland, even for the years 1871 and 1901.

The fact that Northern Ireland, a small community, does not have a consociational system does not in itself prove that smallness is not conducive to consociationalism. Lijphart (1975) tries to rescue the condition of smallness by proposing a limit: "It is a plausible generalization that smallness is conducive to consociational democracy only to a certain limit. And Northern Ireland may be well below this minimum" (p. 101). The case of New Brunswick, however, which is half the size of Northern Ireland, belies this argument. It is better, perhaps, to conclude simply that while smallness may be conducive to cooperation, it is evidently not always sufficient.

4. *Acceptability of Grand Coalition.* Consociational democracy has become closely identified with nations in which the grand coalition form of government is widely accepted as a normative model. As a consequence, the "Dutch" model of coalition government is seen as a necessary condition for elite cooperation, and the "British" model of one-party government is seen as a barrier to consociationalism. Lijphart (1969) has lamented "the strength of the British system as a normative model even in fragmented political systems, where the model is inappropriate and undermines the attempt to achieve political stability by consociational means" (p. 222). The absence of popular acceptance for the Dutch model of coalition government in Northern Ireland is thus interpreted as a sign of the importance of this condition. Lijphart (1975) concludes: "In this respect, Northern Ireland is again in the worst pos-

sible position. The Protestant majority is passionately attached to its tie
with Great Britain, and Britain also provides them with the normative
standards of governmental organization" (p. 100).

The case of New Brunswick appears to throw into question the validity of the proposition that the acceptance of the norm of grand coalition
is essential to the establishment of elite cooperation. Such cooperation
has been built into the British model used in New Brunswick, by permitting each bloc entry into the political party which forms the government. The fundamental issue is essentially the willingness of each bloc to
share political power with the other—whether this takes place within
one party, or within a multi-party coalition. Northern Ireland could con-
ceivably have constructed a "coalescent" government without giving up
the British model, had the Unionist leaders been willing to admit Catholics into the Unionist Party. The essential limitation in Northern Ireland
has not been the acceptance of the British rather than the Dutch model,
but rather the refusal to accept that Catholics should participate in government, no matter what the political arrangements.

9. Conclusion

The advantages of the methodological approach which Eckstein (1966) has described as the "theoretical case study" are that it provides a means of testing and refining a theoretical model, and that it illuminates specific empirical cases. Its application to this study thus has two benefits. First, it provides insight into the theory of political stability. Second, it contributes to our understanding of New Brunswick and Northern Ireland.

POLITICAL STABILITY

The comparison of two communities is not in itself a conclusive test of a political theory, but it does permit the refinement of some of the principal variables. In the cases of New Brunswick and Northern Ireland, the results of the comparison are consistent with the hypothesis that cross-cutting cleavages and elite cooperation are necessary conditions for political stability in a fragmented community. Further, the comparison also provides evidence as to the likely workings of the principal variables, and the linkages between them (see Fig. 11).

Both New Brunswick and Northern Ireland are fragmented communities, that is, they are both subdivided into self-contained blocs, each with its own social organizations—schools, political parties, newspapers, leisure associations. But while both communities are fragmented, they do not both have congruent cleavages. This must be emphasized since social fragmentation and congruent cleavages have often been equated

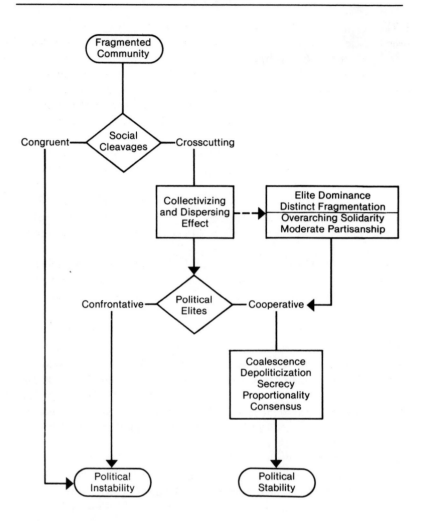

Fig. 11. Chart of the probable relationship between social fragmentation and political stability.

(e.g. Lijphart, 1968a). In Northern Ireland, the ethnic and class divisions have been relatively congruent with the Protestant-Catholic cleavage. But, in New Brunswick, both the religious and class cleavages cut across the English-French divide.

Studies of the effects of crosscutting cleavages in homogeneous cultures have generally concerned themselves with the psychological effects of "crosspressures" on the individual voter (see, for example, Sperlich,

1971). It is evident, however, that crosscutting cleavages have much broader structural effects which, as in the case of New Brunswick, facilitate the resolution of conflict and thus contribute to political stability. First, there is the "dispersing" effect. Conflicts along the different cleavages become largely dissociated from each other, and are consequently less severe. They tend to be single-issue rather than multi-issue conflicts. Thus, while a conflict between Protestants and Catholics in Northern Ireland is based simultaneously on religious, national, economic, and political issues, in New Brunswick it is largely limited to religious differences. Second, there is the "collectivizing" effect. The crosscutting cleavages tend to foster alliances across the community's line of fragmentation, thereby providing both a restraint on interbloc conflict and a common ground for negotiation. Both effects, by facilitating the resolution of conflict, deter the accumulation of hostility and mistrust.

New Brunswick and Northern Ireland also differ in terms of the behaviour of their political elites. While the elites have considerable autonomy in their choice of strategies, comparison of these two communities suggests that certain conditions are conducive to cooperation, rather than confrontation. Some of these conditions increase the capacity and others the predisposition of elites to cooperate. Elite dominance, for example, contributes to their capacity to pursue a strategy of cooperation by allowing them greater room to manoeuvre. In Northern Ireland—where this condition is absent—those leaders who wish to "build bridges" have been unable to carry their followers with them, and have subsequently been succeeded by more militant leaders. Distinct lines of fragmentation, similarly, increase the ability of elites to bridge the divide between the blocs. Potential conflict at the mass level is restricted by lack of contact, and the onus for communication is placed squarely on the elites. Overarching national solidarity, on the other hand, contributes to the predisposition of elites to work together in order to resolve mutual grievances and to preserve the political system. Moderate partisanship is also an important factor encouraging elite cooperation. Because there is a floating vote, and because political loyalties overlap the line of fragmentation, the elites tend to avoid narrow sectarian appeals in order to find policies acceptable to supporters from other blocs. It is noteworthy that conditions such as a multiple balance of power, an external threat, or the acceptability of grand coalition, proposed elsewhere by Lijphart (1968a, 1969, 1977), have not been necessary to bring about elite cooperation in New Brunswick.

The cases of New Brunswick and Northern Ireland stand as convincing confirmation of Lijphart's proposition that cooperative elites are necessary for the maintenance of political stability in a fragmented community. The primary element of this cooperation is coalescence, that is, the formation of a broadly based multi-party coalition (see Daalder, 1974; Lehmbruch, 1975; Lijphart, 1977). But some revision must be made to this concept. In New Brunswick there have been no multi-party coalitions since 1917. The cabinets have been coalescent in the sense that they bring together leaders from both blocs, but this takes place within a one-party government. Clearly, then, the representative parliamentary cabinet is an adequate functional substitute for grand coalition. It may quite well be, as Barry (1975a, 1975b) has suggested, that it is the willingness of the elites to cooperate, rather than the particular institutional arrangements, that is the essential prerequisite. In this regard, the failure of the 1974 coalition in Northern Ireland points to the inadequacy of the institutional arrangements by themselves.

In addition to coalescence, elite cooperation has been implemented in New Brunswick by a variety of other strategies which serve to reduce the competition between the blocs. In contrast to the elites in Northern Ireland, those in New Brunswick have adopted strategies which include depoliticizing communal issues, conducting negotiations in secret, allocating resources proportionally, and establishing bipartisan consensus. In spite of the obvious utility of these practices themselves, it is nevertheless the attitude of conciliation and constraint that is the most salient feature of this behaviour. This attitude is aptly summed up in the New Brunswick phrase *bonne entente*—an expression which provides a vivid contrast to the Northern Ireland slogans "Not an Inch" and "No Surrender."

NEW BRUNSWICK
> Indeed, we in New Brunswick exemplify the mutual tolerance and understanding that could well be emulated more fully in our sister provinces, in any bicultural nation, and in the disturbed world councils of today. (Robichaud, 1961, p. 25)

As befits a community with a long history of political stability, change comes slowly in New Brunswick. On the surface there is little reason to expect that, as the province enters the 1980s, the age-old tradition of *bonne entente* will be any less prominent. Cooperation has characterized New Brunswick politics for over a century, and may last a hundred years more. Nevertheless, events in recent years suggest possible changes in the major cleavages and, perhaps most importantly, in elite behaviour.

New Brunswick has been particularly fortunate that its major cleavages have traditionally cut across the line of fragmentation. The crosscutting of the religious and ethnic cleavages is unlikely to change —although the gradually decreasing salience of the religious cleavage may reduce its impact. But the crosscutting class cleavage is more susceptible to modification. More than any other major cleavage, its pattern can be altered by the economic and social programs of the government. Should the inequalities between the two blocs widen, so would the risk of Acadians becoming an "ethnic class." At present, there are countervailing pressures—some of which widen the inequalities, others of which would close them.

Economically, there is a tendency toward increased disparity because of the more rapid industrialization in the English south relative to the Acadian north. This regional difference has been encouraged by the government's policy of establishing southern cities such as Saint John and Moncton as development centres. Consequently, there is a disproportionately higher concentration of Acadians in the primary sector of the economy—a sector with less employment security and lower pay scales. On the other hand, the centralization and reorganization of the education system has gone a long way to eliminating inequities in the quality of education. The development of French-language schools, as well as the growth of post-secondary institutions such as the Université de Moncton and the Institut de Technologie de Bathurst, is closing the gap between the educational attainment of French- and English-speaking New Brunswickers. This is likely to be reflected in the occupations and the incomes of the two blocs.

Politically, the New Brunswick Official Languages Act, passed in 1969, has made a contribution to reducing inequities: it has assisted Acadians by opening up new opportunities in the civil service—the largest employer in the province—and it has guaranteed Acadians government services in their own language. But these improvements have nevertheless fallen short of expectations. In 1979, a decade after the act was passed, only 15 percent of those in the senior positions of the civil service—the deputy ministers, assistant deputy ministers, and directors—were francophones (Société des Acadiens du Nouveau Brunswick, 1979). Similarly, the level of government services available in French continues to be much inferior to that available in English, in spite of the legal guarantees. The lack of French-language personnel, not only in the upper ranks, but also among the secretarial staff, strongly favours the use of English. Thus, for example, while both English and French languages have equal legal status, in 1978–79, only 6 percent of the trials in the province's Supreme Court, Appeal Court, and County Court were heard in French (Patenaude, 1979). The existence of such inequalities within the public domain increases the likelihood that Acadians will perceive themselves as second-class citizens.

  While there have been no dramatic changes in the behaviour of the elites, there is nevertheless strong evidence that the long-standing tradition of elite cooperation is slowly being eroded. This may be attributed partially to the failings of one-party government, and partially to the weakening of elite dominance. The success of the system of one-party government in fostering coalescence depends upon the ability of the government party to elect leaders from both blocs. Thus, a party that lacks broad support has difficulty in forming a representative cabinet. Traditionally, the Liberal Party has been the dominant party in New Brunswick—and it is that party which has been the most successful in attracting support from both ethnic blocs. Since 1970, however, the Conservatives have formed the government and this party—which is closely identified with the English—has had difficulty in securing substantial Acadian representation. Following the 1978 election, for example, the Conservatives elected twenty-six English members, but only four Acadians. This greatly hinders coalescence, although it does not necessarily spell its doom. Cooperation between the cabinet and non-elected Acadian leaders still continues.

  A more serious threat to the tradition of cooperation lies in the recent challenges to the traditional Acadian leadership, challenges that also bring into question the policy of English-French partnership. These have their origins in three recent developments. First, there is a growing feeling of dissatisfaction, particularly among the more politicized Acadians, with the seemingly modest accomplishments of the traditional leaders in improving both the status of the French language and the Acadian input in government. Second, the success of the Parti Québécois which, through the skilful exploitation of ethnic nationalism, won the 1976 election in the neighbouring province of Quebec, has provided many Acadians with an eloquent example of the advantages of an aggressive nationalist leadership. Third, there is a new Acadian professional class emerging, drawn from occupations within the expanding public sector, which aspires to a more prominent leadership role, within the community as a whole, and within the French-speaking bloc in particular. This rising new class has organized outside the traditional political parties. In 1971, for example, it gave birth to the Parti Acadien, a nationalist party which seeks to replace the Liberal Party as the political spokesman for the Acadian bloc. While the party received only 3 percent of the Acadian vote in 1974, this increased to 10 percent in 1978, and is likely to grow further in the future. Perhaps more important, however, is the accession of the new leadership to increasing prominence in the major Acadian institutions, notably the Société des Acadiens du Nouveau-Brunswick.

The new Acadian leadership prefers confrontation to cooperation. Cooperation is seen as the route to cultural assimilation, and confrontation as the means to defend the Acadian identity. In this view, Acadian interests can be best met by aggressively asserting demands for linguistic equality and cultural autonomy. Competition is one element of this new strategy. While the traditional elites used the Liberal Party as a vehicle for coalition with the English, the new elites use the Parti Acadien as a vehicle for competing with them. Politicization is a second element. Rather than avoid ethnic controversy, the new leaders emphasize that Acadian interests are distinctly different, and attempt to subordinate all political questions to these differences. Jean-Guy Finn (1979) sums up the new strategy:

This new conception of political relations with the majority takes various forms. It manifests itself among other things by the creation of an ethnic party, by the fostering of local crises around questions such as education or the working language in certain municipalities, by the delivery of ultimatums to the provincial political authorities, by the holding of press conferences under the auspices of nationalist associations and by a written and spoken journalism which never misses the opportunity to cover events in such a way as to bring out the ethnic connotations. (pp. 16–17)

The major goal of the new elites is to increase the political autonomy of the Acadian bloc. In the immediate future this means a more rapid development of parallel English and French institutions. The Société des Acadiens du Nouveau-Brunswick (1977), for example, has demanded the establishment of "a progressive duality without territorial distinction," including the creation of "parallel institutions in all domains and above all in the sectors most affecting Acadian life (economics, education, culture)" (p. 81). This duality has been largely attained in the area of education where there is a parallel structure beginning at the level of the deputy ministers and extending down to the separate English and French schools. Many Acadians now desire to extend this example to the other sectors of the society. In the longer run, this may mean the creation of a completely separate political community. Since 1977, the major policy objective of the Parti Acadien has been the establishment of a separate Acadian province. In 1979, at the national convention of the Société des Acadiens du Nouveau-Brunswick, almost half the delegates polled favoured the creation of an autonomous Acadian territory.

The creation of parallel English-French institutions is not inconsistent with either elite cooperation or political stability. Indeed, the development of increased fragmentation—through the establishment of dual institutions—is a factor conducive to political stability. First, it reduces competition by increasing each bloc's autonomy in governing its own affairs; second, it places the onus on the elites by discouraging contact between the blocs at the mass level. Nevertheless, there is a certain danger in the methods employed to obtain this goal—namely, the use of confrontation. By politicizing the ethnic division, tensions in the community are greatly increased. Should the Parti Acadien be successful in polarizing the party system along English-French lines, Acadians might find their access to political power cut off, given the existing system of one-party government and the minority position of Acadians. The present coalition between English and French leaders within the traditional parties assures Acadians of participation in government. A breakdown of this coalition resulting from a bloc vote for the Parti Acadien would risk creating a polarized assembly on the Northern Ireland model, that is, a permanent English government and a permanent French opposition.

In spite of the cracks appearing in New Brunswick's *bonne entente*, the strength of the tradition of cooperation should not be underestimated. It is now more than a century since English and French, Protestants and Catholics first joined together in a coalition cabinet aimed at reducing conflict in the community. The habit of such cooperation, now deeply engrained, is unlikely to be broken overnight. It is also almost two centuries since New Brunswick was founded as a distinct community. Both English and French have worked together to build this community; and they are likely to continue working together to preserve it.

NORTHERN IRELAND

Here we are in this small country of ours, Protestant and Catholic, committed by history to live side by side. No solution based on the ascendancy of any section of our community can hope to endure. Either we live in peace, or we have no life worth living. (O'Neill, 1969, p. 200)

Since the collapse of the coalition executive in 1974, Northern Ireland has been at an impasse. Instability has become the normal and accepted state of affairs. Political violence, although much below the peak levels of 1972, has continued unabated. No negotiated settlement has been found—nor is likely to be found in the near future—to the constitutional stalemate. While the British government has made regular biennial attempts to bring the opposing political leaders to the negotiating table, these efforts have all ended in failure: neither bloc is willing to compromise its position. The 1975 constitutional convention was dissolved in 1976 without any consensus being reached. Political talks to negotiate interim devolution were suspended in early 1978 when the Protestant leaders withdrew. A second constitutional conference, in 1980, was thwarted before it began by the refusal of the Official Unionist Party — the largest party representing Protestant opinion — to attend its proceedings.

Northern Ireland is clearly suffering from its inheritance of congruent cleavages. The cumulation of animosities deriving from differing national and religious identities is one of the fundamental reasons for the seemingly intractable character of the conflict. It increases the tension between the blocs and acts as a barrier to negotiation and reconciliation. Catholics, as represented by the Social Democratic and Labour Party (SDLP), insist on the recognition of an "Irish dimension" — in other words, a role for the Republic of Ireland in the governing of Northern Ireland — as a precondition to any political settlement. Protestants, as represented by the various unionist parties, are equally adamant that there be no weakening of the ties with Great Britain. For a time, during the mid-1970s, it appeared that these competing national loyalties — Irish and British — might be superseded by an overarching identification with Ulster. Among Protestants, in particular, frustration with British direct rule and military intervention gave new impetus to the idea of an independent Northern Ireland state. This culminated in 1977 in the foundation of a new political party, the Ulster Independence Party, seeking support from both Protestants and Catholics. The independence movement was short-lived, however. The SDLP's Irish nationalism, and the Unionist Party's British nationalism, are once again as strong as ever.

The congruence of the class cleavage has also been an important barrier to reconciliation. In the words of former Prime Minister Terence O'Neill, the Northern Ireland problem is unlikely to be resolved so long as Protestants are the "haves," and Catholics the "have-nots" ("Glimmer of hope for Ulster," 1977). Over the past decade, however, many of the political inequalities have been reduced. Reform of the local government system — including universal adult suffrage and the single transferable vote — has almost doubled Catholic representation on the local councils. Following the 1977 elections, Catholics controlled eight of the twenty-six councils — a dramatic increase over the pre-1973 situation. Further, the British government has assured that Catholics are represented on the increasingly important regional boards, responsible for administering education, libraries, health, and social services.

Nevertheless, there is no conclusive evidence that the socio-economic position of Catholics has improved. An effort has been made by the Northern Ireland Housing Executive, established in 1971, to reduce the large disparities in housing conditions, but this has been greatly hampered by the extremely low quality of the existing housing stock, and by the reluctance of many inhabitants to be displaced to new housing estates. There is evidence that Catholics have attained a state of parity with Protestants in terms of educational achievement (Osborne and Murray, 1978), but it is not educational differences which have been the major cause of economic inequalities. The problem has been primarily the privileged access of Protestants into the most prestigious industries, including the civil service. Hence the much higher unemployment rate among Catholics, and their disproportionate concentration in low-status occupations. It is significant, for example, that, in 1975, 78 percent of Catholics (but only 17 percent of Protestants) believed that "one of the main causes of the troubles is the lack of job opportunities for Roman Catholics because Protestants are given preference" (Miller, 1978). If the gap between Protestants and Catholics has since begun to close, it may be due not to a great improvement in the Catholic position but, unfortunately, to the economic decline in the Protestant-dominated industries. By 1980, unemployment in Northern Ireland exceeded 11 percent, a partial consequence of setbacks in the shipbuilding and textile industries. The deteriorating economic situation could give rise to a class alliance cutting across the religious division, and united by common issues such as unemployment and low wages. But the sole precedent for such an alliance—the Outdoor Relief strike of 1932—was relatively short-lived.

The political elites have not, even in recent years, deviated from their traditional behaviour. If anything, the Protestant and Catholic leaders have become more intransigent since the early 1970s. For a time the intervention of the British government and the introduction of proportional representation fragmented the political leadership. But since 1976 the Official Unionist Party and the Democratic Unionist Party have consolidated their leadership of the Protestant bloc, and the SDLP has monopolized leadership of the Catholic bloc. The SDLP demand is twofold: first, the recognition of an Irish dimension by vesting responsibility for Northern Ireland in a joint British-Irish partnership; second, the instauration of a coalition executive that includes the SDLP as a precondition to any devolution of power to Northern Ireland. The Unionist demands are diametrically opposite: first, the guarantee that British rule in Northern Ireland will continue—without any Irish participation; second, the recognition of the principle of majority government rather than institutionalized power sharing. In both the 1975 and the 1980 constitutional conferences, the political leaders have contented themselves with categorical restatements of these positions. There has been no serious effort to negotiate with opponents or to seek out a compromise solution.[1] This undoubtedly reflects the continuing fear of the leaders that any compromise would undermine their own leadership—they would be unable to carry their followers with them.

The search for a compromise political settlement has centred on the possibility of increasing the powers of the parliamentary committees within a new assembly. This would provide a vehicle for elite coalescence without necessarily abandoning the British model of one-party government. A similar reform of the Northern Ireland House of Commons was recommended by Prime Minister Brian Faulkner in 1971, but the recommendation came too late to be effective—the House was suspended shortly afterward. At the 1975 constitutional convention, the United Ulster Unionist Council (UUUC) proposed, similarly, that new powers be given to committees composed of equal numbers of government and opposition members which would, in some cases, be under opposition chairmanship. This might permit greater Catholic participation in the governing process. But it has been opposed by the SDLP, which insists that power-sharing must also take place at the executive level. The Alliance Party has taken the Unionist proposition one step further by recommending that the committee chairmen be responsible for the administration of government departments and for the introduction of legislation in the assembly ("Party's submission to the convention," 1975). This would give the chairmen the equivalent of ministerial responsibility and thus, in effect, would establish a multi-party government. Needless to say, this has been opposed by the unionist parties who insist that the SDLP be excluded from the executive.

Aside from any differences in principle, a primary barrier to a negotiated settlement is the absence of either trust or goodwill between the opposing leaders. The SDLP is not willing to settle for less than a coalition executive, fearing that Catholics would otherwise be totally excluded from political power. In justifying these fears the SDLP can point not only to the exclusively Protestant rule from 1920 until 1972, but also to current Protestant dominance in local government. In spite of their relatively limited powers, a large number of the councils elected in 1977

---

1. A major exception occurred in 1975 when William Craig, leader of the Vanguard Unionist Party (VUP), proposed a temporary coalition with Catholics as an emergency measure. Craig subsequently suffered a rapid loss of political support, however. In 1978, the VUP was dissolved. And in 1979 he lost his seat in the British House of Commons.

have consistently excluded the Catholic minority from positions of influence, whether on council committees or on statutory boards. The unionists, on the other hand, fear not only the loss of their traditionally privileged position but also the consequences of sharing power with those they believe to be enemies of the state: Catholics could use political power to bring about a united Ireland. The intransigence of both blocs is made more palatable because of the alternative which wins by default: direct rule by Britain. It is not the preferred solution but neither is it the worst. For Catholics, it precludes domination by Ulster Protestants; for Protestants, it precludes union with Catholic Ireland.

While direct rule is not the aspiration of either Protestants or Catholics, each failure by the political leaders to negotiate a new settlement has made it more permanent. Ironically, although direct rule is an imposed solution, it has some advantages as a consociational device. Specifically, it reduces confrontation between the blocs. By vesting executive power in a Secretary of State for Northern Ireland, assisted by five ministers—none of whom are from Northern Ireland—competition between Protestants and Catholics for political power is substantially diminished. Regardless of which party has been in power at Westminster, the governing of Northern Ireland has been based on interparty consensus. Political decisions have been further depoliticized by the delegation of administrative power to a wide range of area boards and statutory bodies. These include the Health and Social Services boards, the Education and Library boards, and the Northern Ireland Housing Executive. Thus, contentious matters, such as housing policy, are removed from the political arena where they were previously the subject of Protestant-Catholic competition, to be decided impartially, according to non-sectarian criteria. Perhaps even more significant is the fact that appointments to these boards are made with a view to obtaining proportionality. While the local councils are able to nominate 30 to 40 percent of the members, the British government assures that the boards are broadly representative of all sections of the community.

In the absence of any negotiated agreement between Northern Ireland's leaders, it is the British government that will determine the political solution. In all probability, this means continued direct rule. Ironically, while Northern Ireland's politicians have consistently pursued a strategy of confrontation, current British policy emphasizes one of cooperation. If it is successful in diminishing Protestant-Catholic political competition, such a strategy will likely reduce the level of violence. But it is improbable that enduring political stability can be achieved without the voluntary cooperation of Protestant and Catholic leaders—an event which still appears to be a long way off.

Appendix A

The National Election Study and the Northern Ireland Loyalty Survey

Much of the survey data for this study comes from the National Election Study and the Northern Ireland Loyalty Survey. The National Election Study was made available by the Canadian Consortium for Social Research. The data were originally collected by Harold Clarke, Jane Jenson, Lawrence Leduc, and Jon Pammett. The Northern Ireland Loyalty Survey was made available by the Inter-University Consortium for Political and Social Research. These Northern Ireland data were originally collected by Richard Rose.

The National Election Study was a multi-stage stratified cluster sample of Canadian electors drawn from the 1974 electoral lists. The completion rate for the interviews was 63 percent. Within this national sample, there were 134 New Brunswick respondents. The interviewing of the New Brunswick respondents took place between 25 August and 21 December 1974, with 52 percent of the interviews completed before 15 September, and 87 percent before 13 October. The interviews were conducted in twenty-three polling divisions, in four of the ten federal constituencies. The design for the National Election Study is described in detail by Leduc, Clarke, Jenson, and Pammett (1974).

The Northern Ireland Loyalty Survey was a multi-stage stratified random sample of 1,500 households drawn from the 1968 electoral lists. The completion rate was 86 percent, resulting in a total of 1,291 respondents. Interviewing of the respondents took place between March and August 1968, with most of the interviews completed before 12 July. Interviews were conducted in thirty of the forty-eight Northern Ireland constituencies. (While there were fifty-two constituencies in Northern Ireland, four were "non-geographical," representing graduates of Queen's University.) The design for the Northern Ireland Loyalty Survey is described in detail by Rose (1971).

Appendix B

*Occupational Stratification in
New Brunswick and Northern Ireland*

The analysis of occupational stratification in this study is based largely upon unpublished data from the 1971 censuses. The New Brunswick data, supplied by Statistics Canada, consisted of 498 occupational groups, broken down by ethnic origin and sex. The Northern Ireland data, provided by the Northern Ireland Census Office, consisted of 222 occupational groups, broken down by religious denomination and sex.

The Northern Ireland occupations were classed according to the Hall-Jones scale of occupational prestige (Hall and Jones, 1950; Moser and Hall, 1954). The Hall-Jones scale is an empirical classification of key occupations according to their social status, as ranked by a sample of British respondents. More than 600 ranked occupations have been grouped into seven classes, each class containing occupations of proximate rank (Oppenheim, 1966). There is sufficient similarity between the occupations within each class that descriptive labels can be applied; for example, the lowest category is composed largely of "unskilled manual" occupations, while the highest contains largely "professional" occupations. Use of such terms, however, should not obscure the fact that the classification is based upon social status, rather than the nature of the work. In this study, the seven-class Hall-Jones scale was reduced to five classes by combining certain of the non-manual classes (see Table 52).

The New Brunswick occupations were classed according to a scale constructed specifically for this study in the same manner as the Hall-Jones scale. Seven occupational classes were constructed, using the results of a Pineo and Porter (1973) study, in which a sample of Canadian respondents ranked more than 200 occupations according to social standing. The Canadian rankings were sufficiently similar to the British results for it to be possible to use the same descriptive titles. Nevertheless, the different prestige ranking of occupations in

Table 52
Classification of Selected Occupations by Social Status

New Brunswick	Northern Ireland
Class 1: Professional, managerial	
Accountant (1)	Accountant (1)
Civil engineer (1)	Civil engineer (1)
	Commercial traveller (3)
Elementary school teacher (3)	Primary school teacher (3)
Graduate nurse (2)	Nurse (3)
Minister of religion (2)	Clergyman, minister (2)
Physician (1)	Medical practitioner (1)
Class 2: Lower grade non-manual	
Barber (5a)	Hairdresser (5a)
	Cashier (5a)
Commercial traveller (5a)	
Construction foreman (4)	Engineering foreman (4)
	Caretaker (5a)
Office clerk (5a)	Clerk (5a)
Policeman (5a)	Policeman (5a)
	Shop salesman (5a)
Typist (5a)	Typist (5a)
	Waiter (5a)
Class 3: Skilled manual	
Baker (5b)	Baker (5b)
Bus driver (5b)	Bus driver (5b)
Carpenter (5b)	Carpenter (5b)
Construction electrician (5b)	Electrician (5b)
	Cook (5b)
Machinist (5b)	
Motor vehicle mechanic (5b)	Motor mechanic (5b)
	Painter (5b)
Pipefitter, plumber (5b)	Plumber (5b)
	Cab driver (5b)
Class 4: Semi-skilled manual	
Cashier (6)	
Cook (6)	
Driver-salesman (6)	Roundsman (6)
	Agricultural worker (6)
File clerk (6)	
	Machine tool operator (6)
Painter (6)	
Truck driver (6)	Driver of road goods vehicle (6)
Class 5: Unskilled manual	
Construction labourer (7)	Building and contracting labourer (7)
Farm worker (7)	
Janitor (7)	
Longshoreman (7)	Dock labourer (7)
Sales clerk (7)	
Street vendor (7)	Street vendor (7)
Taxi driver (7)	
Waiter (7)	

Note: The number in parentheses indicates the rank of the occupation if classed according to the seven-class Hall-Jones scale.

the two communities means that the same occupation sometimes falls within different classes. The differing classification of similar occupations in the two communities is illustrated in Table 52.

R eferences

Acadian society to consider steps for "equality" in N.B. 1976. *Telegraph-Journal* (Saint John), 28 April, p. 5.

Akenson, D. H. 1973. *Education and enmity: The control of schooling in Northern Ireland, 1920–1950.* Newton Abbot, England: Published for the Institute of Irish Studies of the Queen's University of Belfast by David & Charles Ltd.

Almond, G. A. 1956. Comparative political systems. *Journal of Politics* 18: 391–409.

Almond, G. A., and Powell, G. B. 1966. *Comparative politics: A developmental approach.* Boston: Little, Brown & Co.

Almond, G. A., and Verba, S. 1965. *The civic culture: Political attitudes and democracy in five nations.* Boston: Little, Brown & Co.

Arthur, P. 1974. *The People's Democracy, 1968–1973.* Belfast: Blackstaff Press.

Aunger, E. A. 1975. Religion and occupational class in Northern Ireland. *Economic and Social Review* 7: 1–18.

Ayling, V. 1976. Colorful ceremony opens LOBA convention. *Telegraph-Journal* (Saint John), 23 April, p. 3.

Baker, W. M. 1974. Squelching the disloyal Fenian-sympathizing brood: T. W. Anglin and Confederation in New Brunswick, 1865–66. *Canadian Historical Review* 55: 167–87.

Balthazar, L., and Despland, M. 1966. *Relations entre culture et religion au niveau de l'éducation dans trois régions du Canada.* Report prepared for the Royal Commission on Bilingualism and Biculturalism, Ottawa.

Banks, A. 1971. *Cross-polity time series data.* Cambridge, Mass.: M.I.T. Press.

Barkley, J. M. 1959. *A short history of the Presbyterian Church in Ireland.* Belfast: Presbyterian Church in Ireland.

Barkley, M. 1971. The Loyalist tradition in New Brunswick: A study in the growth and evolution of an historical myth. Master's thesis, Queen's University (Kingston).

Barritt, D. P., and Carter, C. F. 1972. *The Northern Ireland problem: A study in group relations*. 2nd ed. London: Oxford University Press.

Barry, B. M. 1970. *Sociologists, economists and democracy*. London: Macmillan.

Barry, B. M. 1975a. The consociational model and its dangers. *European Journal of Political Research* 3: 393–412.

Barry, B. M. 1975b. Review article: Political accommodation and consociational democracy. *British Journal of Political Science* 5: 477–505.

Baudry, R. 1960. Les rapports ethniques dans les provinces maritimes. In M. Wade, ed., *La dualité canadienne*. Toronto: University of Toronto Press.

Baudry, R. 1966. *Les Acadiens d'aujourd'hui*. Report prepared for the Royal Commission on Bilingualism and Biculturalism, Ottawa.

Beckett, J. C. 1948. *Protestant dissent in Ireland, 1687–1789*. London: Faber & Faber.

Beckett, J. C. 1966a. *The making of modern Ireland, 1603–1923*. London: Faber & Faber.

Beckett, J. C. 1966b. *A short history of Ireland*. 3rd ed. London: Hutchinson.

Bell, J. B. 1974. *The secret army: A history of the I.R.A.* Cambridge, Mass.: M.I.T. Press.

Bernard, A. 1945. *L'Acadie vivante*. Montreal: Editions du Devoir.

Birrell, W. D., Hillyard, P. A. R., Murie, A. S., and Roche, D. J.D. 1972. *Housing in Northern Ireland*. University Working Paper, no. 12. London: Centre for Environmental Studies.

Black, G. F. 1946. *The surnames of Scotland*. New York: New York Public Library.

Blalock, H. M., Jr. 1970. *Toward a theory of minority-group relations*. New York: Capricorn Books.

Boal, F. W. 1970. Social space in the Belfast urban area. In N. Stephens and R. Glasscock, eds., *Irish geographical studies in honour of E. Estyn Evans*. Belfast: Queen's University.

Boal, F. W. 1971. Territoriality and class: A study of two residential areas in Belfast. *Irish Geography* 6: 229–48.

Bourassa, H. 1914. *Ireland and Canada*. Montreal: Imprimerie Le Devoir.

Boyd, A. 1970. *Holy war in Belfast*. 2nd ed. Tralee, Ireland: Anvil Books.

Boyd, A. 1972. *Brian Faulkner and the crisis of Ulster Unionism*. Tralee, Ireland: Anvil Books.

Boyle, K., Hadden, T., and Hillyard, P. 1975. *Law and state: The case of Northern Ireland*. London: Martin Robertson.

Bradley, A. G. 1932. *The United Empire Loyalists*. London: Thornton Butterworth.

Brebner, J. B. 1927. *New England's outpost: Acadia before the conquest of Canada*. New York: Columbia University Press.

Brown, W. 1965. *The King's friends*. Providence, R.I.: Brown University Press.

Buckland, P. 1973. *Ulster Unionism and the origins of Northern Ireland, 1886–1922*. Dublin: Gill & Macmillan.

Budge, I., and O'Leary, C. 1973. *Belfast: Approach to crisis*. London: Macmillan.

Bunting, W. 1895. *History of the St. John's Lodge F. & A.M. of Saint John, New Brunswick.* Saint John, N.B.: J. A. McMillan.

Burns, R. B. 1968. D'Arcy McGee and the Fenians. In M. Harmon, ed., *Fenians and Fenianism.* Dublin: Scepter Books.

Cadieux, J. 1965. Les Acadiens sont relativement pauvres. *Revue Economique* (Moncton) 3: 2–5.

Cadieux, J. 1966. *Etude sur le bilinguisme et le biculturalisme dans la région de Moncton, Nouveau-Brunswick.* Report prepared for the Royal Commission on Bilingualism and Biculturalism, Ottawa.

Cairns, A. C. 1971. The living Canadian constitution. In J. P. Meekison, ed., *Canadian federalism: Myth or reality.* 2nd ed. Toronto: Methuen.

Caloren, F. 1973. Unemployment: A new analysis. In D. I. Roussopoulos, ed., *Canada and radical social change.* Montreal: Black Rose Books.

Calvert, H. 1968. *Constitutional law in Northern Ireland.* London: Stevens & Sons.

Camp, D. 1970. *Gentlemen, players and politicians.* Toronto: McClelland & Stewart.

Campaign for Social Justice in Northern Ireland. 1969. *The plain truth.* Dungannon, Northern Ireland.

Campbell, A., Converse, P. E., Miller, W. E., and Stokes, D. E. 1960. *The American voter.* New York: John Wiley & Sons.

Canada, Dominion Bureau of Statistics. 1873–1971. *Census of Canada.* 75 vols. Ottawa: Queen's Printer.

Canada, Dominion Bureau of Statistics. 1923–71. *Vital Statistics.* 49 vols. Ottawa: Queen's Printer. (Published annually.)

Canada, Royal Commission on Bilingualism and Biculturalism (A. Laurendeau and A. D. Dunton, chairmen). 1967. *Education.* Vol. 2. Ottawa: Queen's Printer.

Canada, Statistics Canada. 1971. *Occupations: List of occupation codes and titles.* Ottawa: Information Canada.

Canada, Statistics Canada. 1972. *The Labour Force, 1972.* Ottawa: Information Canada. (Published annually.)

Canada, Statistics Canada. 1972–76. *Vital Statistics: Deaths.* 5 vols. Ottawa: Information Canada.

Canada, Statistics Canada. 1973. *Annuaire du Canada, 1973.* Ottawa: Information Canada. (Published annually.)

Canada, Statistics Canada. 1973–77. *Census of Canada, 1971.* 9 vols. Ottawa: Information Canada.

Canadian Parliamentary Companion. 1862–97. 22 vols. Ottawa: Citizen Printing.

Canadian Parliamentary Guide. 1898–1975. 78 vols. Ottawa: (Published annually.)

Canadian Who's Who. 1969. Vol. 11. Toronto: Trans-Canada Press.

Carroll, J. 1972. Moncton could become proving ground for Canadian biculturalism. *Globe and Mail* (Toronto), 1 March, p. 9.

Central power of Ulster Unionism. 1970. *Newsletter of the Campaign for Social Justice in Northern Ireland,* 15 August, p. 12.

Chambers, A. 1975a. Brooks can't remember insurance sale details. *Daily Gleaner* (Fredericton), 24 July, p. 15.

Chambers, A. 1975b. Patronage still flourishes in government insurance purchasing. *Daily Gleaner* (Fredericton), 23 July, p. 1.

Chambers, A. 1975c. Tabled letter links Smith with McMinniman's contract. *Daily Gleaner* (Fredericton), 12 December, p. 11.

Chubb, B. 1970. *The government and politics of Ireland.* Stanford, Cal.: Stanford University Press.

Coleman, J. S. 1957. *Community conflict.* New York: Free Press.

Colvin, I. 1936. *The life of Lord Carson.* 2 vols. London: Gollancz.

A conversation with Fred Arsenault. 1971. *Mysterious East,* March/April, pp. 15–17.

Coser, L. A. 1964. *The functions of social conflict.* New York: Free Press.

Countering the violence. 1974. *Ulster Commentary,* December, p. 16.

Curtis, E. 1936. *A history of Ireland.* London: Methuen.

Curtis, J. 1971. Voluntary association joining: A cross-national comparative note. *American Sociological Review* 36: 872–80.

Cyr, R. 1964. *La Patente.* Montreal: Editions du Jour.

Daalder, H. 1974. The consociational democracy theme. *World Politics,* 26: 604–21.

Dahl, R. A. 1961. *Who governs? Democracy and power in an American city.* New Haven, Conn.: Yale University Press.

Dahl, R. A. 1967. *Pluralist democracy in the United States: Conflict and consent.* Chicago: Rand McNally & Co.

Dahrendorf, R. 1959. *Class and class conflict in industrial society.* Stanford, Cal.: Stanford University Press.

Darby, J. 1976. *Conflict in Northern Ireland: The development of a polarized community.* Dublin: Gill & Macmillan.

Darby, J., and Morris, G. 1974. *Intimidation in housing.* Belfast: Northern Ireland Community Relations Commission.

Dawson, R. M., and Ward, N. 1963. *The government of Canada.* 4th ed. Toronto: University of Toronto Press.

December fatalities. 1977. *The Northern Irish Fortnight: An independent review,* 14 January, p. 19.

De la Garde, R. 1966. *Utilisation de la langue française au Nouveau-Brunswick.* Report prepared for the Royal Commission on Bilingualism and Biculturalism, Ottawa.

DeMerchant, E. B. 1976a. Bilingualism sparks hot debate. *Telegraph-Journal* (Saint John), 28 May, pp. 1–2.

DeMerchant, E. B. 1976b. Liberals question road work. *Telegraph-Journal* (Saint John), 13 May, p. 5.

DeMerchant, E. B. 1976c. Patronage: How bad, how much? *Telegraph-Journal* (Saint John), 24 April, p. 1.

De Paor, L. 1971. *Divided Ulster.* 2nd ed. Harmondsworth: Penguin Books.

Deutsch, K. W. 1954. *Political community at the international level: Problems of definition and measurement.* Garden City, N.Y.: Doubleday.

Deutsch, R., and Magowan, V. 1973, 1974. *Northern Ireland, 1968–1973: A chronology of events.* 2 vols. Belfast: Blackstaff Press.

Devlin, B. 1969. *The price of my soul.* London: Pan Books.

Dewar, M. W., Brown, J., and Long, S. E. 1967. *Orangeism: A new historical appreciation.* Belfast: Grand Orange Lodge of Ireland.

Dillon, M., and Lehane, D. C. 1973. *Political murder in Northern Ireland*. Harmondsworth: Penguin Books.

Dion, P., Even, A., and Hautecoeur, J. P. 1969. *Le bilinguisme à la Commission d'énergie du Nouveau-Brunswick*. 2 vols. Moncton, N.B.: Institut de Recherches en Sciences Sociales.

Di Palma, G. 1973. *The study of conflict in western society: A critique of the end of ideology*. Morristown, N.J.: General Learning Press.

Does detention curb violence? 1973. *Times* (London), 21 October, p. 4.

Dofny, J., and Rioux, M. 1962. Les classes sociales au Canada français. *Revue Française de Sociologie* 3: 290–300.

Donnison, D. 1973. The Northern Ireland civil service. *New Society*, 5 July, pp. 8–10.

Doyle, A. T. 1976. *Front benches and back rooms*. Toronto: Green Tree.

Driedger, E. A., comp. 1974. *A consolidation of the British North America Acts, 1867 to 1965*. Ottawa: Information Canada.

Dubé's expenses under microscope. 1976. *Telegraph-Journal* (Saint John), 13 April, p. 3.

Easton, D., and Dennis, J. 1967. The child's acquisition of regime norms: Political efficacy. *American Political Science Review* 61: 25–38.

Eckstein, H. 1966. *Division and cohesion in democracy: A study of Norway*. Princeton, N.J.: Princeton University Press.

Eckstein, H. 1971. *The evaluation of political performance: Problems and dimensions*. Sage Professional Papers in Comparative Politics, no. 01–017. Beverly Hills: Sage Publications.

Editor & Publisher Co. 1974. *International Year Book, 1974*. New York: Author. (Published annually.)

Edwards, O. D. 1968. Ireland. In O. D. Edwards, ed., *Celtic nationalism*. London: Routledge & Kegan Paul.

Egan, B., and McCormack, V. 1969. *Burntollet*. London: E. R. S. Publishers.

Eliot, T. S. 1949. *Christianity and culture*. New York: Harcourt, Brace & Co.

Elliott, S. 1973. *Northern Ireland parliamentary election results, 1921–1972*. Chichester, England: Political Reference Publications.

Ellis, W. 1974. Wilson's assurance on power-sharing attacked. *Irish Times* (Dublin), 13 September, p. 8.

Etzioni, A. 1965. *Political unification: A comparative study of leaders and forces*. New York: Holt, Rinehart & Winston.

Even, A. 1970. Le territoire pilote du Nouveau-Brunswick ou les blocages culturels au développement économique. Doctoral dissertation, Université de Rennes.

Even, A. 1971. Domination et développement au Nouveau-Brunswick. *Recherches Sociographiques* 12: 271–318.

Fédération des Francophones hors Québec. 1977. *Les héritiers de Lord Durham*. 2 vols. Ottawa: Author.

Financial critic charges reckless public spending. 1975. *Daily Gleaner* (Fredericton), 27 June, p. 1.

Finn, J.-G. 1972. Développement et persistance du vote ethnique: Les Acadiens du Nouveau-Brunswick. Master's thesis, University of Ottawa.

Finn, J.-G. 1979. Les conséquences du comportement d'une minorité en politique: Le cas des Acadiens du Nouveau-Brunswick. *Vie Française* 33: 7–19.

Fisk, R. 1975. *The point of no return: The strike which broke the British in Ulster.* London: André Deutsch.

Fisk, R., and Tendler, S. 1974. Mr. Faulkner resigns after British refusal to negotiate. *Times* (London), 29 May, p. 1.

FitzGerald, G. 1972. *Towards a new Ireland.* London: Charles Knight & Co.

Fitzpatrick, P. J. 1972. The politics of pragmatism. In M. Robin, ed., *Canadian provincial politics.* Scarborough, Ont.: Prentice-Hall.

Fraser, M. 1973. *Children in conflict.* London: Secker & Warburg.

Gallagher, F. 1957. *The indivisible island: The history of the partition of Ireland.* London: Gollancz.

Ganong, W. F. 1904. A monograph on the origins of settlement in the province of New Brunswick. *Proceedings and Transactions of the Royal Society of Canada* 10 (2, Ser. 2): 1–185.

Ganong, W. F. 1933. The Loyalist settlements in New Brunswick. In *Loyalist souvenir, 1783–1933.* Fredericton, N.B.: New Brunswick Historical Society.

Gesner, A. 1847. *New Brunswick; with notes for emigrants.* London: Simmonds & Ward.

Gill, C. 1964. *The rise of the Irish linen industry.* Oxford: Clarendon Press. (Originally published, 1925.)

Glimmer of hope for Ulster. 1977. *Edmonton Journal,* 20 October, p. 22.

Gluckman, M. 1969. *Custom and conflict in Africa.* New York: Barnes & Noble.

Godin, T. 1951. Les origines de l'Association Acadienne d'Education. *Revue d'Histoire de l'Amérique Française* 5: 186–92.

Gray, T. 1972. *The Orange Order.* London: Bodley Head.

Great Britain, Central Statistical Office. 1974. *Annual Abstract of Statistics, 1974.* London: H.M. Stationery Office. (Published annually.)

Great Britain, Office of Population Censuses and Surveys. 1970. *Classification of occupations, 1970.* London: H.M. Stationery Office.

Great Britain, Parliament. 1912. Census of Ireland, 1911: Province of Ulster. In *Accounts and Papers.* Vol. 116, Cd. 6051. London: H.M. Stationery Office.

Griffiths, N. S. 1973. *The Acadians: Creation of a people.* Toronto: McGraw-Hill Ryerson.

Gurr, T. R. 1968. A causal model of civil strife: A comparative analysis using new indices. *American Political Science Review* 62: 1104–24.

Gurr, T. R., and McClelland, M. 1971. *Political performance: A twelve-nation study.* Sage Professional Papers in Comparative Politics, no. 01–018. Beverly Hills: Sage Publications.

Hall, J., and Jones, D. C. 1950. The social grading of occupations. *British Journal of Sociology* 1: 31–55.

Happy birthday 'tit Louis. 1970. *Mysterious East,* July, pp. 4–8.

Harbinson, J. F. 1973. *The Ulster Unionist Party, 1882–1973.* Belfast: Blackstaff Press.

Harris, R. 1972. *Prejudice and tolerance in Ulster. A study of neighbours and "strangers" in a border community.* Manchester: Manchester University Press.

Hastings, M. 1970. *Barricades in Belfast: The fight for civil rights in Northern Ireland.* New York: Taplinger.

Hatfield, M. 1975. H. H. Pitts and race and religion in New Brunswick politics. *Acadiensis* 4: 46–65.

Hautecoeur, J.-P. 1971. Variations et invariance de *l'Acadie* dans le néo-nationalisme acadien. *Recherches Sociographiques* 12: 259–70.

Hautecoeur, J.-P. 1972. L'Acadie: Idéologies et société. Doctoral dissertation, Université Laval.

Hayes, M. N. 1967. Some aspects of local government in Northern Ireland. In E. Rhodes, ed., *Public administration in Northern Ireland*. Londonderry: Magee University College.

Heslinga, M. W. 1962. *The Irish border as a cultural divide*. Assen: Van Gorcum.

Holohan, R. 1974. Wilson pledge to S.D.L.P. on north. *Irish Times* (Dublin), 11 September, p. 1.

Hoogerwerf, A. 1968. Review of *The politics of accommodation: Pluralism and democracy in the Netherlands* by A. Lijphart. *American Political Science Review* 62: 1349–51.

Hubert, J. 1963. Dans l'Acadie de 1963 la langue n'est plus la gardienne de la foi. *Magazine Maclean*, February, pp. 11, 35.

Hunter, J. A. 1971. Population changes in the Lower Roe Valley, 1831–1861. *Ulster Folklore* 17: 61–69.

Independent Television Authority. 1970. *Religion in Britain and Northern Ireland*. London: Author.

International Labour Office. 1974. *International Year Book of Labour Statistics, 1974*. Geneva: Author. (Published annually.)

Isles, K. S., and Cuthbert, N. 1957. *An economic survey of Northern Ireland*. Belfast: H.M. Stationery Office.

Jennings, C. 1974. Strange strategy in a one-man election war. *Globe and Mail* (Toronto), 16 November, p. 8.

Jones, E. 1957. Belfast. In T. W. Moody and J. C. Beckett, eds., *Ulster since 1800*. London: British Broadcasting Corporation.

Kelly, H. 1972. *How Stormont fell*. Dublin: Gill & Macmillan.

Kelly, J. 1970. Secrets of Orange Lodge meetings. *Newsletter of the Campaign for Social Justice in Northern Ireland*, 15 August, p. 6.

Kennedy, D. 1967. Catholics in Northern Ireland, 1926–1939. In F. MacManus, ed., *The years of the great test*. Cork: Mercier Press.

Knight, J. 1974. *Northern Ireland: The elections of 1973*. London: Arthur McDougall Fund.

Kornhauser, W. 1959. *The politics of mass society*. New York: Free Press.

Kriesberg, M. 1949. Cross-pressures and attitudes: A study of the influence of conflicting propaganda on opinions regarding American-Soviet relations. *Public Opinion Quarterly* 13: 5–16.

Krueger, R. R. 1970. The programme for equal opportunity in New Brunswick. In W. E. Mann, ed., *Social and cultural change in Canada*. Vol. 2. Toronto: Copp Clark.

Krueger, R. R., and Koegler, J. 1975. *Regional development in northeast New Brunswick*. Toronto: McClelland & Stewart.

Landry, G. 1975. Trois groupes préconisent une école française unilingue à Grand-Sault. *L'Evangéline* (Moncton), 4 November, p. 5.

Lane, R. E. 1959. *Political life*. Glencoe, Ill.: Free Press.

Lawrence, R. J. 1965. *The government of Northern Ireland: Public finance and public services, 1921–1964*. London: Oxford University Press.

Lawrence, R. J. 1966. Local government in Northern Ireland: Areas, functions and finance. *Journal of the Statistical and Social Inquiry Society of Ireland* 21: 14–23.

Lawrence, R. J., Elliott, S., and Laver, M. J. 1975. *The Northern Ireland general elections of 1973.* London: H.M. Stationery Office.

Lazarfeld, P. F., Berelson, B., and Gaudet, H. 1968. *The people's choice: How the voter makes up his mind in a presidential campaign.* 3rd ed. New York: Columbia University Press.

Lebel, R. 1967. Cliffhanging contest expected in today's election in New Brunswick. *Globe and Mail* (Toronto), 23 October, p. 8.

LeBlanc, E. 1963. *Les Acadiens: La tentative de génocide d'un peuple.* Montreal: Editions de l'homme.

LeBlanc, J. C. 1972. Equalizing educational opportunity in New Brunswick, 1955–1967. Master's thesis, University of Alberta.

LeBlanc, R. A. 1967. The Acadian migrations. *Cahiers de Géographie de Québec* 11: 523–41.

Leduc, L., Clarke, H., Jenson, J., and Pammett, J. 1974. A national sample design. *Canadian Journal of Political Science* 7: 701–8.

Lehmbruch, G. 1975. Consociational democracy in the international system. *European Journal of Political Research* 3: 377–91.

Leslie, P. M. 1969. The role of political parties in promoting the interests of ethnic minorities. *Canadian Journal of Political Science* 2: 419–33.

Leyburn, J. G. 1962. *The Scotch-Irish: A social history.* Chapel Hill: University of North Carolina Press.

Lijphart, A. 1968a. *The politics of accommodation: Pluralism and democracy in the Netherlands.* Berkeley and Los Angeles: University of California Press.

Lijphart, A. 1968b. Typologies of democratic systems. *Comparative Political Studies* 1: 3–44.

Lijphart, A. 1969. Consociational democracy. *World Politics* 21: 207–25.

Lijphart, A. 1971a. Comparative politics and the comparative method. *American Political Science Review* 65: 682–93.

Lijphart, A. 1971b. Cultural diversity and theories of political integration. *Canadian Journal of Political Science* 4: 1–14.

Lijphart, A. 1975. Review article: The Northern Ireland problem; cases, theories and solutions. *British Journal of Political Science* 5: 83–106.

Lijphart, A. 1977. *Democracy in plural societies: A comparative exploration.* New Haven and London: Yale University Press.

Lijphart, A. 1979. Consociation and federation: Conceptual and empirical links. *Canadian Journal of Political Science* 12: 499–515.

Lipset, S. M. 1963. *Political man: The social bases of politics.* Garden City, N.Y.: Anchor Books.

Lipset, S. M., and Rokkan, S. 1967. *Party systems and voter alignments.* New York: Free Press.

Little, J. I. 1972. New Brunswick reaction to the Manitoba schools' question. *Acadiensis* 1: 43–58.

Long, S. E. 1972. *Rather be an Ulsterman.* Dromara, Northern Ireland: Slieve Croob Press.

Lorwin, V. R. 1971. Segmented pluralism: Ideological cleavages and political cohesion in the smaller European democracies. *Comparative Politics* 3: 141–75.

Losier, D. 1977. The Acadians. Address to the World University Service of Canada, Ottawa, 14 January.

Lyons, F. S. L. 1948. The Irish Unionist Party and the devolution crisis of 1904–5. *Irish Historical Studies* 6: 1–22.

Lyons, F. S. L. 1971. *Ireland since the famine*. London: Weidenfeld & Nicolson.

MacIntyre, A. 1974. Irish mythologies. *New Statesman*, 3 May, pp. 626–27.

MacLysagt, E. 1969. *The surnames of Ireland*. Shannon: Irish University Press.

MacNaughton, K. F. C. 1947. *The development of the theory and practice of education in New Brunswick, 1784–1900*. University of New Brunswick Historical Studies, no. 1. Fredericton, N.B.: University Press.

MacNutt, W. S. 1951. New Brunswick's age of harmony: The administration of Sir John Harvey. *Canadian Historical Review* 32: 105–25.

MacNutt, W. S. 1963. *New Brunswick: A history, 1784–1867*. Toronto: Macmillan.

Magee, J. 1970. *The teaching of Irish history in Irish schools*. Belfast: Northern Ireland Community Relations Commission.

Mallory, J. R. 1957. Cabinet government in the provinces of Canada. *McGill Law Journal* 3: 195–202.

Mansergh, P. N. S. 1936. *The government of Northern Ireland: A study in devolution*. London: George Allen & Unwin.

Mansergh, P. N. S. 1965. *The Irish question, 1840–1921*. London: George Allen & Unwin.

Manzer, R. 1974. *Canada: A socio-political report*. Toronto: McGraw-Hill Ryerson.

Marrinan, P. 1973. *Paisley: Man of wrath*. Tralee, Ireland: Anvil Books.

Marx, K., and Engels, F. 1955. *The communist manifesto* (S. H. Beer, ed.). Northbrook, Ill.: A. H. M. Publishing. (Originally published, 1848.)

Marx, K., and Engels, F. 1971. *Ireland and the Irish question* (R. Dixon, ed.). Moscow: Progress Publishers.

Matheson, R. E. 1909. *Special report on the surnames in Ireland*. Dublin: H.M. Stationery Office.

McCann, E. 1974. *War and an Irish town*. Harmondsworth, England: Penguin Books.

McCluskey, P. 1971. Editorial. *Newsletter of the Campaign for Social Justice in Northern Ireland*, 27 March, pp. 1–4.

McRae, K. D. 1974. Consociationalism and the Canadian political system. In K. D. McRae, ed., *Consociational democracy: Political accommodation in segmented societies*. Toronto: McClelland & Stewart.

Metzger, C. H. 1962. *Catholics and the American revolution*. Chicago: Loyola University Press.

Miller, R. 1978. *Attitudes to work in Northern Ireland*, Belfast: Fair Employment Agency.

Mitchell, W. C. 1963. Interest group theory and "overlapping memberships": A critique. Paper presented at the annual meeting of the American Political Science Association, New York, September.

Moser, C. A., and Hall, J. R. 1954. The social grading of occupations. In D. V. Glass, ed., *Social mobility in Britain*. London: Routledge & Kegan Paul.

National Opinion Polls. 1967. Discrimination: Strongest support for legislation among Nationalists. *Belfast Telegraph*, 13 December, p. 3.

National Opinion Polls. 1974. Seven in ten back executive and power-sharing. *Belfast Telegraph*, 19 April, p. 11.

New Brunswick, Chief Electoral Officer. 1967. Eligible voters. Unpublished manuscript, Fredericton, N.B.

New Brunswick, Chief Electoral Officer. 1974. *Report: Twenty-eighth general election*. Fredericton, N.B.: Author.

New Brunswick, Department of Agriculture. 1973. *Credit Unions of New Brunswick, 1972–1973*. Fredericton, N.B.: Author. (Published annually.)

New Brunswick, Department of Education. 1971. *Annual Report of the Minister of Education, 1971*. Fredericton, N.B.: Author. (Published annually.)

New Brunswick, Department of Education. 1974. *New Brunswick School Directory, 1974–1975*. Fredericton, N.B.: Author. (Published annually.)

New Brunswick, Department of Labour and Manpower. 1974. *Directory of Labour Organizations in New Brunswick*. Fredericton, N.B.: Author. (Published annually.)

New Brunswick Housing Corporation. 1968. Urban Development and Housing. Brief presented to the Federal Task Force on Housing and Urban Development, Ottawa, 12 November.

New Brunswick Liberal Party. Unpublished biographical records. New Brunswick Legislative Library.

New Brunswick, Office of the Economic Advisor. 1965. Community inventory survey. Unpublished manuscript, Fredericton, N.B.

Noel, S. J. R. 1976. Patrons and clients in Canadian politics. Paper presented at the annual meeting of the Canadian Political Science Association, Quebec, 31 May.

Nordlinger, E. A. 1972. *Conflict regulation in divided societies*. Occasional Papers in International Affairs, no. 29. Cambridge, Mass.: Harvard University Centre for International Affairs.

Northern Ireland, Commission appointed by the Governor of Northern Ireland (Lord Cameron, chairman). 1969. *Disturbances in Northern Ireland*. Belfast: H.M. Stationery Office.

Northern Ireland, General Register Office. 1973–74. *Census of population, 1971: County report*. 7 vols. Belfast: H.M. Stationery Office.

Northern Ireland, Information Service. 1973. *Ulster year book, 1973*. Belfast: H.M. Stationery Office. (Published annually.)

Northern Ireland, Information Service. 1976. *Facts at your fingertips, July 1976*. Belfast: Author.

Northern Ireland, Ministry of Health and Local Government. 1961. *Proposals for dealing with unfit houses*. Belfast: H.M. Stationery Office.

Northern Ireland, Ministry of Home Affairs. 1967. Analysis of local government electorate. Unpublished manuscript, Belfast.

Northern Ireland, Review Body on Industrial Relations (W. G. H. Quigley, chairman). 1974. *Industrial relations in Northern Ireland*. Belfast: H.M. Stationery Office.

Northern Ireland, Tribunal of Inquiry (L. Scarman, chairman). 1972. *Violence and civil disturbances in Northern Ireland in 1969*. 2 vols. Belfast: H.M. Stationery Office.

O'Brien, C. C. 1972. *States of Ireland*. London: Hutchinson.

O'Connor, F. 1974. UUUC triumph modified only by Maguire. *Irish Times* (Dublin), 12 October, p. 11.

O'Cuiv, B. 1951. *Irish dialects and Irish-speaking districts*. Dublin: Institute of Advanced Studies.

O'Farrell, P. 1971. *Ireland's English question: Anglo-Irish relations, 1534–1970*. London: Batsford.

O'Neill, T. 1969. *Ulster at the crossroads*. London: Faber & Faber.

Oppenheim, A. N. 1966. *Questionnaire design and attitude measurement*. London: Heinemann.

O'Rahilly, T. 1932. *Irish dialects: Past and present*. Dublin: Browne & Nolan.

Osborne, R. D. 1977. *An industrial and occupational profile of the two sections of the population in Northern Ireland*. Belfast: Fair Employment Agency.

Osborne, R. D., and Murray, R. C. 1978. *Educational qualifications and religious affiliation in Northern Ireland*. Belfast: Fair Employment Agency.

Ouellet défendra les droits des Francophones. 1975. *L'Evangéline* (Moncton), 8 September, p. 8.

Le Parti Acadien. 1972. Petit-Rocher, N.B.: Parti Acadien.

Party's submission to the convention. 1975. *Alliance*, October, pp. 1–2.

The past two weeks. 1971. *Fortnight: An independent review for Northern Ireland*, 9 July, pp. 18–19.

Patenaude, P. 1979. La protection linguistique des Acadiens et une nouvelle constitution pour le Canada. In E. Michaud, ed., *L'avenir politique du peuple acadien*. Edmundston: Société des Acadiens du Nouveau-Brunswick.

Pierce, R. 1973. *French politics and political institutions*. New York: Harper.

Pineo, P. C., and Porter, J. 1973. Occupational prestige in Canada. In J. E. Curtis and W. G. Scott, eds., *Social stratification: Canada*. Scarborough, Ont.: Prentice-Hall.

Poole, M. A., and Boal, F. W. 1973. Religious residential segregation in Belfast in mid-1969: A multi-level analysis. In B. C. Clark and M. B. Gleave, eds., *Social patterns in cities*. London: Institute of British Geographers.

Poulin, P. 1969. *Les francophones de la cité de Bathurst*. Bathurst, N.B.: Collège de Bathurst.

Powell, G. B. 1970. *Social fragmentation and political hostility: An Austrian case study*. Stanford, Cal: Stanford University Press.

Power-sharing executive agreed. 1973. *Ulster Commentary*, December, pp. 8–9, 11.

Prenter, S. 1970. The religious difficulty under Home Rule. In S. Rosenbaum, ed., *Against Home Rule: The case for the Union*. Port Washington, N.Y.: Kennikat Press. (Originally published, 1912.)

Reaney, P. H. 1958. *A dictionary of British surnames*. London: Routledge & Kegan Paul.

Richard, P.-E. 1975. The N.B. government's little weakness. *Telegraph-Journal* (Saint John), 27 December, p. 5.

Rioux, M. 1965. Conscience ethnique et conscience de classe au Québec. *Recherches Sociographiques* 4: 23–32.

Robichaud, L.-J. 1961. The Acadian outlook. In C. F. MacRae, ed., *French Canada today*. Sackville, N.B.: Mount Allison University Publications.

Robidoux, F., ed. 1907. *Conventions nationales des Acadiens*. Vol. 1. Shediac, N.B.: Imprimerie du Moniteur Acadien.

Rokkan, S. 1970. *Citizens, elections, parties*. Oslo: Scandinavian University Books.

Rose, R. 1971. *Governing without consensus: An Irish perspective*. Boston: Beacon Press.

Rose, R. 1976. *Northern Ireland: Time of choice*. Washington, D.C.: American Enterprise Institute for Public Policy Research.

Ross, E. A. 1920. *Principles of sociology*. New York: Century Co.

Rothman, S. 1960. Systematic political theory: Observations on the group approach. *American Political Science Review* 54: 15–33.

Rousseau, J. 1971. Black's Harbour. *Mysterious East*, December, pp. 3–6.

Rumilly, R. 1955. *Histoire des Acadiens*. 2 vols. Montreal: Fides.

Rummel, R. 1963. Dimensions of conflict behavior within and between nations. *General Systems Yearbook* 8: 1–50.

Rutan, G. F. 1965. Northern Ireland under Ulster Unionist rule: The anti-movement political system, 1920–1963 (Doctoral dissertation, University of North Carolina, 1964). *Dissertation Abstracts* 26: 1748. (University Microfilms No. 65-9055.)

Savage, D. C. 1961. The origins of the Ulster Unionist Party, 1885–6. *Irish Historical Studies* 12: 185–208.

Savoie, A. 1961. The Acadians: A dynamic minority. In C. F. MacRae, ed., *French Canada today*. Sackville, N.B.: Mount Allison University Publications.

Savoie, R. 1969. La répression en Acadie. *Liberté* 11: 54–57.

Scarrow, H. A. 1962. *Canada Votes*. New Orleans: Hauser Press.

Scott, F. E. 1973. Persuasion in the Northern Ireland civil rights movement, 1964–1970 (Doctoral dissertation, Purdue University, 1972). *Dissertation Abstracts International* 33: 6820A. (University Microfilms No. 72-21268.)

Senior, H. 1966. *Orangeism in Ireland and Britain*. London: Routledge & Kegan Paul.

Senior, H. 1972. *Orangeism: The Canadian phase*. Toronto: McGraw-Hill Ryerson.

Simeon, R., and Elkins, D. J. 1974. Regional political cultures in Canada. *Canadian Journal of Political Science* 7: 397–437.

Simmel, G. 1964. [*Conflict*] (K. H. Wolff, trans.) and [*The web of group-affiliations*] (R. Bendix, trans.). New York: Free Press. (Originally published, 1908 and 1922.)

Sinclair, T. 1970. The position of Ulster. In S. Rosenbaum, ed., *Against Home Rule: The case for the Union*. Port Washington, N.Y.: Kennikat Press. (Originally published, 1912.)

Sissons, C. B. 1959. *Church and state in Canadian education*. Toronto: Ryerson Press.

Social Democratic and Labour Party. 1972. Towards a new Ireland. In *The future of Northern Ireland: A paper for discussion*. Belfast: H.M. Stationery Office.

Société des Acadiens du Nouveau-Brunswick. 1977. *Les héritiers de Lord Durham: Nouveau-Brunswick*. Ottawa: Fédération des Francophones hors Québec.

Société des Acadiens du Nouveau-Brunswick. 1979. *Le projet collectif acadien en rapport avec le pouvoir politique*. Edmundston: Author.

Sperlich, P. W. 1971. *Conflict and harmony in human affairs: A study of cross-pressures and political behavior*. Chicago: Rand McNally & Co.

Spigelman, M. S. 1975. Race et religion: Les Acadiens et la hiérarchie catholique irlandaise du Nouveau-Brunswick. *Revue d'Histoire de l'Amérique Française* 29: 69–85.

Stanley, G. F. G. 1972. The Caraquet riots of 1875. *Acadiensis* 2: 21–38.

Stevens, G. 1975. Expensive promises in N.B. *Globe and Mail* (Toronto), 11 October, p. 6.

Stewart, A. T. Q. 1967. *The Ulster crisis*. London: Faber & Faber.

Sunday Times Insight Team. 1972. *Northern Ireland: A report on the conflict.* New York: Vintage Books.

Sunderland, Preston, Simard & Associates Limited. 1972. *Greater Moncton Metropolitan Plan: Social Studies.* Vol. 3. Author.

Surette, P. 1974. Les Acadiens et la campagne électorale provinciale de 1935 au Nouveau-Brunswick. *Cahiers de la Société Historique Acadienne* 5: 200–224.

Table of casualties. 1978. *Fortnight: An independent review for Northern Ireland*, 20 January, p. 11.

Thorburn, H. G. 1961. *Politics in New Brunswick.* Toronto: University of Toronto Press.

Thorburn, H. G. 1965. *The political participation of the French-speaking population of New Brunswick.* Report prepared for the Royal Commission on Bilingualism and Biculturalism, Ottawa.

Thorburn, H. G. 1966. *Ethnic participation and language use in the public service of New Brunswick.* Report prepared for the Royal Commission on Bilingualism and Biculturalism, Ottawa.

Thorburn, H. G. 1971. French in the New Brunswick civil service: Ethnic participation and language use. *Canadian Ethnic Studies* 3: 23–54.

Toner, P. M. 1967. The New Brunswick separate schools issue, 1864–1876. Master's thesis, University of New Brunswick, 1967.

Tonnies, F. 1957. [*Community and society*] (C. P. Loomis, ed. and trans.). East Lansing, Mich.: Michigan State University Press. (Originally published, 1887.)

Tremblay, M.-A. 1962. L'état des recherches sur la culture acadienne. In F. Dumont and Y. Martin, eds., *Situation de la recherche sur le Canada français.* Quebec: Presses de l'Université Laval.

Truman, D. B. 1971. *The governmental process: Political interests and public opinion.* 2nd ed. New York: Alfred A. Knopf.

Turgeon, O. 1928. *Un tribut à la race acadienne: Mémoires, 1871–1927.* Montreal: G. Ducharme.

United Nations, 1974. Department of Economic and Social Affairs. *Demographic Yearbook, 1973.* New York: Author. (Published annually.)

United Nations, World Health Organization. 1948–64. *Annual Epidemiological and Vital Statistics.* 14 vols. Geneva: Author. (Published annually.)

United Nations, World Health Organization. 1965–75. *World Health Statistics Annual: Vital statistics and causes of death.* 10 vols. Geneva: Author. (Published annually.)

United States, Bureau of the Census. 1974. *Statistical Abstract of the United States, 1974.* Washington, D.C.: Author. (Published annually.)

Urquhart, M. C., and Buckley, K. A. 1965. *Historical statistics of Canada.* Toronto: Macmillan.

Verba, S. 1965. Organizational membership and democratic consensus. *Journal of Politics* 27: 467–97.

Wade, M. 1961. Two French Canadas: Quebec and Acadia. In C. F. MacRae, ed., *French Canada today.* Sackville, N.B.: Mount Allison University Publications.

Wade, M. 1974. Commentary: *Québécois* and *Acadien*. *Journal of Canadian Studies* 9: 47–53.

Wall, M. 1967. *The penal laws, 1691–1760*. Dublin: Dublin Historical Association.

Walker, T. 1924. The Grand Lodge of New Brunswick. In O. Sheppard, ed., *Freemasonry in Canada*. Hamilton, Ont.: Osborne Sheppard.

Wallace, M. 1971. *Northern Ireland: Fifty years of self-government*. Newton Abbot, England: David & Charles.

Weber, M. 1968. *Economy and society*. New York: Bedminster Press.

Weisberg, H. F. 1974. Models of statistical relationship. *American Political Science Review* 68: 1638–55.

Whalen, H. J. 1963. *The development of local government in New Brunswick*. Fredericton, N.B.: Queen's Printer.

Wharton, J. H., ed. 1975. *Canadian Legal Directory, 1975*. Toronto: Author. (Published annually.)

Wheare, K. C. 1953. *Federal government*. 3rd ed. London: Oxford University Press.

Whitaker, J. 1869–1976. *An Almanack*. 108 vols. London: J. Whitaker & Sons.

Who's Who. 1969. Vol. 121. London: A. & C. Black.

Who Was Who. 1897–1970. 6 vols. London: A. & C. Black.

Whyte, J. H. 1971. *Church and state in modern Ireland, 1923–1970*. Dublin: Gill & Macmillan.

Wilbur, R. 1971. New Brunswick's francophones: A self-inflicted genocide. *Mysterious East*, March/April, pp. 4–11.

Williams, R. M., Jr. 1947. *The reduction of intergroup tensions: A survey of research on problems of ethnic, racial, and religious group relations*. New York: Social Science Research Council.

Woodward, C. A. 1976. *The history of New Brunswick provincial election campaigns and platforms, 1866–1974*. Toronto: Micromedia.

Wright, E. C. 1955. *The Loyalists of New Brunswick*. Fredericton, N.B.: Author.

Wright, F. 1973. Protestant ideology and politics in Ulster. *European Journal of Sociology* 14: 213–80.

Wright, Q. 1951. The nature of conflict. *Western Political Quarterly* 4: 193–209.

Index